The Course of Knowledge

A 21st Century Theory

by
Dr. Alex Bennet
Dr. David Bennet
with Dr. Joyce Avedisian

Mountain Quest Institute

MQIPress (2018)
Frost, West Virginia
ISBN 978-1-949829-24-2

The Knowledge Series

In this book we explore *the course of knowledge*. Just as a winding stream in the bowls of the mountains curves and dips through ravines and high valleys, so, too, with knowledge. In a continuous journey towards intelligent activity, context-sensitive and situation-dependent knowledge, imperfect and incomplete, experientially engages a changing landscape in a continuous cycle of learning and expanding.

MQIPress
Frost, West Virginia
303 Mountain Quest Lane, Marlinton, WV 24954
United States of America
Telephone: 304-799-7267

eMail: alex@mountainquestinstitute.com
www.mountainquestinstitute.com
www.mountainquestinn.com
www.MQIPress.com
www.Myst-Art.com

ISBN 978-1-949829-24-2

Graphics by Fleur Flohil

Table of Contents

Figures

In Appreciation

We are so appreciative of the times within which we live! Conversations crisscross a global world, and we can see glimmers of knowledge moving toward intelligent activity. Neuroscience continues to explore the power of the human mind/brain, a microcosm of the Universal brain. Science and Spirituality are colliding as the exploration of Quantum theory opens to the potential of All That Is.

We are so blessed. We live on a beautiful farm in the middle of the Allegheny Mountains of West Virginia, with many of our children around us, and dear friends who visit us often, all of whom are supportive of our work. They are such an important part of our lives and our learning. Thank you all for being you.

And from all three of us, a special thank you to all of our families and friends, and deep appreciation to our colleagues. We love you all.

Alex Bennet, David Bennet and Joyce Avedisian

Foreward

Knowledge is at the core of what it is to be human, the substance which informs our thoughts and determines the nature and course of our actions. Our growing focus on, and understanding of, knowledge and its consequent actions is changing our relationship with the world. Because **knowledge determines the quality of every single decision we make**, it is critical to learn about and understand what knowledge is. Meta-knowledge—or knowledge about knowledge—is essential to our ability to efficiently and effectively manage information and apply knowledge. This book *lays the groundwork for exploring* different ways of understanding, creating, sharing, and working with knowledge.

We explore a theory of knowledge that is both pragmatic and biological. Pragmatic in that it is based on taking effective action, and biological because it is created by humans via patterns of neuronal connections in the mind/brain. It has only been in the past few decades that cognitive psychology and neuroscience have begun to seriously explore our unconscious mental life; and even more recently that we have begun to relate knowledge to both the conscious and unconscious workings of the mind/brain. This new learning includes the recognition that conscious experience, thought and action are influenced by unconscious concepts, memories and other mental constructs, mostly inaccessible to our own conscious awareness and somehow independent of voluntary control (Eich et al., 2000). Research in neuroscience is also digging deeper into the understanding of the emotions, working memory and the unconscious processing that occurs within the mind and throughout the body.

Since knowledge is what makes our actions successful, it is critical that we tap into the best knowledge possible to help us achieve our goals and dreams, both as individuals and as participants in a global world. We live in a complex world that is shifting and changing with every breath we take. Now that we understand more about the way our mind/brain works, we realize that knowledge is created (and re-created) for the moment at hand (see Chapter 9). The mind/brain is an associative patterner (see Chapter 7). In the multidimensional unconscious processes, the association of incoming information with internal information is a powerful form of learning. We as humans—continuous learners anticipating the outcome of our decisions and actions—are **verbs, not nouns**, ever expanding and maneuvering our way through life as we continuously learn and work to create a better future.

So, we ask: How do we make best use of this process for ourselves, our organizations and our world? The search for an answer leads to thinking beyond what is described as ordinary consciousness towards what we will call extraordinary consciousness, *with knowledge the currency of our journey.* Life is indeed a journey! We are in a continuous cycle of knowledge creation such that every moment offers the opportunity for the emergence of new and exciting ideas, all waiting to be put in service to an interconnected world.

Ordinary consciousness represents the customary or typical state of consciousness or awareness, that which is common to everyday usage, or of the usual kind. For example, Polanyi sees tacit knowledge as *not part* of one's ordinary consciousness (Polanyi, 1958); thus, tacit knowledge resides in the unconscious. See Chapter 4 for a in-depth treatment of tacit knowledge. From a pragmatic perspective, we often don't know what we know (Bennet & Bennet, 2004). *So, we ask: How do we purposefully and consciously draw upon our tacit knowledge?* See Chapter 5.

Extraordinary consciousness would be considered special, exceptional, and outside of the usual or regular state of consciousness. This means a heightened sensitivity to, awareness of and connection with our unconscious mind, together with its memory and thought processes. For example, to access tacit knowledge an individual needs to move from ordinary consciousness to extraordinary consciousness, acquiring a greater sensitivity to information available in the unconscious. There are ways to accomplish this. See Chapter 5.

An aspect of extraordinary consciousness is tapping into our sense of knowing. Each of us has had the surprising experience of pulling up ideas and solutions from seemingly nowhere. *So, we ask: Where do these ideas and solutions come from? What is the relationship between knowledge and knowing?* The concepts of ordinary consciousness and extraordinary consciousness are introduced in-depth in Chapter 5 and come up again in our discussion of wisdom in Chapter 11. The relationship of knowledge and knowing is addressed in Chapter 12.

The journey toward achieving extraordinary consciousness begins with building a new understanding of knowledge, that is, developing meta-knowledge. No, we don't intend to throw the baby out with the bath water ... we don't throw away the historical concepts of knowledge; rather, we take what makes sense and incorporate it into new frames of reference in the context of the 21st century. These frames of reference are tied to emerging values in a new era of connectivity and mental capability, what we refer to as **the Golden Age of Humanity**.[1]

Through the past 20 years we have engaged in extensive research—much of it experiential in nature—which has led us to break through life-long perceived limits and sift and expand our beliefs about life and the world of which we are a part. Right up front we offer the following assumptions:

Assumption 1: Knowledge itself is neither true nor false, and its value in terms of good or poor is difficult to measure other than by the outcomes of its actions.

Knowledge includes a special form of information and all information is energy; how it is used determines its value. Hence, good knowledge would have a high probability of producing the desired and anticipated outcome, and poor knowledge would have a low probability of producing the expected result. For complex situations, the quality of knowledge (from good to poor, relative to each specific situation) may be hard to estimate before the action is taken because of the situation's unpredictability. After the outcome has occurred, the quality of knowledge can be assessed by comparing the actual outcome to the anticipated outcome.

Assumption 2: The human mind is an associative patterner, that is, continuously re-creating knowledge for the situation at hand. Knowledge exists in the human brain in the form of stored or expressed neural patterns that may be selected, activated, mixed and/or reflected upon through thought. Incoming information is associated with stored information. From this mixing process new patterns are created that may represent understanding, meaning and the capacity to anticipate to various degrees the results of potential actions. Thus, knowledge is context sensitive and situation dependent, with the mind continuously growing, restructuring and creating increased organization (information) and knowledge for the moment at hand.

Assumption 3: All knowledge is imperfect and/or incomplete intelligence. Intelligent activity represents a perfect state of interaction where intent, purpose, direction, values and expected outcomes are clearly understood and communicated among all parties, reflecting wisdom and achieving a higher truth. Because the effectiveness of all knowledge is context sensitive and situation dependent, knowledge is shifting and changing in concert with our environment and the demands placed upon us. A large example of this is the discovery of quantum physics, coupled with the realization of the limitations of Newtonian physics, in representing our physical reality. The incompleteness of knowledge that is never perfect serves as an incentive for the continuous human journey of learning and the exploration of new ideas.

Assumption 4: The unconscious mind is multidimensional and, given a healthy mind and body, has a vast store of tacit knowledge available to us. It has only been in the past few decades that cognitive psychology and neuroscience have begun to seriously explore unconscious mental life. Polanyi (1967) felt that tacit knowledge consisted of *a range* of conceptual and sensory information and images that could be used to make sense of a situation or event (Hodgkin, 1991; Smith, 2003). He was right. The unconscious mind is incredibly powerful, on the order of a million times more powerful in processing speed than the conscious stream of thought. *The challenge is to make better use of our tacit knowledge through creating greater connections with the unconscious, building and expanding the resources stored in the unconscious, deepening areas of resonance, and sharing tacit resources among individuals.*

Assumption 5: There are still vast workings of the human mind and its connections to higher-order energies that we do not understand. The limitations we as humans place on our decision-making capacities and capabilities are created from past reference points, that which has been developed primarily through the rationale and logical workings of the mechanical functioning of our mind/brain, an understanding that has come through extensive intellectual effort. Yet we now recognize that knowledge is a living form of information (energy), tailored by our minds specifically for a situation at hand. The totality of knowledge can no more easily be codified and stored than our feelings, nor would it be highly beneficial to do so in a changing and uncertain environment. *Thus, in this book—understanding the limitations of our own perceptions and understanding—we consider and explore areas and phenomena that are beyond old paradigms of knowledge.* This does not mean that we ignore all that we have learned. Hardly! Rather, we recognize that there are many approaches to living, that knowledge takes many forms, and that the way we think and act is our own choice ... an extremely important choice, especially in a complex, uncertain and changing world!

This book expands on a compendium of work written and published through journals and chapters in academic and business books from 2004 through 2014. What all of this work has in common is knowledge. This is the first time it has been pulled together as a 21st century holistic treatment of knowledge. The various chapters are footnoted to reference where key material was first published, and any other locations the original work may be available.

Section I, Laying the Foundation, begins with an introduction that lays the groundwork—and provides working definitions—for the entire book, including an explication of Knowledge (Informing) and Knowledge (Proceeding). The advantage of clear definitions of information and knowledge is the consistency, ease and precision of communication, and potential insights these definitions may provide, perhaps moving our knowledge a bit closer to intelligent activity. Influenced by our years with the US Department of the Navy, we move into a discussion of levels of knowledge in terms of surface, shallow and deep, followed by a chapter on types of knowledge seen from the viewpoint of what knowledge is needed to do a particular type of work, take a particular action or create a desired situation.

Section II, The Voiced and Unvoiced, focuses on that which is voiced and that which is unvoiced, that is, affecting our thought, words and behaviors, possibly outside of our awareness. We begin by exploring the explicit, implicit and tacit dimensions of knowledge. Developing a deeper understanding of tacit, we look at ways to engage our tacit knowledge, moving into the realms of extraordinary consciousness. Recognizing that all knowledge is context-sensitive and situation dependent, Section I ends with an in-depth treatment of context, taking into account and building on the work of McLuhan (1964).

Section III, The Neuroscience of Knowledge, introduces some ideas from the neuroscience side of knowledge, exploring the workings of the mind/brain in relationship to knowledge. We first consider the magnificent mind/brain, then look at social knowledge, and end with investigating the fallacy of knowledge reuse.

Section IV, Values, Wisdom and Knowing, focuses on the human search for value. Introducing values as knowledge, with the same attributes as knowledge, we first explore the relationship of value and values, then reflect on the relationship of knowledge and wisdom. Next is an exploration of the differences between, and overlaps among, knowledge and knowing. Finally, we introduce sub-personalities as knowledge, a critical role knowledge plays in our personal coping with the world and in our expansion of consciousness.

We begin.

Section I
Laying the Foundation

Potential. Choice. Activity.

We define knowledge as *the capacity (potential or actual) to take effective action*. Every day of our lives we are embedded in fields of potential. We are continuously informed from without and within and by uniquely sifting through, focusing, and connecting the stream of information that informs our knowledge and drives our actions. Sometimes we recognize our choices, and sometimes they are beyond our conscious awareness. The knowledge we can create is both triggered by external events and very much determined by our past experiences and current state of learning.

Recognizing that all models are artificial constructs developed to facilitate our understanding and share what we are learning with others, we introduce several frameworks for exploring knowledge. Over the past dozen years these frameworks have proven very useful in both digging deeper into the human capacity for knowledge and in the application of knowledge management initiatives in the public and private sectors.

Polanyi advocated that tacit knowledge consisted of *a range* of conceptual and sensory information and images that could be used to make sense of a situation or event (Hodgkin, 1991). We agree. Thinking of knowledge in terms of levels—surface, shallow and deep (see Chapter 2)—represents a fluctuating continuum very much dependent on the context and situation at hand.

The concept of deep knowledge begs the question: **Does deep knowledge denote a higher level of intelligent activity?** Not necessarily. It represents a deeper exploration of a specific domain or area of knowledge; it does not represent a perfect state of interaction where intent, purpose, direction, values and expected outcomes are clearly understood and communicated among all parties, reflecting wisdom and achieving a higher truth.

In addition to potentially limiting our frame of reference (by choice and focus), an inherent difficulty with deep knowledge is communicating it and having others understand it. Because of this, there is the ever-present danger that the "expert" ceases to interact with others and his/her environment. Perceiving oneself *as* the knowledge instead of the creator and user of knowledge can lead to pushing, directing or ordering—and perhaps even controlling—others' actions because of a perceived superiority. Some of the ways to mitigate such situations is to remain a continuous learner, engage in conversations with experts in other domains, and fully participate in mentoring experiences, staying open to new ways of seeing and thinking ... and remembering that we are a verb, not a noun, ever learning and expanding.

This section includes a short Introduction (Chapter 1); Levels of Knowledge (Chapter 2); and Types of Knowledge (Chapter 3).

Chapter 1
Introduction

This book is all about knowledge. As a functional definition, we consider knowledge as *the capacity (potential or actual) to take effective action* in varied and uncertain situations (Bennet & Bennet, 2004). This is a human capacity that consists of understanding, insights, meaning, intuition, creativity, judgment, and the ability to anticipate the outcome of our actions. While it is not necessary to add "in varied and uncertain situations" to our definition of knowledge, in this introduction we have done so to emphasize the necessary human element in a complex environment. In the future, when biological computing becomes a reality, it may become necessary to revise our definition or perception about knowledge as a human capacity!

The only way that we can influence, and possibly change, our material world is by acting upon it. Such action may or may not result in the desired changes. However, if we understand some aspect of our world—such as an undesirable situation—then we may be able to create and apply the right knowledge (the capacity to take effective action) and thereby improve the situation. Thus, the awareness, importance and application of knowledge becomes critical to our ability to survive and grow and contribute to the larger world.

> Knowledge is the capacity (potential or actual) to take effective action.

There is considerable precedent for linking knowledge and action. In 2005, 34 Knowledge Management (KM) thought leaders spanning four continents participated in an extensive study exploring the field of KM and their passion for the field. When participants were asked to define knowledge, 84 percent *tied knowledge directly to action* or use. See Appendix A for more details. Similarly, emerging from nearly 20 years of APQC's (American Productivity & Quality Center) leading research in the field of knowledge management, O'Dell and Hubert define knowledge from the practical perspective as "information in action" (O'Dell & Hubert, 2011 p. 2).

The Relationship of Data, Information and Knowledge

Exploring the relationship among data, information and knowledge leads us to a discussion of knowledge from a frame of reference based on the universal and the physical reality of information. In his three-volume study of the role of information in the structure of the Universe, the theoretical biologist Tom Stonier proposes that "organization is the physical expression of a system containing information" (Stonier, 1997, p. 14). By organization he means the existence of a non-random pattern of particles and energy fields, or more generally, the sub-units comprising any system. Thus, in the material work organization can be observed in space and time as a physical phenomenon. Stonier considers information (any organized or non-random pattern) to be a basic property of the Universe—as fundamental as matter and energy (Stonier, 1997). Along with Stonier, *we take information to be any non-random pattern or set of patterns*.

All knowledge is comprised of information. By selecting and putting information together, one may be able to create knowledge. Think of a picture puzzle in which each piece fits into the puzzle at a particular place. If all of the pieces are put in their rightful place, we come up with a picture that may be beautiful, and informative. So, it is with knowledge. When the right information is identified and put together in the right way (for the situation at hand), we have created knowledge—the capacity to take effective action. Of course, every situation that we try to deal with, try to change and improve, will require its own picture, that is, its own combination of ideas, interpretations, relationships and actions. If these pieces of information are identified, connected and implemented, they may result in providing the effective action needed to create the desired picture, or, in other words, transform an undesirable situation into a desirable situation.

Data, a subset of information, is factual information organized for analyses. In computer science, it is used to describe numerical or other information represented in a form suitable for processing by computers. The term is also used to represent values derived from scientific experiments (*American Heritage Dictionary*, 1992). While data and information both consist of patterns, they have no meaning until some organism recognizes and interprets the patterns. In other words, meaning comes from the combination of non-random patterns and an observer who can interpret these patterns to create recognition or understanding (Bennet & Bennet, 2008a). *It is only when the incoming patterns from the environment are integrated with the internal neural patterns within our brains that they take on meaning to the individual.* These units of understanding are referred to as "semantic complexes". As Stonier explains,

> ... a semantic complex may be further information-processed as if it were a new message in its own right. By repeating this process, the original message becomes more and more meaningful as, at each recursive step, new semantic complexes are created. As these impinge on even larger areas provided by the internal information environment, whole new and elaborate knowledge structures may be built up—a process which leads to understanding (Stonier, 1997, p. 157).

Thus, knowledge exists in the human brain in the form of *stored or expressed neural patterns that may be activated and reflected upon through conscious thought.* This is a high-level description of the creation of knowledge that is consistent with the neural operation of the brain and is applicable in varying degrees to all living organisms. It took 50 years of research before this process of neuroplasticity (the capability of the external environment and learning to change the internal patterns and structure of the brain) was understood and accepted by the

> Knowledge exists in the human brain in the form of stored or expressed patterns that may be activated and reflected upon through conscious thought.

scientific community. From these findings we now know that our thoughts directly impact the structure of our brain; and the structure of our brain affects our thoughts. We will explore this further in Chapter 7.

The Nature of Knowledge

Knowledge is dependent on context. In fact, it represents an understanding of situations and their context, insights into the relationships within a system, and the ability to identify leverage points and weaknesses to recognize the meaning in a specific situation and to anticipate future implications of actions taken to resolve problems or meet challenges.

Shared understanding, the underlying purpose of communication and a primary goal of knowledge mobilization (Bennet & Bennet, 2007), is taken to mean the movement of knowledge from one person to the other, recognizing that what passes in the air when two people are having a conversation is information in the form of changes in air pressure. These patterns of change may be understood by the perceiver (if they know the language and its nuances), but the changes in air pressure do *not* represent understanding, meaning or the capacity to anticipate the consequences of actions. The perceiver must be able to take these patterns (information) and—interpreting them through context—re-create the knowledge that the source intended. This same phenomenon occurs when information is passed through writing or other communications vehicles. In other words, content and context (information) originating at the source resonate with the perceiver such that the intended knowledge can be re-created by the perceiver. If the subject is simple and familiar to both participants, knowledge sharing (re-creation) may be easy. However, if the subject is complex and the parties do not have common contexts, sharing may be very challenging. There is an in-depth treatment of context in Chapter 6.

Recognizing the nature of knowledge in terms of context sensitivity and situation dependence, it follows that all knowledge is imperfect and/or incomplete, that is, any small shift in the context or situation may require shifting or expanding knowledge, which in turn drives different decisions and actions to achieve the desired outcome(s).

> Knowledge is always partial, that is, imperfect and/or incomplete.

Further, in a complex environment—and all people and organizations are complex adaptive systems—it is impossible to know or even identify all the elements of a system affecting a challenge or situation. Thus, knowledge is always partial (imperfect and/or incomplete), that is, knowledge is the best we can create at the moment of decision for the situation at hand.

Still further, intelligent activity involves engagement in the external reality; and the choices we make and actions we take affect the larger energy field within which we interact. Knowledge grows with use and increases when shared. Thus, through our actions we participate in the expansion of the field, which in turn requires new ways of thinking—new knowledge—for us to be effective. The concept of intelligent activity was introduced in Assumption 3 of the Foreward and is brought in throughout this book where appropriate. The social construction of knowledge is treated in depth in Chapter 8.

As introduced in Assumption 1, since knowledge is neither true nor false, its value is difficult to measure other than by the results of its actions. Hence, good knowledge would have a high probability (P=.9) of producing the desired (anticipated) outcome, and relatively poor knowledge would have a low probability (P=.1) of producing the expected result. It should also be understood that desired outcomes cannot usually be described with high precision. Rather, there is likely to be a cone of acceptable outcomes that have different measures of goodness (see Figure 1-1).

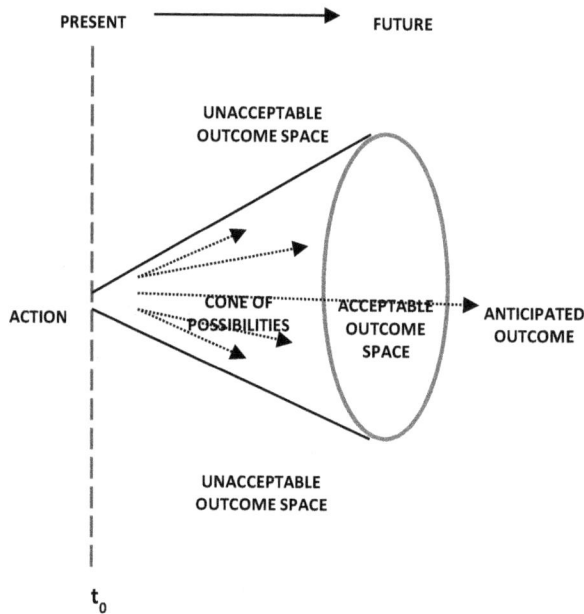

Figure 1-1. *Cone of acceptable outcomes with varying levels of goodness.*

Of course, any attempt to measure the value of *specific* knowledge can be difficult since it becomes entangled with the situation and with the knowledge and actions of all those involved in the situation.

Knowledge (Informing) and Knowledge (Proceeding)

For purposes of clarification, we consider knowledge as comprised of two parts: Knowledge (Informing) and Knowledge (Proceeding) (Bennet & Bennet, 2008b). This builds on the distinction made by Ryle (1949) between "knowing that" and "knowing how" (the *potential* and *actual* capacity to take effective action).

Knowledge (Informing) is the *information (or content)* part of knowledge. While this information part of knowledge is still generically information (organized patterns), it is special because of its structure and relationships with other information. Knowledge (Informing) consists of information that may represent understanding, meaning, insights, expectations, intuition, theories and principles that support or lead to effective action. When viewed separately this is information even though it *may* lead to effective action. It is considered knowledge when used as *part of the knowledge process*. In this context, the same thought may be information in one situation and knowledge in another situation.

Knowledge (Proceeding), represents the *process* and *action* part of knowledge. It is the process of selecting and associating or applying the relevant information, or Knowledge (Informing), from which specific actions can be identified and implemented, that is, actions that result in some level of anticipated outcome. There is considerable precedent for considering knowledge as a process versus an outcome of some action. For example, Kolb (1984) forwards in his theory of experiential learning that knowledge retrieval, creation and application requires engaging knowledge as a process, *not* a product. Bohm reminds us that "the actuality of knowledge is a living process that is taking place right now" and that we are taking part in this process (Bohm, 1980, p. 64). Note that the process our minds use to find, create and semantically mix the information needed to take effective action (i.e., knowledge) is often unconscious and difficult to communicate to someone else; therefore, by definition, tacit.

In Figure 1-2 below, "Justified True Belief" represents the theories, values and beliefs that are generally developed over time and often tacit. "Justified True Belief" is the definition of knowledge credited to Plato and his dialogues (Fine, 2003). The concept is based on the belief that in order to know a given proposition is true you must not only believe it, but must also have justification for believing it. Wilber (1983) says that all valid knowledge—no matter its domain—is essentially similar in structure and has three basic components: injunction, illumination and confirmation. These basic strands of knowledge are:

1. *An instrumental or injunctive strand.* This is a set of instructions simple or complex, internal or external. All have the form: 'If you want to know this, do this.'

2. *An illuminative or apprehensive strand.* This is an illuminative seeing by the particular eye of knowledge evoked by the injunctive strand. Besides being self-illuminative, it leads to the possibility of:

3. *A communal strand.* This is the actual sharing of the illuminative seeing with others who are using the same eye. If the shared vision is agreed upon by others,

this constitutes a communal or consensual proof of *true seeing*. (Wilber, 1983, pp.31-32)

Number 1 looks through the eye of the flesh; number 2 looks through the eye of the mind (the truth can be seen); and number 3 is sharing this proof with others.

Let's explore this process of knowledge. As indicated above, the instrumental or injunctive strand takes the form: "If you want to know this, do this." A simple example would be directions, "If you want to drive to the outlet store, go straight for two blocks and turn right on Jefferson Lane, and the store will be at the end of the block on the left." If the directions are provided in a language that is understandable, then the truth of the directions can be seen. The final strand would be sharing these directions with other to establish communal proof.

While Wilber builds these basic strands of knowledge on Plato's definition of knowledge—justified true belief—these basic strands also work with our definition of knowledge as the capacity (potential or actual) to take effective action. Step 1 is the expression of information in context, step 2 is the proof from the viewpoint of the individual mind in terms of effectiveness, and step 3 is the proof from viewpoint of the communal in terms of effectiveness when shared. Note that step 3 follows the scientific approach requiring repeatability and external validation.

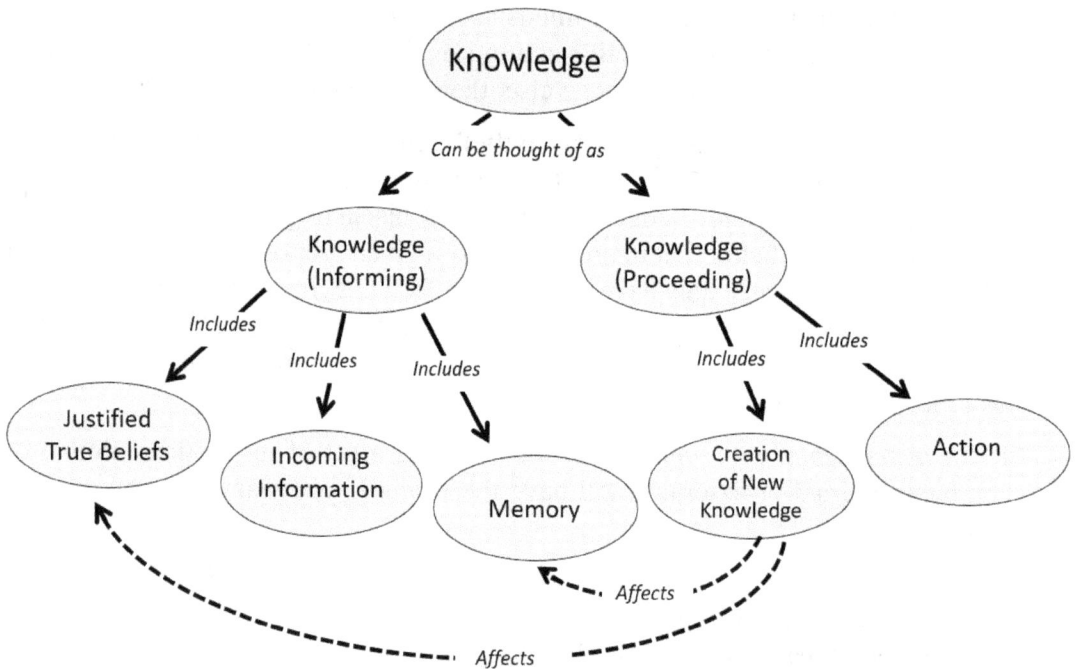

Figure 1-2: *Knowledge (Informing) and Knowledge (Proceeding)*

Note that justified true belief represents an *individual's* truth, that is, whether judging my personal experience or judging the experience of others, the beliefs and values that make up our personal theories, all developed and reinforced by personal life experiences, impact that judgment. Therefore, it is acknowledged that an individual's justified true belief may be based on a falsehood (Gettier, 1963). However, if it is used to take effective action in terms of the user's expectations of outcomes, then *it would be considered knowledge from that individual's viewpoint.* Note that this is only one part of Knowledge (Informing), and that our beliefs and theories are part of the living process described above (Bohm, 1980; Bennet & Bennet, 2008e; 2014). The term "memory" is used as a singular collective and implies all the patterns and connections accessible by the mind occurring before the instant at hand.

As a foundational concept, Knowledge (Informing) and Knowledge (Proceeding) will be used throughout this book as a tool for understanding ever-expanding concepts of knowledge about knowledge.

Chapter 2
Levels of Knowledge[1]

Acknowledging that any framework or model is an artificial construct, we nonetheless propose that it is helpful to consider knowledge in terms of three levels: surface knowledge, shallow knowledge and deep knowledge. The analogy built upon here is that of exploring the ocean. A pontoon or light sail boat catching the wind skims rapidly across the waters without concern for that which lies below in the water; as long as whatever lies below does not come to or affect the surface, it is of little concern to forward movement. For any boat moving in shallow waters, more attention (and some understanding) is required of what is beneath the surface, dependent on the ballast, to ensure forward movement. In deep waters—engaged over longer periods of time—safety and success require a proven vessel, an experienced captain, a thorough understanding of oceanography, a well-honed navigation system sensitive to current flows and dangers of the ocean, and a well-developed intuition sensitive to deep water terrain, currents and so forth. Carrying the metaphor a bit further, whether surfing or moving through shallow or deep waters, a certain amount of skill is involved, although different levels also require somewhat *different* skill sets. The metaphor deals with the level of involvement with what is below the surface. Further, as a ship moves into deep waters there is increased reliance on experience and intuition as unforeseen perturbations move into the situation.

Surface knowledge is predominantly, but not exclusively, information. Answering the question of what, when, where and who, it is primarily explicit, and represents visible choices that require minimum understanding. Further, little action is typically required; it is more of an awareness of *what is* on the part of the receiver.

Surface knowledge in the form of information can be stored in books and computers, and the mind/brain. Much of our everyday life such as light conversations,

> Surface knowledge in the form of information can be stored in books and computers, and the mind/brain.

descriptions and even self-reflection could be considered surface thinking and learning that creates surface knowledge. Perhaps too much of what is taught in schools is focused on awareness and memorization (surface knowledge) with inadequate focus on understanding or meaning. For example, the National Research Council has expressed concern that the U.S. education system teaches students science using a mile wide and inch deep approach (National Research Council, 2000; Oakes & Lipton, 1999). The emphasis is on surface learning, that is, learning that "relies primarily on short term memorization—cramming facts, data, concepts and information to pass quizzes and exams…deep learning asks that we create and re-create our own personal understanding" (Chickering, et al., 2005, pp. 132-133). Chickering and his colleagues discovered that in Scotland, Canada and Australia 90 percent of student learning was surface learning, and felt this figure was similar to that in the United States. This suggests that many future adults may not be prepared to address problems that require deep learning. Further, surface knowledge is frequently difficult to remember and easy to forget because it has little meaning to improve recall, and few connections to other stored memories (Sousa, 2006).

Shallow knowledge is when you have information plus some understanding, meaning and sense-making. *To understand is to make some level of meaning, with meaning typically relating to an individual or organization and implying some level of action. To make meaning requires context.* For example, the statement "John's car hit a telephone pole" is descriptive. If you don't know John, it has minimal meaning (surface knowledge). On the other hand, if John was driving your car it has a deeper meaning to you. That meaning is added by you because the context of that statement has specific significance for you. Meaning is something the individual creates from the received information and their own internal information, a process of creating Knowledge (Proceeding).

Thus, shallow knowledge requires a level of understanding and meaning such that the knowledge maker can identify cohesion and integration of the information in a manner that makes sense. This meaning can be created via logic, analysis, observation, reflection, and even—to some extent—prediction. Using our example, if you know it's your car, you can predict you are going to have to fill out forms, get the car repaired, etc. You make sense of what happened in the situation via integrating it, making it cohesive or self-consistent, and creating the knowledge that gives you meaning and understanding in the sense-making process and lets you know the actions you will have to take.

In an organizational setting shallow knowledge emerges (and expands) through interactions as employees move through the processes and practices of the organization. For example, organizations that embrace the use of teams and communities facilitate the mobilization of knowledge and the creation of new ideas as individuals interact in those groups. This again helps them create and implement the actions they will have to take.

For **deep knowledge** you have to develop understanding and meaning, integrate it, and be able to shift your frame of reference as the context and situation shift. Since Knowledge (Proceeding) must be created in order to know when and how to take effective action, the unconscious plays a large role in this area. The source of deep Knowledge (Proceeding) lies in your creativity, intuition, forecasting experience, pattern recognition, and use of theories (also important in shallow situations). This is the realm of the expert. The expert's unconscious has learned to detect patterns and evaluate their importance in anticipating the behavior of situations that are too complex for the conscious mind to understand. During the lengthy period of practice needed to develop deep knowledge, the expert has often developed an internal theory that guides her Knowledge (Proceeding).

The development of deep knowledge is not an easy task. It takes an intense and persistent interest and dedication to a specific area of learning, knowledge and action.

> The development of deep knowledge takes an intense and persistent interest and dedication to a specific area of learning, knowledge and action.

An individual must "live" with their field of expertise and at the same time—in a process of continuous learning—focus on the details and contexts of every specific experience, asking questions and analyzing what went right, what went wrong and why, leads to uncovering relationships and patterns that over time become the unconscious bedrock of expertise, that is, deep knowledge. Gathering relevant information and combining it in chunks builds up a wide range of patterns to draw from when encountering a new or unusual situation. Gathered through what is called *effortful practice*, much of this knowledge resides within the unconscious and surfaces only when the individual takes an action or makes a decision based on "feel" or "intuition." Nevertheless, deep knowledge usually provides the best solution to a complex problem.

Each learning experience builds on its predecessor by broadening the sources of knowledge creation and the capacity to create knowledge in different ways. When an individual has deep knowledge, more and more of their learning will continuously build up in the unconscious. In other words, in the area of focus, knowledge begets knowledge. The more that is understood, the more that can be created and understood.

Levels of Learning

Two of the modes in Kolb's experiential learning cycle are referred to as internal reflection and comprehension (Kolb, 1984). Internal reflection is where understanding and meaning are created and includes some intuition based upon past experience of logic, analysis and causality. Comprehension includes creativity, insights, forecasting future results based upon specific actions, problem-solving, intuition, and logical analysis.

When you have internal reflection—when you look for understanding, meaning and sense-making—you look from a particular frame of reference. Underlying each frame of reference are specific, often unconscious assumptions and presuppositions that may need to be surfaced and evaluated from a critical thinking perspective. At the shallow knowledge level, you might need to consciously shift reference frames. Shifting reference frames occurs most often at the shallow level of knowledge, where the individual stands back and says "maybe I'm using the wrong logic or analysis approach," and "I need to look at this situation from a different perspective." At the deep level this shifting would likely be automatic and occur without conscious awareness.

The value of shifting your frame of reference can be demonstrated by the monk on the mountain problem. One morning a monk decides to go for a walk up a mountain. He starts at 8 AM at the beginning of the path. He walks up the mountain at various speeds (always following the path), stops and has lunch, continues up the mountain and reaches the end of the path at the top of the mountain at 4 PM. He decides he's too tired to walk back down the mountain that evening, so he camps out at the top of the mountain. The next morning at exactly 8 AM he starts walking down the path, continues walking at various speeds, stops and has lunch, continues on down the mountain and arrives at his original starting point at exactly 4 PM on the second day. The problem is to provide a convincing explanation that there is *some point* on the monk's path that he will *cross at exactly the same time on each day*. Note that you do not have to know or state where that point is located on the path. This problem is quite difficult from the story's common frame of reference, that is, thinking of a single monk walking up and down the mountain on two different days. However, there is another frame of reference which might make the solution clearer.[2]

Interestingly enough, in shallow knowledge there is some forecasting, problem-solving, logic and all of those other aspects found in the comprehension phase of Kolb's experiential learning model. Note that although all four modes (experience, internal reflection, comprehension and action) are experienced at every level, it is the amount of each mode that varies among the surface, shallow and deep levels. Internal reflection is predominantly conscious. The comprehension part of deep knowledge is predominantly unconscious (tacit knowledge). We can take each of these two modes and look at what is surface, shallow and deep to get a perspective on the content. Figure 2 includes brief descriptors of experience, learning (internal reflection and comprehension), knowledge and action.

LEVEL	SYSTEMS	EXPERIENCE	LEARNING	KNOWLEDGE	ACTIONS
SURFACE	SIMPLE SYSTEMS	Immediate Awareness Sense-making	Awareness Memorizing Understanding	Kn(Informing) Information Conscious	Remembering Communicating Acting
+	+	+	+	+	+
SHALLOW	COMPLICATED SYSTEMS	Feeling Relational Intuitive	Causality Coherence Meaning-making	Kn(Proceeding) Conscious Causality	Explaining Anticipating Problem-solving
+	+	+	+	+	+
DEEP	COMPLEX SYSTEMS	Attuned Embodied Spiritual	Effortful practice Insights Intuition Lived experience	Kn(Proceeding) Mostly unconscious Pattern detection	Creating Intuiting Predicting

Figure 2-1. *Brief descriptors of systems, experience, learning (internal reflection and comprehension), knowledge and action in terms of surface, shallow and deep.*

Complexity of Situations

Recall that knowledge is defined as the ability (potential or actual) to take effective action. Clearly, the effectiveness of action is highly dependent on the specific situation in which specific knowledge is applied. Thus, we now apply our analogy to decision-making and action after first building an understanding of the levels of the complexity of a situation.

Something catches your attention. It could be something not quite right, a problem, or perhaps an opportunity requiring some decision and action. In order to understand the level of knowledge needed for decision-making and action, the first question to ask is what is the level of the situation: Is it a simple situation? Is it complicated? Or is it complex, or some combination?

A simple situation is one that has knowable and predictable patterns of behavior. There are few elements involved in a situation and simple relationships exist among those elements. Easily fixed mistakes would fall into this category. If it's simple, and the solution is not apparent, that is, the information needed to solve the problem does not work, then either the wrong information is available and being used or perhaps the frame of reference needs to be shifted.

While a complicated situation also has knowable and predictable patterns of behavior, the number of interrelated parts and connections among the parts is so large that there may be some difficulty in identifying cause and effect relationships. A complicated situation requires information and

> In complicated situations, the number of related parts and connections among the parts is so large that there may be some difficulty in identifying cause and effect relationships.

shallow knowledge, implying that causality can be identified and understood. Good knowledge of the specific domain of causality related to the situation is needed. Then, by logical analysis, systematic investigation, and deductive processes the situation at hand can be corrected as desired. An example of a complicated system would be a television set.

Again, however, the frame of reference and set of assumptions underlying the approach to a solution may significantly impact success. When a solution cannot be found to a complicated situation, it usually means that either insufficient or wrong information or inadequate knowledge is being used. Multiple perspectives may need to be considered as well as a review of implicit and explicit assumptions and presuppositions. Here also is where multiple individuals working collaboratively may find solutions more effectively and efficiently than a single individual. This is the concept upon which collaborative advantage is built. Given adequate information, complicated problems should be solvable, although deep knowledge may be required to do so. This is not the case for complex problems.

In a complex situation the patterns of behavior are difficult (and sometimes impossible) to understand and predict. The large number of interrelated parts have nonlinear relationships, time delays, and feedback loops; thus, while the situation has some degree of order, it has too many elements and relationships to understand in simple analytic or logical ways (Bennet & Bennet, 2004). In the extreme, the landscape of a complex situation is one with multiple and diverse connections with dynamic and interdependent relationships, events and processes. As Axelrod states, "The hard reality is that the world in which we must act is beyond our understanding" (Axelrod & Cohen, 1999, p. xvii).

A quality of complex situations is the emergence of behaviors, patterns or conditions as a product of the interactions and relationships among the various aspects of the situation and the environment in which the situation is occurring. Organizational examples of such emergence are trust, attitudes and culture. Emergence is discussed further below.

When a problem is highly complex, deep knowledge is needed to deal with the situation and its complexities, its history, and, where possible, its patterns. Such knowledge can only be created by lived experience and intense concentration of the unconscious to develop an appreciation for the patterns involved in the situation. This is needed to develop possible solutions and to anticipate future pattern directions that will support and produce the desired outcome.

> When a problem is highly complex, deep knowledge is needed to deal with the situation and its complexities, history and patterns.

An example of a complex problem is knowledge conservation, the issues involved with a large portion of the workforce reaching retirement age. What kind of knowledge needs to be considered? What level of knowledge is not available from other sources? When dealing with surface level problems information systems, common sense, guidance documents or a simple conversation with a colleague can typically resolve the issue. When considering shallow knowledge, you need to look at what kind of decisions, actions and situations the departing individual dealt with: Were decisions causally determined? What processes were used? What information was necessary? How did this individual go about making decisions? Logic, cause and effect, communication, mentoring, and coaching are all processes that work well for gathering surface knowledge. While the requisite knowledge may be implicit, it can usually be made explicit if you ask the right questions and know what to look for.

Deep knowledge is the most difficult knowledge to share. It takes two individuals who have similar backgrounds, developing a good relationship through mentoring or coaching, and asking the right questions. Sharing deep knowledge takes time, patience and dedicated effort. This means that such conversations need to be planned well before the retiring person leaves. Ron Dvir (2006) with the Futures Center in Tel-Aviv, Israel, uses the phrase *knowledge moments* to describe the intersection of people, places, processes and purpose. Knowledge moments can be facilitated and nurtured. For example, conversations, stories and dialogues occur informally as we move through meetings and lunch-time training experiences as well as through large socially-structured events such as knowledge fairs and town halls.

Complexity of Making Decisions

So how do surface, shallow and deep knowledge and learning help the decision-maker? Recognizing the level of the situation (simple, complicated, complex) allows one to anticipate the level of experience, learning and knowledge needed to take effective actions to solve the problem. It also guides the decision-maker to ask the right questions and to recognize which approaches are not likely to work and which frames of reference may yield the desired payoff.

When sharing or conserving knowledge that is going out the door, it is critical to ensure that both parties are communicating at the same knowledge level. Finding the right questions to ask can help the transfer process. What questions can best elicit the knowledge that is needed at each level? What kinds of tools are appropriate to conserve knowledge at each level?[3] How long does it take to develop each level of knowledge? How does the loss of each level of knowledge engaged by this individual affect the organization's mission? How many other individuals in the organization need this knowledge? *The language, meaning, comprehension, level of intuition, frame of reference and presuppositions regarding a specific area of knowledge all come into play and can enhance, inhibit, or sabotage any attempt to share knowledge via the medium of information.*

Ashby's law of requisite variety (Ashby, 1964) implies that any decision you make must allow more flexibility in implementation than the variability of the situation you are influencing. Thus, a simple situation with few elements and relationships would require a simple decision solution set whereas a complicated situation would usually require a larger solution set, and a complex situation an even larger one. A simple decision might answer the questions: What days do we get off this month? Is my paycheck accurate? The answers to these questions require surface knowledge, routine knowledge based on what, when, where and how. In exploring the hierarchy of product development decisions, Clausing (1994) indicates that most of these decisions are made on the basis of experience. That body of experience includes analyses, handbooks, computerized records and other depositories. Most of the decisions made in organizations are at this level (see Figure 3). As Clausing says, "In developing a complex product, there may be 10 million decisions; most of them are within the grasp of individuals equipped with these tools" (Clausing, 1994, p. 57). These decisions would be at the surface and shallow level, that is, require those levels of knowledge. However, the more critical decisions, approximately 25% of an organization's decisions, are at the shallow level (Bennet & Bennet, 2008a). Finally, there is that small group of strategic decisions (5%) that require even more attention. Most often these do not lie within the grasp of a single individual. For these decisions, Clausing feels that, "collective experience properly concentrated is sufficient. The right multifunctional team using a disciplined approach can make good decisions" (Clausing, 1994, p. 57). [NOTE: We would tend to say this a bit differently, that is, collective experience properly concentrated *may be* sufficient.]

In terms of the current discussion, this level of decisions would likely require deep knowledge regarding the design, engineering, and production of complicated products. It would also require an understanding of the language and basics of systems and complexity theory in order to predict how the people and organization will react to system changes. For example, systems and complexity thinking can support leader and stakeholder understanding of demand, competition, product interrelationships, cultural changes, and market shifts. This understanding can also provide ideas for influencing complex situations. Three examples are boundary management, sense and respond, and seeding.

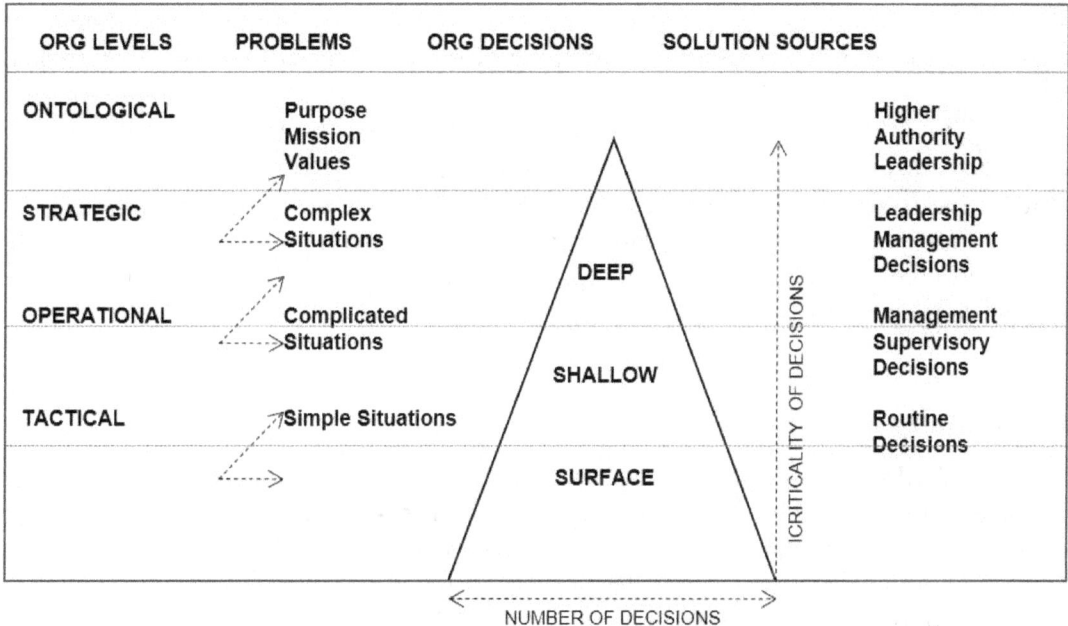

Figure 2-2. *Characterization of organizational knowledge needs. Routine decisions made in organizations are at the surface level. Decisions requiring deep knowledge are much fewer, and tend to be more critical.*

Complex system behavior is usually very sensitive to boundary conditions because that is where the energy comes from that keeps it alive and in disequilibrium. For example, if a vendor is providing medium quality products to a manufacturing plant, the buyer may change the boundary conditions (purchase price, delivery schedule, quantity, etc.) to press the vendor to improve quality, forcing the problem into the vendor's system. Changing the information, funding, people, material, or knowledge that goes into or out of a complex situation will impact its internal operation and behavior.

Sense and respond is another strategy to deal with complex situations. This is a testing approach where the situation is observed, then perturbed, and the response studied. This begins a learning process that helps the decision-maker understand the behavior of the situation. Using a variety of sensing and perturbations provides the opportunity to dig into the nature of the situation before taking strong action. This tactic is often used by new managers and senior executives who wait, watch and test the organization before starting any change management actions.

Seeding is a process of nurturing emergence. Since emergent properties arise from multiple nonlinear interactions among agents of the system (people), it is rarely possible to design a set of actions that will result in the exact solution desired. However, such actions may influence the system in a way that the desired emergent properties, outcomes, or something close to them, will emerge. *Emergence is not random.* It is the result of the interaction of a variety of elements and, if we cannot predetermine the exact emergent property such as a specific culture, we may be able to create a culture that is acceptable—or at least as good as—the one we desired. If we can find the right *set of actions* to move a problem in the right direction, we may be able to guide the situation toward the intended outcome. Such a journey is the decision strategy. (See Bennet & Bennet, 2013 for a depth treatment.)

> Since emergent properties arise from nonlinear interactions among agents of the system, it is rarely possible to design a set of actions that will result in the exact solution desired.

Complexity of Actions

Surface, shallow and deep can also be used to describe the complexity of actions. Surface actions would be common everyday actions such as opening a door, running, or turning on a light switch. Shallow actions would be where an individual deliberately sets about doing something that initially requires practice but becomes relatively easy as it is mastered over some period of time. Examples would be machining metal parts or driving a crowded four-lane highway during rush hour.

Deep action refers to actions based on deep knowledge and deep learning. A well-known example would be the transfer of tacit knowledge involved with bread-making (Nonaka & Takeuchi, 1995). A similar example would be that of an apprentice learning to build a violin. In both cases, not only would the individual have to work with a mentor long enough to embed the same actionable movements as the expert, but that individual would have to develop an understanding of how and why these movements were applied. Karl Weick's study of expert firefighters fighting fires is another example of what is suggested by deep action (Weick, 1995). See Chapters 4 and 5 for an extensive treatment of tacit knowledge.

An example of a complex problem would be to change an organization into a knowledge centric, adaptable, sustainable organization operating within a changing, uncertain, complex environment. This example is not an unusual challenge for large organizations struggling to survive in a global competitive environment. Deep knowledge is needed to understand and know how to deal with organizational culture, workers, managers and leaders. The environment (including the organization's customers) would need to be well understood. Patterns of change would need to be anticipated and integrated with new ideas, roles and structures to create the needed adaptability and sustainability. A deep sensitivity to the organizational history and management reactions to changes in their roles and responsibilities would need to be considered in order to construct an effective change management program. While this list goes on, it is clear that only a strong team of individuals with deep knowledge in a number of areas and a large network of trusted relationships could successfully move an organization toward knowledge centricity.

The Net Generation

Expansion of shallow knowledge is an area of strength for the younger generation of knowledge workers. This knowledge (as a potential or actual capacity) prepares knowledge workers for a changing and uncertain future by expanding areas of thought and conversation beyond a bounded functional and operational area of focus. Thus, new areas of interest are discovered, ideas expanded, and judgment and decisions made from a broader scale.

> Shallow knowledge prepares knowledge workers for a changing and uncertain future by expanding areas of thought and conversation beyond a bounded functional and operational area of focus.

A nominal representation of this shift from a primary focus on surface knowledge in 2000 to a primary focus on shallow knowledge in 2020 is represented in Figure 2-3. The representation on the left (Graph 1) is based on studies in education, organizations and complexity (Bennet & Bennet, 2010; Chickering et al., 2005; Clausing, 1994; National Research Council, 2000; Oakes & Lipton, 1999). The representation on the right (Graph 2) is speculative based on the anticipated social aspects of developing shallow knowledge. As knowledge workers communicate and learn via the Internet, they gain more shallow knowledge. As the environment continues to become more complex (and perhaps fragile), more people will develop the deep knowledge needed to make the right decisions and take effective action. Thus, there is also an increase in the amount of deep knowledge needed (and developed) to co-evolve with an increasingly CUCA [increasing change, uncertainly, complexity and the resulting anxiety] environment.

The implications of continuous social interactions (conversation and dialogues) across an expanded global network (capacity) are that, when needed, knowledge workers will have the ability to develop context and generate ideas around a specific issue at hand (capability). Further, swimming around and diving up and down in the global shallows—which are filled with diversity of views, perspectives, concepts and cultures—spurs on greater creativity and more significant innovation than surface swimming. Because of growing up globally connected, knowledge workers coming of age in the global world are mentally stimulated by interactions involving diverse views, perspectives, concepts and cultures and are not bounded by local ideas.

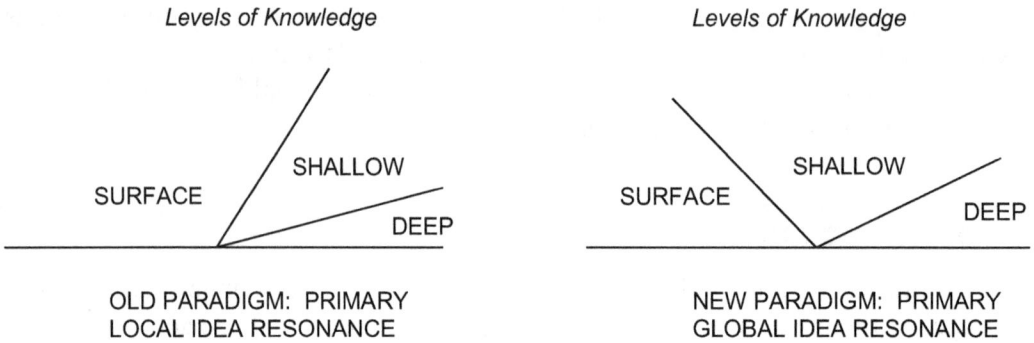

Levels of Knowledge

SHALLOW

SURFACE

DEEP

OLD PARADIGM: PRIMARY
LOCAL IDEA RESONANCE

Levels of Knowledge

SHALLOW

SURFACE

DEEP

NEW PARADIGM: PRIMARY
GLOBAL IDEA RESONANCE

Graph 1. A nominal graph illustrating the historic (2000) level of knowledge achieved by knowledge workers. Note that these levels are consistent with the level of decisions made in an organization (Bennet and Bennet, 2008c).

Graph 2. A nominal graph illustrating the future (2020) level of knowledge achieved by knowledge workers. The increase in shallow knowledge is a result of consistent expanded interactions via social media.

Figure 2-3. *Nominal shift in focus of levels of knowledge from 2000 to 2020.*

As introduced earlier, developing deep knowledge in a specific domain requires bounding an area of interest, and focusing on that domain over time to develop lived experience and expertise. In contrast, shallow knowledge requires context, whether that context applies to a specific domain, connects domains, or crosses domains. While one does not necessarily preclude the other, by definition deep knowledge requires a commitment of time and focus *around a specific domain* which will likely allow less time and focus for developing breadth of thought and following other interests.

Creativity and innovation thrive on different ideas and ways of looking at things and flourish from connecting different streams of thought. From cross domain stimulation of an open mind, new and often unsought patterns can emerge. A key here is "open mind", that is, a mind not "limited" (whether purposefully or otherwise) to a specific direction or bounded domain of knowledge. "Open mind" describes a knowledge worker co-evolving with the CUCA environment and searching out relationships between the mission/vision/purpose/values of their organizational alliance and the potential offered within their environmental opportunity space. They are seeking that window of opportunity in terms of space and time in a turbulent environment.

Simultaneously, because this new social way of being, thinking and acting taps into a huge diversity of experience, there is also an increased appreciation of difference, and with it comes tolerance. Immersion coupled with conversation and dialogue is quite the opposite of the Cold War isolation approach. As thoughts are exchanged and built upon there is a value statement that moves into the exchange. (See Chapter 10 for an in-depth treatment on knowledge and values.) The U.S. Department of the Navy (DON) identified this in their Knowledge Management change agent's strategy focused on the growth of knowledge and sharing. See Figure 11-1 in Chapter 11. While not supported by the social media of today, as a strategy this model encouraged interactions across large relationship networks and sharing and learning across organizational boundaries. When connectedness increases there is

> When connectedness increases, there is a heightened awareness of the potential value of knowledge, leading motivated individuals and organizations to advance new concepts even further, engendering the rise of social responsibility.

also heightened awareness or consciousness of the potential value to a larger audience, leading motivated individuals and organizations to advance these concepts even further, engendering the rise of social responsibility (Porter et al., 2002; Bennet & Bennet, 2004). This shift appears consistent with what is occurring in the Net Generation.

Final thoughts

We began this chapter surfing with ideas, and then slowly made connections that moved us into shallow waters. After defining knowledge as grounded in action, this chapter suggests areas and levels of knowledge that provide for a more detailed understanding and application of knowledge. The relationships between the complexity of situations, the complexity of making decisions and the complexity of actions were then related to the surface, shallow and deep levels of knowledge and of learning.

Some overarching patterns have emerged. At the surface level, the focus is on **Knowledge (Informing)**, that is, facts, data, concepts and other information that can be memorized and applied, and captured and stored in technology systems for processing and reference. At the shallow level, the focus is on **social interactions** through, for example, conversations, dialogues, debates, and the flow of ideas that emerges in communities and teams. At the deep level, the focus is on the learning from **effortful practice and lived experience** that creates **Knowledge (Proceeding)**. The overarching theme at the organizational level would be **organizational learning**. This three-level model provides a common taxonomy that couples nicely with the strategic, operational and tactical levels in organizations. At the same time, the process relationships between experience, learning, knowledge and action highlights the influence each factor has on the other. Further, the breakdown of systems into the classic three areas of simple, complicated and complex appears to carry over into the three corresponding levels (surface, shallow and deep) as applied to learning and knowledge.

What does all this mean?

For most of the history of the human species, knowledge has been considered as justified true belief. This resulted in numerous interpretations with little basis for agreement. Grounding knowledge in action permits a measure of knowledge by measuring the degree of effectiveness of the results or measuring the probability of achieving the effectiveness of results in a given application. Analyzing characteristics such as Knowledge (Informing) and Knowledge (Proceeding), and identifying differences in levels and content of knowledge, offers the opportunity for a fine-grained analysis. This analysis can be used to ask relevant questions about specific levels of knowledge. It also enables managers to recognize the scope and depth of knowledge available to maximize problem solving, decision-making and action in simple, complicated and complex situations. Further, it permits knowledge developers to tailor learning and knowledge to improve knowledge sharing and conservation. While additional research may uncover a finer grained analysis of knowledge which allows even more specificity (or optimization), this may be the first step toward that end.

Chapter 3
Types of Knowledge in Terms of Roles[1]

In any specific application there may be several areas of knowledge that need to be considered in order to take action. These areas or types of knowledge can be grouped or organized according to similarities and differences, what could be called a knowledge taxonomy. As a framework for recognizing and working with knowledge, the following taxonomy offers a useful grouping for understanding different types of knowledge from the viewpoint of what knowledge is needed to do a particular type of work or take a particular action.

The categories in this taxonomy include: Kmeta, Kresearch, Kpraxis, Kaction, Kdescription, Kstrategic and Klearning (see Figure 3-1). Taken together, these types of knowledge play different roles in understanding situations and taking actions. Each of these types is discussed separately below.

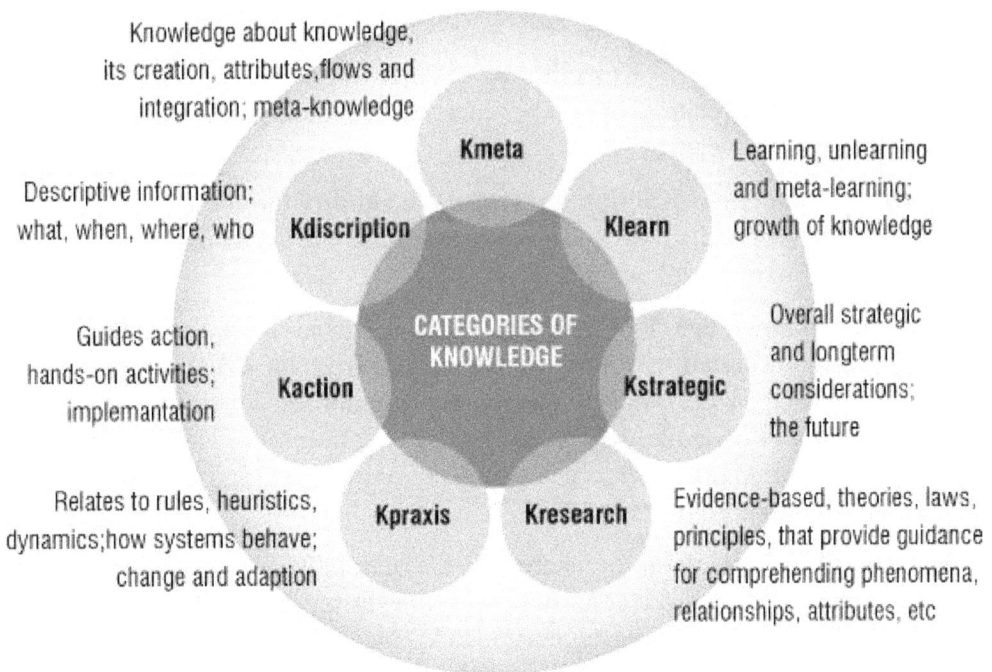

Figure 3-1. *A knowledge taxonomy for grouping types of knowledge from the viewpoint of what knowledge is needed to do a particular type of work or take a particular action (Bennet & Bennet, 2007).*

Meta-knowledge, **Kmeta**, represents the capacity to understand, create, assimilate, leverage, sculpt and apply various types of information and knowledge. Since most complex situations contain several disciplines and categories of knowledge, our use of Kmeta (knowledge about knowledge) also includes the ability to bring different types of knowledges together. William Whewell, in his 1840 synthesis, *The Philosophy of the Inductive Sciences*, spoke of consilience as "…a 'jumping together' of knowledge by the linking of facts and fact-based theory across disciplines to create a common groundwork of explanation" (Wilson, 1998, p. 8). E. O. Wilson also uses consilience to mean, "The explanations of different phenomena most likely to survive … those that can be connected and proved consistent with one another." (Wilson, 1998, p. 53) In making sense of complex situations, the consilience of different frames of references and knowledge categories may provide the best understanding for developing a solution.

> In making sense of complex situations, the consilience of different frames of references and knowledge categories may provide the best understanding for developing a solution.

Evidence based knowledge, **Kresearch**, includes theoretical as well as empirical knowledge and represents the fundamental concepts that explain *why* things happen. Such knowledge serves as a guide for setting expectations and possibilities and provides the user a level of confidence.

Pragmatic knowledge, **Kpraxis**, represents the practical understanding of situations and *how* they change or *can* be changed. Much pragmatic knowledge is tacit, experiential and intuitive.

Knowledge in action, **Kaction**, represents the ability to take specific actions that achieve the desired result. It includes understanding the *local* context and situation within which the action is taken.

Descriptive knowledge, **Kdescription**, is information that informs the *what, who, when* and *where* of a situation. As can be understood from the discussion of knowledge offered by Stonier (1992), all knowledge is composed of information, but all information is *not* knowledge. Knowledge is information that, when combined in the mind (associated or *complexed)*, creates understanding, meaning and, where action is involved, the anticipation of its outcome.

The role of **Kstrategic** is to ensure that the actions taken are in consideration of their long-term impact and are consistent with the strategy, identity, and values of the organization. While this is a high-level type of knowledge (and thinking), note that this refers to the information, processes and patterns used to apply other information, processes and patterns in a strategic way. This means that many different types of knowledge can be used strategically.

The role of **Klearning** includes individual, group and organizational learning. This focus is to ensure that as a situation or process unfolds, individuals learn from each other and, when appropriate, build organizational learning into a task outcome to ensure that the organization is capable of adapting to future changes in the environment.

The above seven categories can be considered as a useful spectrum of knowledge areas, sometimes overlapping and often having gaps between them. They are selected for their usefulness in the problem solving, decision-making, execution and feedback learning processes, particularly when dealing with complex situations. An individual or members of a team or organization may have expertise in one, several, or none of these categories and the knowledge needed will depend on the content, context and desired outcome of the situation/problem. The more complex the situation, the more categories of knowledge may be needed for the individual or team to be successful.

> The more complex the situation, the more categories of knowledge may be needed for the individual or team to be successful.

In the discussion of Kstrategic above, it was noted that this type of knowledge refers to the information, processes and patterns used to apply other information, processes and patterns in a strategic way. In other words, many different types of knowledge can be used strategically. The concepts of tactical, operational and strategic information and knowledge are often used in organizations. These three concepts can be correlated to the levels of knowledge (surface, shallow, and deep). For example, strategic knowledge would emphasize deep knowledge because of the complexity of forecasting the future environment and creating a strategy to ensure organizational sustainability into the future. A successful strategy would require creative ideas and practices with flexibility built into implementation. Operational management would require primarily surface knowledge during normal operations when the environment was stable. However, when disruptions occurred in the environment or within the organization, managers and leaders with deep knowledge in the areas where the disruptions impacted the organization and its future would be called upon. Tactical implementation, under stable conditions, would require mostly surface knowledge, with shallow knowledge available for equipment failures, or changes in technology or core processes. All of the above descriptions are simplifications of reality and are provided to highlight the differences and range of needs of the levels of knowledge in a typical organization.

Knowledge Mobilization

Knowledge Mobilization (KMb) is an action journey within an identified action space, combining theoretical knowledge (Kresearch) with praxis (Kpraxis) through the collaboration of multiple stakeholders having a common goal. Within that space, KMb is a process of creating value or a value stream through the creation, assimilation, leveraging, sharing and application of knowledge (Kaction).

The government of Canada embraced KMb through its Knowledge Impact on Society program which was designed to move knowledge from the researcher to the citizens, with KMb complementing—and becoming as important as—the research itself. Observing the KMb process from a bird's eye view (see Figure 3-2), we can identify three major forces for success, with each of these forces representing individuals or teams and the knowledge they possess. Recognizing that in reality there is no beginning and no end, we begin our discussion with the researchers who have deep knowledge of the research findings (Kresearch) and are usually found in universities or research institutions. These are the people who generate and tailor theories.

The second significant force in the KMb process is the practitioner, who typically has strong knowledge of change management and how to get things done. This

> The three major forces in the Knowledge Mobilization process are researchers, practitioners and the individuals or teams throughout the community at the point of action.

pragmatic "how to" knowledge is primarily shallow in nature, that is, it requires the context gained through interactions (dialogue, mimicry, questions and answers, shared language, etc.) to successfully mobilize. The third major force is those individuals or teams throughout the community at the point of action where local actions are taken to change behavior and create opportunities. Community leaders possess experiential knowledge and a strong understanding of their local culture, its beliefs and values. This knowledge in action is primarily surface in nature.

In Figure 3-2, the three outer ovals represent the three primary forces involved in the KMb process (researchers, practitioners and community members). The other three ovals represent their corresponding knowledge brought to the KMb process. The traditional flow of the process is from the researcher to the practitioner to the community member. This flow of knowledge is from the theory of the researcher to the pragmatic knowledge of the practitioner to knowledge-in-action of the community member. While this flow is essential to KMb, so, too, is the simultaneous flow of knowledge from community member to practitioner to researcher as well as direct flows among researchers and community members where it makes sense. The challenge is to facilitate: (1) this flow of knowledge, (2) the transformation of knowledge from theory to action and back, and (3) the interactions necessary among the three groups to nurture that flow. As can be seen, it is critical to understand the differences between the types of knowledge necessary at each part of the process in order to mobilize the knowledge that is needed and "take effective action".

Let's look at a hypothetical example. Researchers discover a simple process involving natural food combinations and positive attitudes that can eliminate cancer. Alternative medicine practitioners and nutritionists are a part of the trials and, along with advocacy groups, strive to mobilize this information across their communities (patients, schools, community groups, etc.). Deep knowledge (Kresearch) has been translated into shallow knowledge (Kpragmatic) which in turn is translated into surface knowledge (Kaction). The end of cancer.

Staying with the KMb approach, the eight steps in the generic model start with a situation that has been matched to research findings (Figure 3-3.) These steps are:

1. Situation (problem, issue, opportunity) identified. (Kdescriptive)
2. Information gathered about/from the situation and its context. (Kdescriptive)

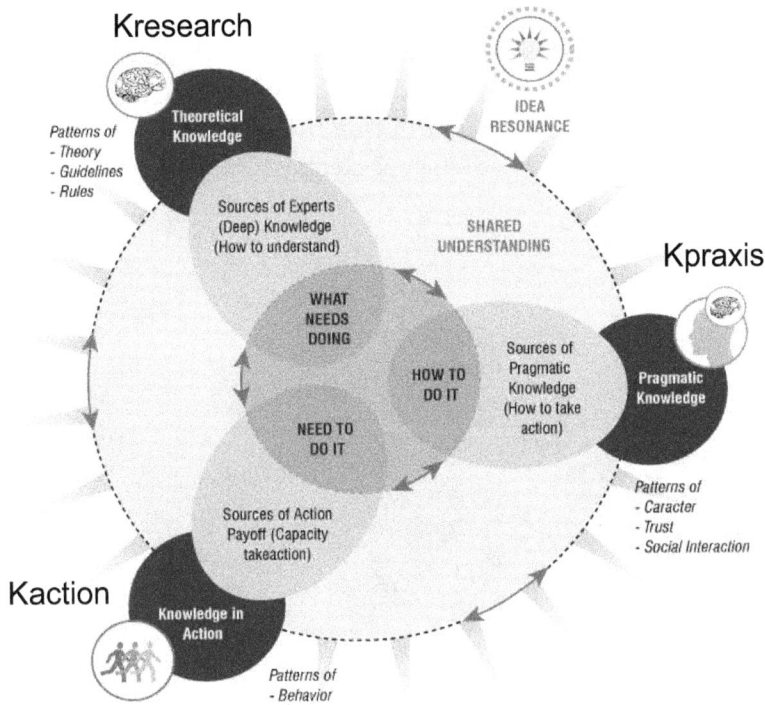

Figure 3-2. *The KMb process and knowledge flows.*

3. Understanding generated from the information, experience and other multiple related sources. (Kmeta)

4. Theoretical knowledge considered in the context of the situation. (Kresearch)

5. Pragmatic knowledge from practical experience, similar situations, and systems understanding of the target community integrated with (1) through (4) above. (Kpraxis)

6. Action or a set of actions taken. (Kaction)

7. New situation emerges from these actions. (Kdescriptive)

8. Feedback provides the opportunity to assess the effectiveness of actions toward achieving the desired goal and the opportunity to change or supplement those actions as needed. (Klearning)

As shown in the figure, these eight steps move through the focus areas of problem identification to problem understanding to problem solving to decision-making, implementation and action learning. A primary type of knowledge is connected to each step of the model. Note that while this model has been couched in terms of an identified "problem", this process would also apply to an identified opportunity. Throughout this process research findings are being explored in the context of the situation, other theoretical knowledge and the pragmatic knowledge of community stakeholders.

This brief treatment of KMb—a much larger approach than can be presented here—is intended to provide an example of the types of knowledge that need to be translated and mobilized in order to achieve a desired outcome. For an in-depth treatment of KMb see *Knowledge Mobilization in the Social Sciences and Humanities: Moving from Research to Action* (Bennet & Bennet, 2007).

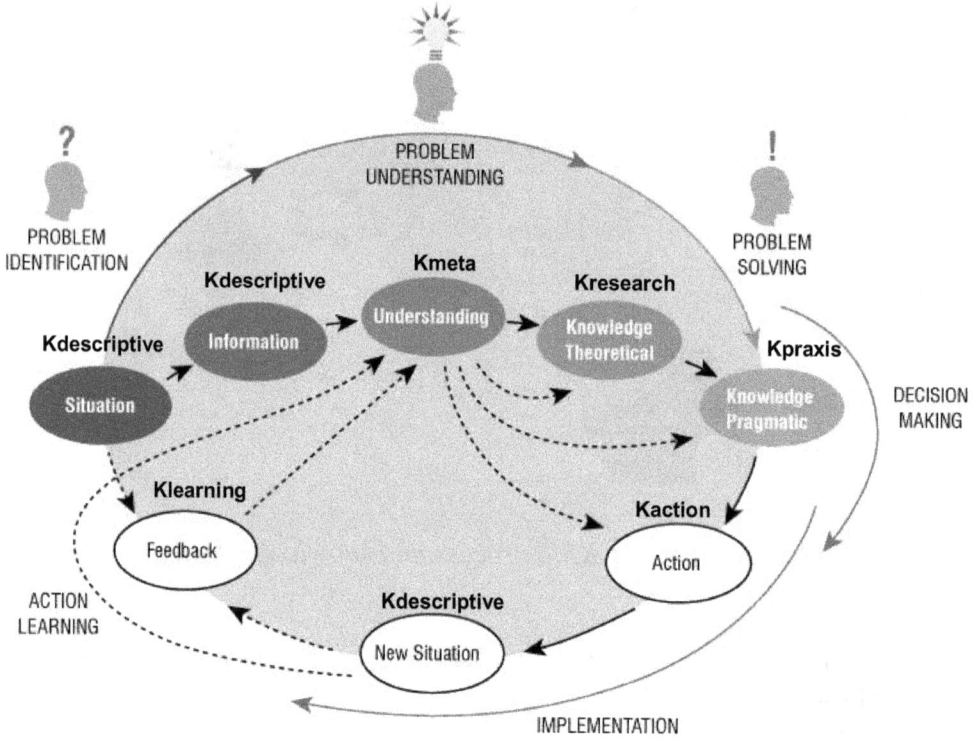

Figure 3-3. *The eight steps of the generic KMb process.*

In summary, this chapter provides a framework for recognizing and working with types of knowledge and the roles they play in facilitating a particular type of work, taking a particular action, and achieving a desired outcome. One or more areas can be used depending on the content, context and desired outcome of the situation/problem. For example, KMb combines theoretical knowledge (Kresearch) with the "how to" knowledge of practitioners (Kpraxis) with experiential knowledge at the point of action (Kaction) to create a value process and achieve the common goal of multiple stakeholders. Further, it is possible for a decision-maker or an organization—or a country—to become so focused on a specific type of knowledge that they devalue other types of knowledge. Intelligent action demands a balance, that is, an understanding of all the knowledges at play in a specific situation coupled with a perfect state of interaction where intent, purpose, direction, values and expected outcomes are clearly communicated and understood among all parties, reflecting wisdom and achieving a higher truth.

Section II
The Voiced and Unvoiced

As thoughts grow into thought forms (the process of creativity and innovation) and knowledge drives actions, much of that thought and knowledge is occurring in our unconscious, that is, it is not in our awareness. The terms explicit, implicit and tacit (see Chapter 4) are useful in clarifying and understanding the ability to express knowledge. Much like our levels of knowledge and consistent with Polanyi's work, these terms describe aspects of a fluctuating continuum (*a range*) rather than a rigid classification schema. We choose to use these terms in support of this fluctuating continuum.

Residing in the unconscious and by definition not able to be voiced, tacit knowledge is of specific interest. We may or may not have conscious awareness of this knowledge; hence the now-famous dictum "We don't know what we know." As we explore how to engage tacit knowledge, we **introduce the concept of extraordinary consciousness**, a heightened sensitivity to, awareness of, and connection with our unconscious mind, together with its memory and thought processes.

Recognizing that all knowledge is context sensitive and situation dependent, and the important role of knowledge sharing in our knowledge journey toward intelligent activity, we explore the power of context. Given that context supports a specific meaning, the more relevant clues added to the content, the higher the resonance of shared understanding. In exploring eight avenues of context we adopt McLuhan's intent, that is, "... not to offer a theory of communication but *to probe the effects of anything and everything we use in dealing with the world around us*, including language" (Gordon, 1997, p. 328). In this new century where we are beginning to understand the power of the mind/brain and the unconscious, we expand that intent to read *to probe the effects of anything and everything we use in dealing with the world around us, **and with the world within us**.*

> Given that context supports a specific meaning, the more relevant clues added to the content, the higher the resonance of shared understanding.

This section includes Explicit, Implicit and Tacit Dimensions (Chapter 4); Engaging Tacit Knowledge (Chapter 5); and Living through Context (Chapter 6).

Chapter 4
Explicit, Implicit and Tacit Dimensions[1]

In order to focus on tacit knowledge let's develop a common understanding of what it is and what it isn't. By the latter part of the 20th century the push to understand knowledge and its value to organizations had spread across a number of disciplines with the result that concepts of explicit, implicit and tacit knowledge began to emerge in both the academic organizational literature and the popular press. Our interpretation of each of these concepts is described briefly below.

Explicit knowledge is the process of calling up information (patterns) and processes (patterns in time) from memory that can be described accurately in words and/or visuals (representations) such that another person can comprehend the knowledge that is expressed through this exchange of information. This has historically been called declarative knowledge (Anderson, 1983). Emotions can be expressed as explicit knowledge in terms of changes in body state. As Damasio notes, "Many of the changes in body state—those in skin color, body posture, and facial expression, for instance—are actually perceptible to an external observer" (Damasio, 1994, p. 139). Often these changes to the body state represent part of an explicit knowledge exchange (Bennet and Bennet, 2007a). Examples would be turning red with embarrassment or blushing in response to an insensitive remark.

Implicit knowledge is a more complicated concept, and a term not unanimously agreed-upon in the literature. This is understandable since even simple dictionary definitions—which are generally unbiased and powerful indicators of collective preference and understanding—show a considerable overlap between the terms "implicit" and "tacit," making it difficult to differentiate the two. We propose that a useful interpretation of *implicit knowledge* is knowledge stored in memory of which the individual is *not immediately aware*. While this information is *not readily accessible*, it may be pulled up when triggered (associated). Triggering might occur through questions, dialogue or reflective thought, or happen as a result of an external event. In other words, implicit knowledge is knowledge that the individual *does not know* they have, but is self-discoverable! However, once this knowledge is surfaced, the individual *may or may not* have the ability to adequately describe it such that another individual could create the same knowledge; and the "why and how" may remain tacit knowledge.

A number of published psychologists have used the term implicit interchangeably with our usage of tacit, that is, with implicit representing knowledge that once acquired can be shown to effect behavior but is not available for conscious retrieval (Reber, 1993; Kirsner et al., 1998). As described in the above discussion of implicit knowledge, what is forwarded here is that the concept of implicit knowledge serves a middle ground between that which can be made explicit and that which cannot easily (if at all) be made explicit. By moving beyond the dualistic approach of explicit and tacit—that which can be declared versus that which can't be declared, and that which can be remembered versus that which can't be remembered—*we posit implicit as representing the knowledge spectrum between explicit and tacit*. While explicit refers to easily available, some knowledge requires a higher stimulus for association to occur yet is not buried so deeply as to prevent access. This understanding is the domain of implicit knowledge.

Calling them interactive components of cooperative processes, Reber agrees that there is no clear boundary between that which is explicit and that which is implicit (our tacit): "There is ... no reason for presuming that there exists a clean boundary between conscious and unconscious processes or a sharp division between implicit and explicit epistemic systems ..." (Reber, 1993, p. 23). Reber describes the urge to treat explicit and implicit (our tacit) as

> The boundary between the conscious and the unconscious is somewhat porous and flexible.

altogether different processes the "polarity fallacy" (Reber, 1993). Similarly, Matthews says that the unconscious and conscious processes are engaged in what he likes to call a "synergistic" relationship (Matthews, 1991). What this means is that the boundary between the conscious and the unconscious is somewhat porous and flexible. Given that caveat, how do we describe tacit knowledge?

Tacit knowledge is the descriptive term for those connections among thoughts that cannot be pulled up in words, a knowing of *what* decision to make or *how* to do something that cannot be clearly voiced in a manner such that another person could extract and re-create that knowledge (understanding, meaning, etc.). An individual *may or may not* know they have tacit knowledge in relationship to something or someone. But even when it *is known*, the individual is unable to put it into words or visuals that can convey that knowledge. We all know things, or know what to do, yet may be unable to articulate *why* we know them, *why* they are true, or even exactly *what they are*. To "convey" is to cause something to be known or understood or, in this usage, to transfer information from which the receiver is able to create knowledge.

Knowledge starts as tacit knowledge, that is, the initial movement of knowledge is from its origins within individuals (in the unconscious) to an outward expression (howbeit driving effective action). What does that mean? Michael Polanyi, a professor of both chemistry and the social sciences, wrote in *The Tacit Dimension* that, "We start from the fact that we can know more than we can tell" (Polanyi, 1967, p. 108). He called this pre-logical phase of knowing tacit knowledge, that is, knowledge that cannot be articulated (Polanyi, 1958).

Tacit and explicit knowledge can be thought of as residing in "places," specifically, the unconscious and conscious, respectively, although both Knowledge (Informing) and Knowledge (Proceeding)—whether tacit or explicit—are differentiated patterns spread throughout the neuronal system, that is, the volume of the brain and other parts of the central nervous system. On the other hand, implicit knowledge may reside in either the unconscious (prior to triggering, or tacit) or the conscious (when triggered, or explicit). See the continuum of awareness of knowledge source/content represented in Figure 4-1 in the discussion of tacit knowledge later in this chapter. Note that there is no clean break between these three types of knowledge.

Knowledge (Proceeding) may be explicit, implicit or tacit. For anything except the simplest knowledge, the process we use to find, create and mix the information needed to take effective action is difficult, if at all possible, to communicate to someone else. Thus, the expertise involved in deciding what actions to take in many situations will almost always be tacit. Team discussions, problem solving and decision-making, while helpful and necessary, must address the emotional, intuitive and embodied aspects as well as relevant data, information, and explicit knowledge of the participants. (A discussion of embodied tacit knowledge is later in this chapter.

As another point of comparison, explicit, implicit and tacit knowledge appear to almost always include both Knowledge (Informing) and Knowledge (Proceeding). As an example of how these three aspects of knowledge can work together, consider the development that occurs as we learn to drive a car. When you first get behind the steering wheel of a car, each action comes slowly and is learned only through practice (trial and error). You are creating explicit knowledge, and able to talk about every action you take. As your experience increases, many things—such as how to brake evenly, how to turn corners in your lane, or how to accelerate smoothly—become automatic. Soon, with practice, many of the aspects of driving become natural, moving them into implicit knowledge. After driving to work for some length of time, you know the road, the car and the traffic patterns so well that you can think about other things and still drive safely. Much of your driving is now tacit knowledge, yet there is always an alert, implicit part that immediately *knows* when something ahead may become a problem. Implicit driving can quickly become explicit if someone in front of you slams on their brakes or a passing car swerves too close to you. Yet when nothing special happens during your trip, you may have no memory of driving the last ten miles!

Relationship with Levels of Knowledge

There are significant differences between the levels of knowledge introduced in Chapter 2 and the explicit, implicit and tacit dimensions of knowledge explicated in this chapter. First and primary is the focus. As described above, the tacit, implicit and explicit dimensions are focused on that which resides in the conscious and that which resides in the unconscious; specifically, the ability to express knowledge (explicit) or inability to express knowledge (tacit), with implicit used to describe knowledge stored in memory of which the individual is not immediately aware, but which may be pulled up when triggered (associated), a moving middle ground between explicit and tacit. In contrast, the levels of knowledge focus on the ease of understanding: simple facts (surface knowledge), the need for shared context (shallow knowledge, also known as social knowledge) and the pattern-recognition of lived experience in a knowledge domain (deep knowledge).

While it is possible to be unable to recall/voice simple facts and yet be able to convey deep knowledge through stories, for example, a larger amount of surface knowledge will be explicit and a larger amount of deep knowledge will be tacit. See Figure 4-1.

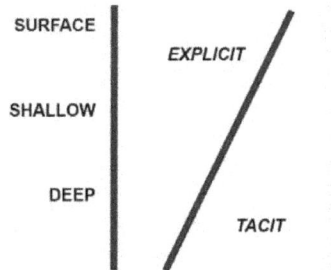

Figure 4-1. *Relationship between levels of knowledge and dimensions of knowledge.*

This relationship between the levels of knowledge and the dimensions of knowledge is because surface knowledge is primarily information, easily accessible and rapidly changing, and largely Knowledge (Informing). In contrast, deep knowledge deals with patterns developed over time, the realm of the expert who has developed an internal knowing based on complex interactions through focused effort in a domain of knowledge. Much of this will be Knowledge (Proceeding), the unique way a decision-maker complexes internal and external Knowledge (Informing) to make decisions and take effective action.

Expanding the Tacit Dimension

Dealing with change, uncertainty and complexity demands deep knowledge, which comes primarily from tacit knowledge (Goldberg, 2005). If tacit is that which cannot be fully shared through communication and is not part of one's ordinary consciousness, then how do we get the knowledge needed to deal with complex problems, dynamic systems or unpredictable events?

The deeper we go into the meaning and characteristics of the concept of tacit knowledge, the more complex it becomes. Nevertheless, as the importance of tacit knowledge grows in support of organizational performance, so must our depth of understanding and the articulation of that understanding. Building on our functional definition of knowledge, *the capacity (potential or actual) to take effective action*, we now explore four aspects of tacit knowledge: embodied, affective, intuitive and spiritual. **Each of these has its own unique characteristics and plays a different role in learning and the implementation of tacit knowledge within individuals and organizations**. The four aspects of tacit knowledge are represented in Figure   4-2 along with explicit and implicit knowledge on the continuum of awareness.

	TACIT Kn				IMPLICIT Kn / EXPLICIT Kn	
	SPIRITUAL	**INTUITIVE**	**AFFECTIVE**	**EMBODIED**	**IMPLICIT Kn**	**EXPLICIT Kn**
	• Based on matters of the soul • Represents animating principles of human life • Focused on moral aspects, human nature, higher development of mental faculties • Transcendent power • Moves knowledge to wisdom • Higher guidance with unknown origin	• Sense of knowing coming from within • Linked to FOR • Knowing that may be without explanation (outside knowledge) • *Why* (evasive or unknown) • 24/7 personal servant of human being • *Why* (unknown)	• Feelings • Generally attached to other types or aspects of knowledge	• Expressed in bodily/material form • Stored within the body (riding bike) • Can be kinesthetic or sensory • Learned by mimicry and behavioral skill training • *Why* (evasive)	• Stored in memory but not in conscious awareness • Not readily accessible but capable of being recalled when triggered • Don't know you know, but self-discoverable • Ability may or may not be present to facilitate social communication. • *Why* (questionable)	• Information stored in brain that can be recalled at will • In conscious awareness • Can be shared through social communication • Can be captured in terms of information (given context) • Expressed emotions (visible changes in body state) • *Why* (understood)

UNCONSCIOUS AWARENESS	*Level of Awareness of*	CONSCIOUS AWARENESS →
	Origins / Content of Knowledge	

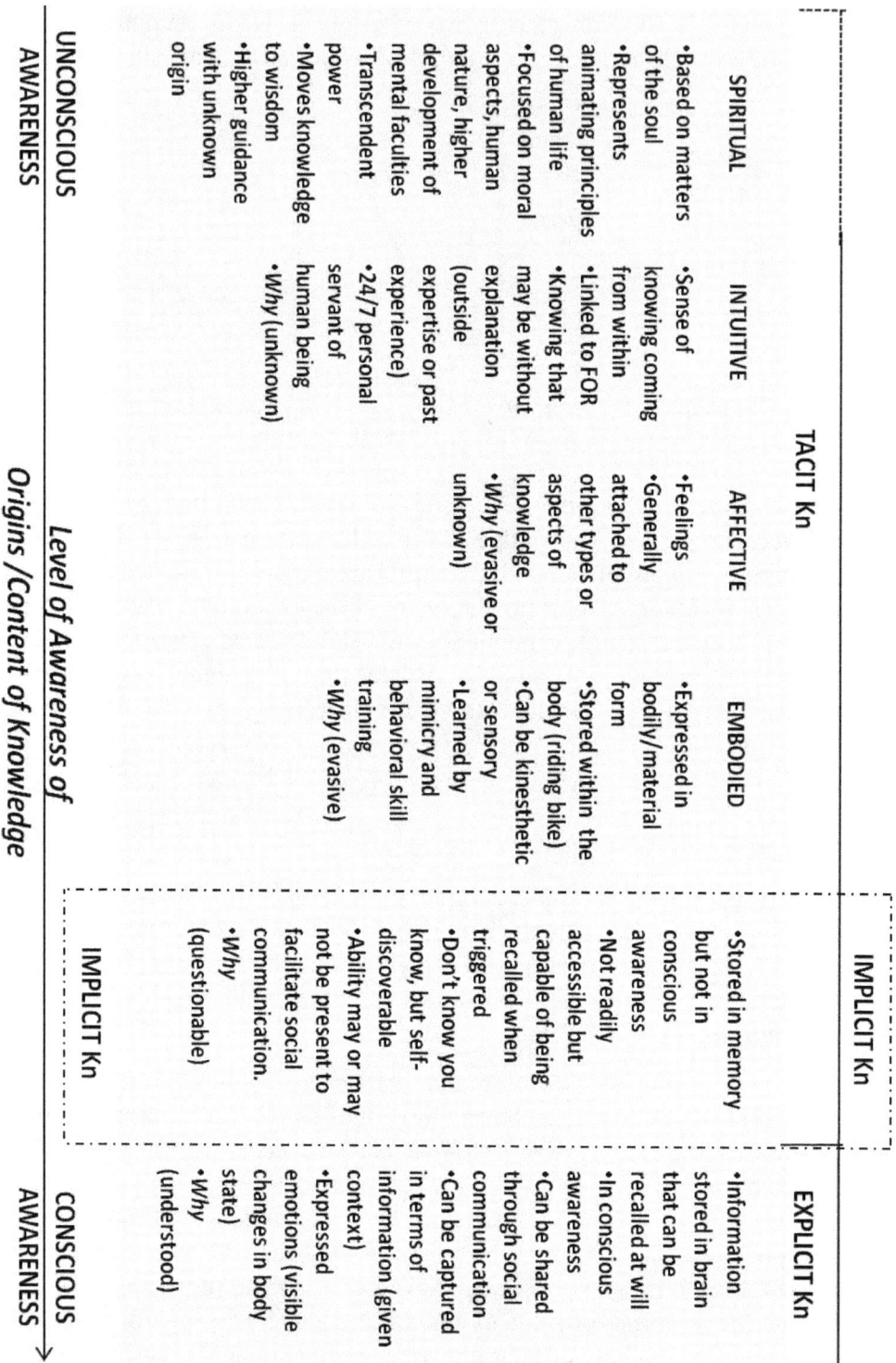

Figure 4-2. *Continuum of awareness of knowledge source/content.*

As our understanding of these aspects grows, techniques for working with tacit knowledge suggest themselves and potential leadership/management actions are suggested.

Embodied tacit knowledge, also referred to as somatic knowledge, can be represented in neuronal patterns stored within the body. It is both kinesthetic and sensory. *Kinesthetic* is related to the movement of the body and, while important to every individual every single day of our lives, is a primary focus for athletes, artists, dancers, kids and assembly-line workers. A commonly used example is knowledge of riding a bicycle. *Sensory*, by definition, is related to the five human senses through which information enters the body (sight, smell, hearing, touch and taste). An example is the smell of burning metal from your car brakes while driving or the smell of hay in a barn. These smells can convey knowledge of whether the car brakes need replacing (get them checked immediately), or whether the hay is mildewing (dangerous to feed horses, but fine for cows). These responses would be overt, bringing to conscious awareness the need to take effective action and driving that action to occur.

Because embodied learning is often linked to experiential learning (Merriam et al., 2006), embodied tacit knowledge can generally be learned by mimicry and behavior skill training. While deliberate learning through study, dialogue or practice occurs at the conscious level, when significant or repeated over time such learning often becomes tacit knowledge. Further, as individuals develop competence in a specific area, more of their knowledge in that area becomes tacit, making it

> Embodied tacit knowledge can be both preventative and developmental.

difficult or impossible for them to explain how they know what they know. The neuronal patterns representing that knowledge become embedded within long-term working memory where they become automatic when needed, but lost to consciousness. Embodied tacit knowledge can be both preventative and developmental. For example, a physical response can warn *not* to do something or move an individual *to do something*. Both of these responses constitute the capacity to take effective action since *not taking an action is an action choice.*

Intuitive tacit knowledge is the sense of knowing coming from inside an individual that may influence decisions and actions; yet the decision-maker or actor cannot explain *how* or *why* the action taken is the right one. Damasio calls intuition, "the mysterious mechanism by which we arrive at the solution of a problem *without* reasoning toward it" (Damasio, 1994, p. 188). The unconscious works around the clock with a processing capability many times greater than that at the conscious level. This is why as the world grows more complex, decision-makers will depend more and more on their intuitive tacit knowledge. But in order to use it, decision-makers must first be able to tap into their unconscious.

Intuitive tacit knowledge can be both Knowledge (Informing) and/or Knowledge (Proceeding), and it may reside in either the potential aspect of taking effective action (knowing how) or the actual aspect of taking effective action (acting). A form of knowing, deep tacit knowledge is created within our minds (or hearts or guts) over time through experience, contemplation, and unconscious processing such that it becomes a natural part of our being—not just something consciously learned, stored, and retrieved (Bennet & Bennet, 2007e). In other words, intuitive tacit knowledge is the result of continuous learning through experience. To develop intuitive skills requires making sure that your experiences are meaningful, that is, having specific objectives in mind such as how to size up situations quickly and develop a good sense of what will happen next (Klein, 2003). It is also important to get immediate and accurate feedback directly related to the context within which a decision was made. Understanding the outcomes of actions and why something did or did not happen helps develop patterns in the unconscious (intuition). According to Klein, to build up expertise requires: (1) feedback on decisions and actions, (2) active engagement in getting and interpreting this feedback (not passively allowing someone else to judge them); and (3) repetitions, which provide the opportunity to practice making decisions and getting feedback (Klein, 2003).

> Understanding the outcomes of actions and why something did or did not happen helps develop patterns in the unconscious.

Affective tacit knowledge is connected to emotions and feelings, with emotions representing the external expression of some feelings. Feelings expressed as emotions become explicit (Damasio, 1994). Feelings that are not expressed—perhaps not even recognized—are those that fall into the area of affective tacit knowledge. From neuroscience research, information coming into the body moves through the amygdala, that part of the brain that is,

> ... important both for the acquisition and for the on-line processing of emotional stimuli ... [with] Its processing encompassing both the elicitation of emotional responses in the body and changes in other cognitive processes, such as attention and memory. (Adolphs, 2004, p. 1026)

It is as incoming information moves through the amygdala that an emotional "tag" is attached. If this information is perceived as life-threatening, then the amygdala takes control, making a decision and acting on that decision before conscious awareness of a threat! Haberlandt (1998) goes so far as to say that there is no such thing as a behavior or thought not impacted by emotions in some way. Even simple responses to information signals can be linked to multiple emotional neurotransmitters. Thus, affective tacit knowledge is attached to other types or aspects of knowledge. For example, when an individual thinks about recent occurrences like an argument or a favorite sports team losing in the Rose Bowl, feelings are aroused. Or recall the internal responses to holding the hard copy of your first book, or your new born child. As Mulvihill states,

> Because the neurotransmitters which carry messages of emotion are integrally linked with the information during both the initial processing and the linking with

information from the different senses, it becomes clear that there is no thought, memory, or knowledge which is 'objective,' or 'detached' from the personal experience of knowing. (Mulvihill, 2003, p. 322)

Feelings as a form of knowledge have different characteristics than language or ideas, but they may lead to effective action because they can influence actions by their existence and connections with consciousness. When feelings come into conscious awareness, they can play an informing role in decision-making, providing insights in a non-linguistic manner and thereby influencing decisions and actions. For example, a feeling (such as fear or an upset stomach) may occur every time a particular action is started which could prevent the decision-maker from taking that action. See Goleman (1995) for an in-depth treatment of the emotions in terms of emotional intelligence.

Spiritual tacit knowledge can be described in terms of knowledge based on matters of the soul. The soul represents the animating principles of human life in terms of thought and action, specifically focused on its moral aspects, the emotional part of human nature, and higher development of the mental faculties (Bennet & Bennet, 2007c). While there is a "knowing" related to spiritual knowledge similar to intuition, this knowing does not include the experiential base of intuition, and it may or may not have emotional tags. The current state of the evolution of our understanding of spiritual knowledge is such that there are insufficient words to relate its transcendent power, or to define the role it plays in relationship to other tacit knowledge. Nonetheless, this area represents a form of higher guidance with unknown origin.

> While there is a knowing related to spiritual knowledge similar to intuition, this knowing does not include the experiential base of intuition, and it may or may not have emotional tags.

In a study in early 2007, representative human characteristics spiritual in nature were identified that contribute to learning (Bennet & Bennet, 2007c). These characteristics were grouped into five general areas: *shifting frames of reference* (represented by abundance, awareness, caring, compassion, connectedness, empathy, openness); *animating for learning* (represented by aliveness, grace, harmony, joy, love, presence, wonder); *enriching relationships* (represented by authenticity, consistency, morality, respect, tolerance, values); *priming for learning* (represented by awareness, eagerness, expectancy, openness, presence, sensitivity, unfoldment, willingness); and *moving toward wisdom* (represented by caring, connectedness, love, morality, respect, service).

The general area of *shifting frames of reference* was intertwined with learning, thinking and acting (Bennet, 2006), covering the external approach (looking from an outside frame of reference) and the internal approach (taking an empathetic perspective which moves the viewpoint from the objective to the subjective). Frames of reference can be focusing and/or limiting, allowing the mind to go deeper in a bounded direction. Shifting frames of reference potentially offer the opportunity to take a multidimensional approach to exploring the world around us and facilitates creativity and innovation. The area of *animating for learning* speaks to the fundamental source of life—learning, the energy used for survival and growth. The area of *enriching relationships* is tied to competence theory (White, 1959), which assumes that it is natural for people to strive for effective interactions with their world. This brings in the two dimensions of spirituality that exist beyond ourselves (other people and the larger energy system/ecosystem perceived as outside the human) with whom we can truly learn to grow in understanding (Nouwen, 1975). *Priming for learning* attributes are considered as those that actively prepare and move an individual toward learning. Wisdom, the highest part of the knowledge spectrum, is considered as forwarding the goal of achieving the common or greater good (Sternberg, 2003) (see Chapter 11). Reflecting on this short study, it would appear that spiritual knowledge would provide a transcendent frame of reference that puts things in relationship to a larger perspective while promoting self-knowledge and learning.

Spiritual knowledge may be the guiding purpose, vision and values behind the creation and application of tacit knowledge. It may also be the road to moving information to knowledge and knowledge to wisdom, i.e., purpose, vision and values are excellent guidelines. Zohar and Marshall describe spiritual tacit knowledge as,

> ... the intelligence with which we address and solve problems of meaning and value, ... place our actions and our lives in a wider-richer meaning-giving context, [and] ... can assess that one course of action or one life-path is more meaningful than another. (Zohar & Marshall, 2000, pp. 2-3)

In the context of this treatment, spiritual tacit knowledge is considered the source of higher learning, helping decision-makers create and implement knowledge that has greater meaning and value for the common good—wisdom. An example of spiritual tacit knowledge that is primarily Knowledge (Proceeding) might be Csikszentmihalyi's concept of flow (Csikszentmihalyi, 1990). Spiritual tacit knowledge that is primarily Kn_I is often referred to as streaming or channeling of information that is outside an individual's personal experience or awareness. An example would be the numerous recorded instances in times of warfare where military personnel under fire have known what actions to take without detailed knowledge of the terrain or enemy troop movement.

Final Thoughts

Similar to the possible interactions among tacit, implicit and explicit knowledge, the four aspects of tacit knowledge can experience considerable interconnections and overlaps. For example, referring to a somatic learning model by Amann, Merriam says that "the spiritual aspect of somatic learning is meaning-making through music, art, imagery, symbols, and rituals and overlaps or intersects with the other three dimensions" (Merriam, et al, 2006, p. 195), which are described as kinesthetic learning, sensory learning and affective learning. While organized differently than the knowledge model presented here, the Amann somatic learning model includes four elements—kinesthetic, sensory, affective and spiritual—as tacit knowledge (Amann, 2003).

As a second example of overlap, affective and embodied somatic states can operate both inside and outside an individual's awareness or consciousness; however, if overlap occurs in the unconscious the results may surface as intuition. Conversely, affective and embodied somatic states are often accompanied by overt somatic markers; for example, a "gut feel." In contrast, intuition comes from the neural network of the reticular activating system. Instead of producing a body-state change (sematic marker), it inhibits the regulatory neural circuits located in the brain core, which can influence behaviors (Damasio, 1994).

It is important to realize that we as decision-makers are holistic in nature, that is, all of the tacit knowledges described above are playing a role in our experiential engagement of life. In an increasingly uncertain and complex environment, to take effective action requires a mix of explicit, implicit and particularly tacit knowledge. The dilemma is that implicit knowledge and tacit knowledge, residing in the unconscious, cannot be readily shared so that individuals and teams can extract information and recreate the knowledge to make decisions and take effective action. The growing criticality of gaining access to this knowledge magnifies the need to understand implicit knowledge and the four aspects of tacit knowledge (embodied, intuitive, affective and spiritual), and intentionally develop vehicles to bring that knowledge into play.

In Chapter 5 we explore specific processes for engaging tacit knowledge and the role of leadership in managing the organizational environment for, and nurturing the creation and utilization of, tacit knowledge in support of sustainable high performance.

Chapter 5
Engaging Tacit Knowledge[1]

It has only been in the past few decades that cognitive psychology and neuroscience have begun to seriously explore unconscious mental life. This includes the recognition that conscious experience, thought and action are influenced by unconscious concepts, memories and other mental constructs inaccessible to conscious awareness and somehow independent of voluntary control (Eich, et al., 2000). At the same time, research in neuroscience is also digging deeper into the understanding of the emotions, working memory and the unconscious processing that occur within the mind, and to some extent throughout the body.

As introduced in the Foreward of this book, Polanyi felt that tacit knowledge consisted of *a range of conceptual and sensory information and images* that could be used to make sense of a situation or event (Hodgkin, 1991). We agree. Two observations that have emerged in the discussion above are: (1) While the terms explicit, implicit and tacit may be useful in clarifying and understanding knowledge, these terms describe aspects of a fluctuating continuum (a range) rather than a rigid classification schema. (2) **In the unconscious mind the association of incoming information with internal information is a powerful form of continuous learning**. Significant gains can be made in the effectiveness of problem solving and decision-making through understanding and stimulating this process. (See Bennet and Bennet, 2013.) *So how do we make best use of this process for our own and our organization's benefit?* The search for an answer leads to thinking beyond what is described as ordinary consciousness towards what we will call **extraordinary consciousness.**

Ordinary consciousness represents the customary or typical state of consciousness, which is common to everyday usage, or of the usual kind. Polanyi sees tacit knowledge as *not part* of one's ordinary consciousness (Polanyi, 1958); thus, tacit knowledge resides in the unconscious. **To access tacit knowledge an individual needs to move from ordinary consciousness to extraordinary consciousness, acquiring a greater sensitivity to information stored in the unconscious**. *Extraordinary consciousness* would be considered special, exceptional, and outside of the usual or regular state of consciousness. This means a heightened sensitivity to, awareness of, and connection with our unconscious mind, together with its memory and thought processes.

The challenge is to make better use of our tacit knowledge through creating greater connections with the unconscious, building and expanding the resources stored in the unconscious, deepening areas of resonance, and sharing tacit resources among individuals. We propose a four-fold action model with nominal curves for building extraordinary consciousness within individuals that includes surfacing tacit knowledge, embedding tacit knowledge, sharing tacit knowledge, and inducing resonance (see Figure 5-1).

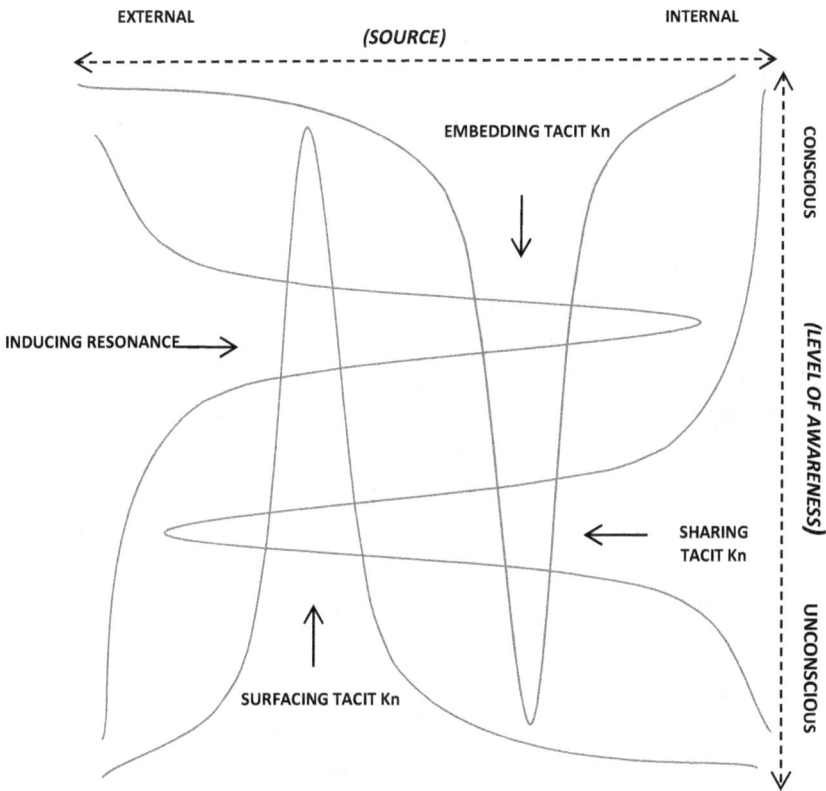

Figure 5-1. *Building extraordinary consciousness within an individual.*

Surfacing Tacit Knowledge

The first approach toward building extraordinary consciousness is *surfacing tacit knowledge*. As individuals observe, experience, study and learn throughout life they generate a huge amount of information and knowledge that becomes stored in their unconscious mind. Even though an individual may have difficulty pulling it up when needed, learning how to access their unconscious—and listen to it—can become a valuable learning resource. Surfacing tacit knowledge is focused on accessing the benefit of that which is tacit by moving knowledge from the unconscious to conscious awareness. Three ways that tacit knowledge can be surfaced are through external triggering, self-collaboration and nurturing.

As represented in Figure 5-1, the process of triggering is primarily externally driven with internal participation. For example, conversation, dialogue, questions, or an external situation with specific incoming information may trigger the surfacing of tacit knowledge needed to respond. The unconscious is aware of the flow of consciousness, available to affect decisions as incoming information is associated with internal information. In these cases we would describe the knowledge surfaced from the unconscious as implicit, with externally-generated information mixing with tacit knowledge in order to create that surfaced implicit knowledge. (See the earlier discussion on implicit knowledge.) Triggering is often the phenomenon that occurs in "sink or swim" situations, where an immediate decision must be made that will have significant consequences.

Although collaboration is generally thought about as interactions among individuals and/or groups, there is another collaboration that is less understood. This is the process of individuals consciously collaborating with themselves. What this means is the conscious mind learning to communicate with, listen to, and trust its own unconscious. In order to build this trust, it is necessary for individuals to first recognize where their tacit knowledge is coming from. Recall that tacit knowledge is created from continuous mixing of external information with internal information. This means that when you trust your unconscious you are trusting yourself, and the semantic complexing of all the experiences, learning, thoughts and feelings throughout your life. Thus, the process of associating (learning) in your unconscious is related to life-long conscious learning experiences (see the section below on embedding tacit knowledge).

One way to collaborate with yourself is through creating an internal dialogue. For example, accepting the authenticity of and listening deeply to a continuous stream of conscious thought while following the tenets of dialogue. Those tenets would include: withholding quick judgment, not demanding quick answers, and exploring underlying assumptions (Ellinor & Gerard, 1998, p. 26), *then* looking for collaborative meaning between what you consciously think and what you feel. A second approach is to ask yourself a lot of questions related to the task at hand. Even if you don't think you know the answers, reflect carefully on the questions, and be patient. Sleeping on a question will often yield an answer the following morning. Your unconscious mind processes information 24/7 and exists to help you survive. It is not a figment of your imagination, nor your enemy.

> One way to collaborate with yourself is through creating an internal dialogue. A second approach is to sleep on it.

Although requiring time, openness and commitment, there are a number of approaches readily available for those who choose to nurture their sensitivity to tacit knowledge. These include (among others) meditation, inner tasking, lucid dreaming, and hemispheric synchronization. Meditation practices have the ability to quiet the conscious mind, thus allowing greater access to the unconscious (Rock, 2004). Inner tasking is a wide-spread and often used approach to engaging your unconscious. Tell yourself, as you fall asleep at night, to work on a problem or question. The next morning when you wake up, but before you get up, lie in bed and listen to your own, quiet, passive thoughts. Frequently, but not always, the answer will appear, although it must be written down quickly before it is lost from the conscious mind. Like meditation, the efficacy of this approach takes time and practice to develop (Bennet & Bennet, 2008e).

Lucid dreaming is a particularly powerful way to access tacit knowledge. The psychotherapist Kenneth Kelzer wrote of one of his lucid dreams:

> In this dream I experienced a lucidity that was so vastly different and beyond the range of anything I had previously encountered. At this point I prefer to apply the concept of the spectrum of consciousness to the lucid dream and assert that within the lucid state a person may have access to a spectrum or range of psychic energy that is so vast, so broad and so unique as to defy classification (Kelzer, 1987).

Another way to achieve sensitivity to the unconscious is through the use of sound. For example, listening to a special song in your life can draw out deep feelings and memories buried in your unconscious. Sound and its relationship to humans has been studied by philosophers throughout recorded history; extensive treatments appear in the work of Plato, Kant and Nietzsche. Through the last century scientists have delved into studies focused on acoustics (the science of sound itself), psychoacoustics (the study of how our minds perceive sound) and musical psychoacoustics (the discipline that involves every aspect of musical perception and performance). Sound (as do all patterns in the mind) has the ability to change and shape the physiological structure of the brain. Neuroscience has slowly begun to recognize the capability of both internal thoughts and external incoming information (including sound) to affect the physical structure of the brain—its synaptic connection strength, its neuronal connections and the growth of additional neurons (Pinker, 2007; Nelson, et al., 2006; Gazzaniga, 2004). This phenomenon called plasticity is independent of an individual's age.

Hemispheric synchronization (bringing both hemispheres of the brain into coherence) can be accomplished through the use of sound coupled with a binaural beat (Bennet & Bennet, 2008g). Inter-hemispheric communication is the setting for brain-wave coherence which facilitates whole-brain cognition, assuming an elevated status in subjective experience (Ritchey, 2003). What can occur during hemispheric synchronization is a physiologically reduced state of arousal, quieting the body *while maintaining conscious awareness* (Mavromatis, 1991; Atwater, 2004; Fischer, 1971; West, 1980; Delmonte, 1984; Goleman, 1988; Jevning, et al., 1992), thus providing a doorway into the unconscious. It is difficult to imagine the amount of learning and insights that might reside therein—and the expanded mental capabilities such access may provide—much less the depth and breadth of experience and emotion that has been hidden there, perhaps making such access a mixed blessing.

Embedding Tacit Knowledge

The second approach toward building extraordinary consciousness is *embedding tacit knowledge*. Although information is continuously going into our unconscious all of the time, only significant things stay in memory—often without our conscious awareness. Said another way, **every experience and conversation is *embedding* potential knowledge in the unconscious as it is associated with previously stored**

information to create new patterns. Thinking about embedding as a process for improving our tacit knowledge can lead to new approaches to learning. In Figure 5-1, we see that embedding is both externally and internally driven, with knowledge moving from the conscious to the unconscious. Embedding knowledge in the unconscious can occur through exposure or immersion, by accident or by choice. Examples would include travel, regularly attending church on Sunday, or listening to opera and imitating what you've heard in the shower every day. Practice moves beyond exposure to include repeated participation in some skill or process, thus strengthening the patterns in the mind. For example, after many years of imitation (practice) look at what Paul Potts, Britain's newest opera singer, accomplished![2]

Creating tacit knowledge occurs naturally and quietly as an individual lives through diverse experiences and becomes more proficient at some activity (such as public speaking) or cognitive competency (such as problem solving). As their scope of experience widens, the number of relevant neuronal patterns increases. As an individual becomes more proficient in a specific area

> Creating tacit knowledge occurs naturally and quietly as an individual lives through diverse experiences and becomes more proficient at some activity or cognitive competency.

through effortful practice, the number of neurons needed to perform the task decreases and the remaining pattern gradually becomes embedded in the unconscious, ergo it becomes tacit knowledge. When this happens, the reasons and context within which the knowledge was created often become hidden from consciousness.

Recognizing the differences among the four aspects of tacit knowledge suggests specific ways to embed knowledge. *Embodied tacit knowledge* requires new pattern embedding for change to occur. This might take the form of repetition in physical training or in mental thinking. For example, embodied tacit knowledge might be embedded through mimicry, practice, competence development or visual imagery coupled with practice. An example of this would be when an athlete training to become a pole vaulter reviews a video of his perfect pole vault to increase his athletic capability. This is a result of the fact that when the pole vaulter performs his perfect vault, the patterns going through his brain while he is doing it are the same patterns that go through his brain when he is watching himself do it. When he is watching the video, he is repeating the desired brain patterns and this repetition strengthens these patterns in unconscious memory. When "doing" the pole vault, he cannot think about his actions, nor try to control them. Doing so would degrade his performance because his conscious thoughts would interfere with his tacit ability.

In the late 1990's, neuroscience research identified what are referred to as mirror neurons. As Dobb's explains,

> These neurons are scattered throughout key parts of the brain—the premotor cortex and centers for language, empathy and pain—and fire not only as we perform a certain action, but also when we watch someone else perform that action (Dobbs, 2007, p. 22).

Watching a video is a cognitive form of mimicry that transfers actions, behaviors and most likely other cultural norms. Thus, when we *see* something being enacted, our mind creates the same patterns that we would use to enact that "something" ourselves. As these patterns fade into long-term memory, they would represent tacit knowledge, both Knowledge (Informing) and Knowledge (Proceeding). While mirror neurons are a subject of current research, it would appear that they represent a mechanism for the transfer of tacit knowledge between individuals or throughout a culture. For more information on mirror neurons, see Gazzaniga, 2004.

Intuitive tacit knowledge can be nurtured and developed through exposure, learning, and practice. Intuitive tacit knowledge might be embedded through experience, contemplation, developing a case history for learning purposes, developing a sensitivity to your own intuition, and effortful practice. Effortful study moves beyond practice to include identifying challenges just beyond an individual's competence and focusing on meeting those challenges one at a time (Ericsson, 2006). **The way people become experts involves the chunking of ideas and concepts and creating understanding through the development of significant patterns useful for solving problems and anticipating future behavior within their area of focus**. A recent study of chess players concluded that "effortful practice" was the difference between people who played chess for many years while maintaining an average skill and those who became master players in shorter periods of time. The master players, or experts, examined the chessboard patterns over and over again, studying them, looking at nuances, trying small changes to perturb the outcome (sense and response), generally "playing with" and studying these *patterns* (Ross, 2006). In other words, they use long-term working memory, pattern recognition and chunking rather than logic as a means of understanding and decision-making. This indicates that by exerting mental effort and emotion while exploring complex situations, knowledge—often problem-solving expertise and what some call wisdom—becomes embedded in the unconscious mind. For additional information on the development of expertise see Ericsson (2006).

An important insight from this discussion is the recognition that when facing complex problems which do not allow reasoning or cause and effect analysis because of their complexity, the solution will most likely lie in studying patterns and chunking those patterns to enable a tacit capacity to anticipate and develop solutions. This was demonstrated in the movie *A Beautiful Mind* staring Russell Crowe as a brilliant mathematician on the brink of international acclaim who becomes entangled in a mysterious conspiracy. For more on the reference to wisdom see Chapter 11.

Affective tacit knowledge requires nurturing and the development of emotional intelligence. Affective tacit knowledge might be embedded through digging deeply into a situation—building self-awareness and developing a sensitivity to your own emotions—and having intense emotional experiences. How much of an experience is kept as tacit knowledge depends upon the mode of incoming information and the emotional tag we (unconsciously) put on it. The stronger the emotion attached to the experience, the longer it will be remembered and the easier it will be to recall. Subtle patterns that occur during any experience may slip quietly into our unconscious and become affective tacit knowledge. For a good explanation of Emotional Intelligence see Goleman (1998).

Spiritual tacit knowledge can be facilitated by encouraging holistic representation of the individual and respect for a higher purpose. Spiritual tacit knowledge might be embedded through dialogue, learning from practice and reflection, and developing a sensitivity to your own spirit, living with it over time and exploring your feelings regarding the larger aspects of values, purpose and meaning. Any individual or organization who demonstrates—and acts upon—their deep concerns for humanity and the planet is embedding spiritual tacit knowledge.

Sharing Tacit Knowledge

The third approach toward building extraordinary consciousness is *sharing tacit knowledge*. In our discussion above on surfacing tacit knowledge, it became clear that surfaced knowledge is new knowledge, a different

> It is not necessary to make knowledge explicit in order to share it.

shading of that which was in the unconscious. If knowledge can be described in words and visuals then this would be by definition explicit. Yet the subject of this paragraph is sharing tacit knowledge. **The key is that it is not necessary to make knowledge explicit in order to share it.**

In Figure 5-1, sharing tacit knowledge occurs both consciously and unconsciously, although the knowledge shared remains tacit in nature. The power of this process has been recognized in organizations for years, and tapped into through the use of mentoring and shadowing programs to facilitate imitation and mimicry. More recently, it has become the focus of group learning, where communities and teams engage in dialogue focused on specific issues and, over time, develop a common frame of reference, language and understanding that can create solutions to complex problems. These solutions may retain "tacitness" in terms of understanding the complexity of the issues (where it is impossible to identify all the contributing factors much less a cause and effect relationship among them). Hence these solutions would not be explainable in words and visuals to individuals outside the team or community. When this occurs, the team (having arrived at the "tacit" decision) will often create a rational explanation of why the decision makes sense to communicate to outside individuals.

Inducing Resonance

The fourth approach toward building extraordinary consciousness is *inducing resonance*. Through exposure to diverse, and specifically opposing, concepts that are well-grounded, it is possible to create a resonance within the receiver's mind that amplifies the meaning of the incoming information, increasing its emotional content and receptivity. In Figure 5-1, inducing resonance is a result of external stimuli resonating with internal information to bring into conscious awareness. When resonance occurs, the incoming information is consistent with the frame of reference and belief systems within the receiving individual. This resonance amplifies feelings connected to the incoming information while also validating the re-creation of this external knowledge in the receiver. Further, this process results in the amplification and transformation of internal affective, embodied, intuitive or spiritual knowledge from tacit to implicit (or explicit). Since deep knowledge is now accessible at the conscious level, this process also creates a sense of ownership within the listener. The speakers are not telling the listener what to believe; rather, when the tacit knowledge of the receiver resonates with what the speaker is saying (and how it is said), a natural reinforcement and expansion of understanding occurs within the listener. This accelerates the creation of deeper tacit knowledge and a stronger affection associated with this area of focus.

An example of inducing resonance can be seen in the recent movie, *The Debaters*. We would even go so far as to say that the purpose of a debate is to transfer tacit knowledge. Well-researched and well-grounded external information is communicated (explicit knowledge) and tied to emotional tags (explicitly expressed). The beauty of this process is that this occurs on *both sides* of a question such that the active listener who has an interest in the area of the debate is pulled into one side or another. An eloquent speaker will try to speak from the audience's frame of reference to tap into their intuition. She will come across as confident, likeable and positive to transfer embodied tacit knowledge, and may well refer to higher order purpose, etc. to connect with the listener's spiritual tacit knowledge. A strong example of this occurs in the Presidential debates. This also occurs in litigation, particularly in the closing arguments, where for opposing sides of an issue emotional tags are used to connect to the jurors and affect their judgment.

Leadership and Tacit Knowledge

Given the definitions, descriptions and characteristics of tacit knowledge presented in Chapter 4 and above, and considering the value of tacit knowledge to an organization, we now turn to the role of leadership in managing the organizational environment for, and nurturing the creation and utilization of, tacit knowledge in support of sustainable high performance. Most organizations face a two-fold problem in this regard. First, the role of tacit knowledge must be recognized and its value to the organization understood and appreciated. Once this occurs, tacit knowledge can be managed to various degrees depending on the knowledge, its context and the organization's culture and leadership. In this context, management does not mean control, rather it refers to taking actions and creating environments in which desirable results can—and will—be achieved.

The value of any specific tacit knowledge may be positive or negative. For example, where tacit knowledge is the capability to maintain a quick response, flexible and high-quality assembly line such as Dell Computer had for a number of years, or Walmart's nation-wide distribution capacity, such tacit knowledge is extremely valuable and very difficult to replicate. However, **when fixed beliefs and habits of decision-making become so internalized that they are unrecognized by their owners, they can perpetuate decisions that no longer relate to a changing environment**. Such knowledge forecasts the decay and possible disappearance of the organization.

Thus, leaders and managers need to create an environment that maximizes the creation and contribution of employee tacit knowledge. This environment would facilitate the recognition and removal of outdated tacit knowledge while creating, modulating and adapting tacit knowledge that can respond to opportunities and demands of an unpredictable market. The role of leaders and managers begins with recognizing, respecting and rewarding productive tacit knowledge, then supporting the surfacing of this knowledge where it makes sense, and encouraging open communications among knowledge workers.

A significant strength of tacit knowledge is in its efficiency and efficacy as internal patterns are combined with incoming information to develop situation-focused responses that are context sensitive and situation dependent. The costs are in overcoming the difficulty of sharing such knowledge with others. Since tacit knowledge is usually deeper than explicit knowledge, it can be more powerful; but when outdated it is much harder to change, usually requiring a transformational learning experience. See Mezirow (1991) for a thorough discussion of this phenomenon.

From a leadership perspective, techniques for *surfacing tacit knowledge* include observing and discussing the role of emotions in decision-making, actions and dialogue; and practicing reflection and self-questioning by individuals when they are using feelings, intuition, or gut feel as guides for decisions or actions. Where embodied sensations arise during an experience, the individual can seek to understand this internal effect, and explore the situation in terms of their own history, frame of reference and the sources of their reactions. In addition, individuals who have developed tacit knowledge through experience can sometimes surface the thinking and understanding underlying that knowledge by getting in touch with their unconscious through self-reflection and inner tasking, questioning their own thinking and looking for underlying patterns in their actions.

Embedding tacit knowledge in an organizational setting serves a number of significant purposes for an organization. In a changing and surprise-prone environment, individuals who have deep knowledge and wide experience related to an area of focus—rich sources of tacit knowledge—are able to quickly respond to a variety of emerging challenges. Another example would be the embedding of tacit knowledge in complex areas vital to corporate survival; for instance, a series of highly efficient processes that give the organization competitive advantage. It is difficult if not impossible for competitors to copy or reproduce complex processes, particularly those that have tacit knowledge embedded within them. Such tacit knowledge is often the sum of the separate (and different) tacit knowledge of many individuals.

From a leader's perspective, ways to embed tacit knowledge include (1) encouraging employees to become aware of what tacit knowledge is and its importance to the organization; and (2) encouraging all employees to improve their competency through the techniques of effortful practice, repetition, and experience that develops a high level of expertise.

Sharing tacit knowledge may occur in communities of practice, interest and learning that have emerged over the last decade as the significance of knowledge to organizational survival was recognized. **Communities provide an excellent environment for questions, dialogues and information exchanges which can bring out the nuances, feelings and insights related to the tacit knowledge of participants.** Von Krogh suggests that the best way to share tacit knowledge is through what is called micro communities of knowledge. These are small teams of five to seven members who are socialized through team projects and come to understand each other through a common language and purpose. This facilitates the surfacing and sharing of meaning and understanding, provided the participants are able to verbalize their unconscious knowledge (Von Krogh et al., 2000). Such communication can never be perfect because tacit knowledge comes with emotions, memories and deeper meanings that may not be known to its owner, and may be truly inaccessible. What can happen is that the listener may receive sufficient information to re-create a significant part of the speaker's knowledge within their own cognitive reality. When this occurs, the listener's perceptions, understanding, and meaning may be close enough for an approximate re-creation of the speaker's tacit knowledge. This learning process is contingent upon the listener being receptive to the information and finding the results compatible with their own knowledge, beliefs and assumptions (see the discussion on resonance above). If this does not occur, the listener may reject what is heard, misinterpret what was said, or have a "disorienting experience" that leads them to question their own beliefs and assumptions through critical analysis—perhaps leading to transformational learning. Clearly, the best transfer will occur if there is a compatible and reinforcing dialogue between the listener and the owner of tacit knowledge, with both parties coming from a common (or similar) frame of reference.

Other ways of sharing tacit knowledge include employees discussing and learning from their own and others experience, feelings and intuition. Leaders can facilitate learning through conversations, dialogues, after-action reviews, reflection and continuous questioning of policies, practices, and historical ways of doing things.

The process of mentoring can stimulate the surfacing, embedding and sharing of tacit knowledge of both individuals involved. **Mentoring is most effective when the individuals have a common context—similar backgrounds, vocabulary and**

outlooks on the organization, particularly in their areas of expertise. If the groundwork for understanding has not been developed, deeper aspects of knowledge cannot connect and grow. It is helpful to provide the mentee with a good set of questions that encourage the expert to reflect on his/her own thinking, feeling and unconscious proclivities. Recall the previous discussion on getting in touch with your own unconscious, and being very sensitive to emotions, hunches, gut feelings, body tenseness, etc. In a healthy mentoring relationship it is important not to let the dialogue stay only on a logical, cognitive plane. While the rational approach is natural in a professional setting, it is the non-rational and non-vocal areas that may lie within the unconscious that are primary domains of interest. *Each of us through experience and expertise develops an internal world that re-presents the history of our learning— although never precisely accurate.* The map is not the territory. Nevertheless, it is just this autobiographical history, plus the situational inputs (as perceived by the mentor), that "wakes up" the non-vocal signs representing tacit knowledge.

> Through experience and expertise, each of us develops an internal world that re-presents the history of our learning—although never precisely accurate.

For best understanding of a mentor's tacit knowledge, the mentee must try to "see" the same situation as the mentor. This is where good communication about the situation can become very helpful, but realize the mentor may not consciously know why he sees what he sees. Also, seeing the same situation differently may open the door to an understanding of differing frames of reference which can be the starting point for exploring why the mentor has the frame of reference she has. This in turn can lead to questions that help the mentee understand his own frame of reference and an exploration of why certain feelings occur and why certain actions are chosen over others. Since the unconscious mind can detect patterns and influence actions without the conscious mind being aware of it, the mentor may be unconsciously detecting patterns in the situation, and acting on his tacit knowledge without being aware of doing so. An alert mentee who is aware of this phenomenon can consciously look for those subtle patterns that the mentor uses to make decisions but does not see.

To establish a base for *inducing resonance* in an organization, leaders need to create a culture that recognizes, understands, appreciates and is aligned with the purpose, mission, vision and values of the organization. Such a culture is then open to resonance of information and knowledge generated by leadership, thought leaders or outside experts who can focus the meaning and intent of their knowledge so that it resonates with employees. When this occurs employee understanding, acceptance and enthusiasm for the knowledge will be significantly enhanced because it is consistent with, and greatly enhances, their personal competency and contribution to the organization. This relationship is the resonance phenomena.

Within the culture described above, ways of facilitating local resonances include setting up formal dialogues, conversations and brainstorming sessions. As a point of caution, too much resonance throughout the workplace may act as a narrow band filter causing the rejection of non-resonant or diverse ideas. This, of course, would stifle innovation, creativity and adaptability to changing world situations. The point made here is the importance of recognizing and honoring resonance on both sides of any issue or question.

Final Thoughts

Knowledge is often treated as a generic concept and has been given many interpretations. In this book we have offered a functional definition that—when coupled with learning theory and neuroscience—leads to a lexicon of types of knowledge, and specific aspects of tacit knowledge. For example, after identifying explicit, implicit and tacit knowledge as part of a fluctuating continuum in Chapter 4, we have decomposed tacit knowledge into four aspects: embodied, affective, intuitive and spiritual. Recognizing that tacit knowledge is by definition not part of one's ordinary consciousness, we began to develop the understanding that since incoming information is continuously associated with internal information (referred to as semantic complexing—the creating of meaning), all knowledge coming into conscious awareness is new knowledge (see Chapter 9).

The recognition that tacit knowledge resides beyond ordinary consciousness led to the search for approaches to identifying extraordinary consciousness, that is, developing a greater sensitivity to information stored in the unconscious in order to facilitate the management and use of tacit knowledge. Surfacing, embedding and sharing tacit knowledge were discussed as approaches for mobilizing tacit knowledge in support of individual and organizational objectives. The importance of extraordinary consciousness became clear as we discussed these approaches. In addition, it was forwarded that participating in or exposing ourselves to situations that induce resonance engages our personal passion in developing deeper knowledge and expanded awareness of that knowledge. Finally, we suggested some actions that leaders and managers could take to maximize the value of tacit knowledge to their organizations.

> The recognition that tacit knowledge resides beyond ordinary consciousness led to the search for approaches to developing a greater sensitivity to information stored in the unconscious.

Changing and uncertain times require new ways of thinking and new ways of acting. We can take good actions only if we can make good decisions. We can make good decisions only if we have good understanding. We can have good understanding only if we have good knowledge. We can have good knowledge only if we know how to learn. Since much of our information and knowledge is tacit, this needs to become the focus of our learning and decision-making. Our knowledge of tacit knowledge is crucial to our future. We all have much learning to do in this area. *What better resource than our minds to co-evolve with and contribute to our world?* This treatment offers a single drop in an ocean of possibilities.

Chapter 6
Living through Context[1]

Knowledge is situation-dependent and context sensitive, and with this realization a shift began in the way we share knowledge built on an understanding of intent through content and context. Exploring context offers a significant contribution to building theories of meaning in terms of shared knowledge.

This chapter explores the multiple and varied contexts involved in the movement of knowledge from a source to a perceiver. Building on the definitions of information and knowledge set forth in the beginning of this book, we begin this chapter with a definition of context before launching into the context avenues in our model. Throughout this chapter the relationships of the conscious and unconscious mind to the different context avenues are addressed and their impact on the sharing of knowledge considered.

The Power of Context

The innate ability to evoke meaning through understanding—to evaluate, judge and decide—is what distinguishes the human mind from other life forms. This ability enables us to discriminate and discern—to see similarities and differences, form patterns from particulars, and create and store knowledge purposefully. In this human process to create meaning and understanding from external stimuli, *context shapes content*. We have heard this phrase so many times over the past few years that we have no idea who said it first, but it is another one of those thoughts that captures the imagination. **While the content of the external stimuli may be constant, when you change the context the meaning can be entirely different!** For example, the simple statement "Let's get together" could *mean* "sometime," or some specific time set earlier or later in a conversation or assumed because of the subject of the conversation, or could possibly be a nice thing to say without any real intent behind it. This brings us to the power of context to influence knowledge sharing.

In our first paragraph we reiterated that knowledge was context sensitive. The word "context" comes from the Latin stem of *contexere* which translates as "weave together." While it can loosely be defined as a set of circumstances, the *Oxford English Dictionary* also provides, "The part or parts immediately preceding or following a passage or word as determining or helping to reveal its meaning; the surrounding structure as determining the behavior of a grammatical item, speech, sound, etc." (*Oxford English Dictionary*, 2002, p. 501) *The greater the context, providing it is coherent and relevant, the greater the number of related patterns generated by the context that offer the potential to create shared understanding.* In our example above, that could mean adding, "… before school tomorrow morning in the library" to "Let's get together." If this exchange was among members of the opposite sex accompanied by a wink and smile or a soft tone of speech, an even more significant context accompanies the words. If these same words were an exchange between a mentor and student who is having difficulty with a subject (where both individuals are aware of a major test the student has the following morning), and if the words are delivered firmly and with urgency, an entirely different shared understanding would occur. **Given that context supports a specific meaning, the more relevant clues added to the content the higher the resonance of shared understanding**.

Realizing that any model is an artificial construct, we propose eight primary avenues of context that may directly impact the content of a message. While we will focus on one part of a conversation between two individuals to explore these avenues, each context could be considered from the viewpoints of the source (S) and the perceiver (P) based on their perceptions of the interaction that is occurring. Each of these contexts could also be extrapolated across to written and virtual texts. For example, this includes the choice of words and sentence structure in a virtual resource,

> Through experience and expertise, each of us develops an internal world that re-presents the history of our learning—although never precisely accurate.

the tone of the writing, the impact of visual approaches in support of text, or the feelings present from past interactions with the originator of the text. Further, as represented by the well-known McLuhan-originated meme (*the medium is the message*) (McLuhan, 1964) and touched on below, the specific medium of communication directly affects the content, and each context will potentially relate differently to the various mediums of exchange. The key word here is "affect." McLuhan did not seek to "isolate the concepts behind the words but to integrate them as perceptions." (Gordon, 1997, p. 305) In other words, *understanding the medium and the perceiver's interaction with the medium provides a greater opportunity to interpret and integrate the intent of the message with the perceptions of the receiver* (the perceiver).

Since the initial publication of McLuhan's ground-breaking work over 40 years ago, he has grown to be recognized as a principal contributor to the field of communications; volumes and volumes of explication of, and argument about, his work have been published, perhaps realizing the intent of McLuhan's efforts. As Gordon so eloquently states, "McLuhan's object is not to offer a theory of human communication, but to *probe the effects of anything and everything we use in dealing with the world around us*, including language." (Gordon, 1997, p. 328) As we explore the avenues of the context model below, we adopt McLuhan's intent and—in this new century where we are beginning to understand the power of the mind/brain and the unconscious—would expand that intent to include: *and with the world within us*.

The Context Avenues

While we will focus on one side of an exchange from a source to a perceiver—the traditional hierarchal model of communication—there is nonetheless a feedback loop occurring during this exchange. The context avenues model explicated below captures the layers of context from the viewpoint of this single point of exchange, the shared understanding (the "what"), and does not include the full richness of the "why" that produces the exchange, which is beyond the scope of this chapter. Note that feedback of some nature is always present (the perceiver cannot be completely passive), that conversations are social experiences, and that in a participative relationship an immediate reversal of roles will occur when the perceiver responds. However, for the sake of ease of discussion we are limiting the focus to a direct, one-way event.

It is also recognized that in our face-to-face example there are the physical characteristics related to sound that influence what humans perceive as they listen. Specifically, these are the loudness or amplitude, the pitch or frequency and the tonal quality or wave-form. And since different people hear best at different frequencies, this might also contribute to *what* is heard, and *how* it is heard, with implications on the meaning transferred. That said, we now move into the eight avenues of context in our model as visualized in Figure 6-1.

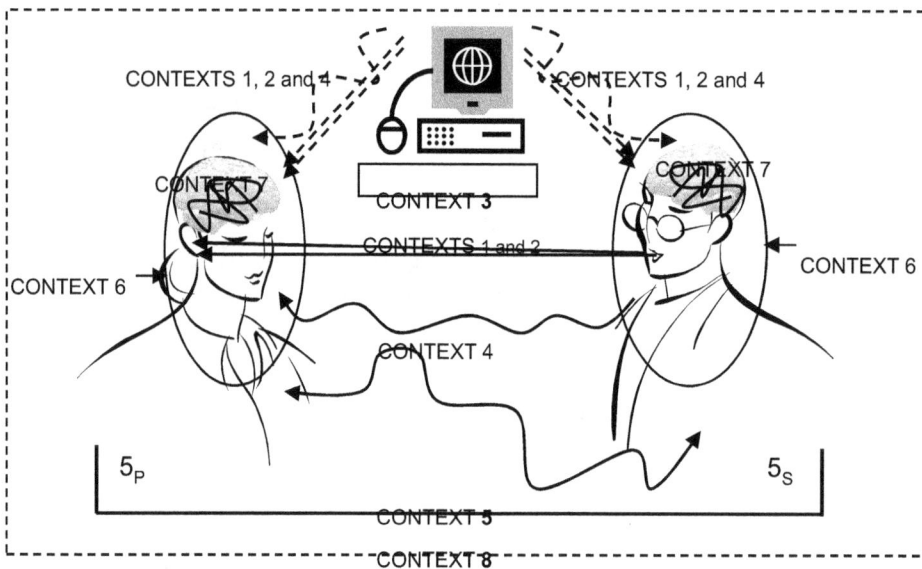

Figure 6-1. *Visualization of the eight avenues of context.*

Context 1 focuses on the content itself: the specific nouns and verbs selected, the adjectives and adverbs used in the primary expression, and the structure of the sentence that support this expression.

Context 2 is the setting or situation surrounding the content of information; that is, the words and structure of the words expressed before and after the primary expression that provide further explication of the intent of content.

Contexts 1 and 2 are informational in nature and directly tied to the use and rules of language. Syntax is the body of rules used by/in sources when combining words into sentences. Syntax is often taken for granted in those who have grown up with a native language (residing in the unconscious), but syntax will be different from region to region and must be learned by those coming from a different native language. There are also morphological rules (regulating the formation of words); semantic rules (determining interpretations of words and sentences); phonological rules (dealing with allowable patterns of sounds); and phonetic rules (determining pronunciation of words and sentences) (Baker, 1989). These rules facilitate the ability of the perceiver to understand the words and structure of the words of the source. They are also sensitive to region and must be learned when acquiring the language in use (in our case English) as a second language. For native speakers these rules reside primarily in the unconscious.

> Contexts 1 and 2 are informational in nature and directly tied to the use and rules of language.

In terms forwarded by Nonaka and Takeuchi (1995), contexts 1 and 2 are explicit, and the transfer process from the source to the perceiver is primarily that of internalization by the perceiver (from explicit to tacit). Internalization has served as a primary form of learning since the advent of the alphabet. Before development of the alphabet, the visual sense along with the tactile was primary in facilitating understanding and supporting the work process and tool formation crucial to human evolution. (Fekete, 1977, p. 214) McLuhan observed that the visual sense became "powerfully privileged by the alphabet. As a new technology, the alphabet required a new set of habits that carried over from reading to virtually every area of human thought and endeavor." (Gordon, 1997, p. 303) McLuhan refers to language as "mankind's first technology for *extending consciousness*." (McLuhan, 1964, p. 57) The term technology is used in the anthropological sense, meaning "the body of knowledge available to a civilization that is of use in fashioning implements, practicing manual arts and skills, and extracting or collecting materials" (*American Heritage Dictionary*, 1992, p. 1843).

Taking another perspective on structure—and noting that the most commonly used symbol in the written English language is the space between words--Stonier contends that "the absence of structure within a structure may carry information as real as the structure itself" (Stonier, 1997, p. 23). He provides the following insight:

> Holes and spaces within an organized structure may comprise a significant part of the organization of that structure, and hence contain information ... The information content of such holes or spaces is entirely dependent upon the organization and behavior of the structures or systems which surround them. This demands that there exists information which can exist only as long as there exists a context or structure—a form of information which appears to disappear the moment the structure disappears. (Stonier, 1997, p. 23)

This observation leads us to consideration of the absence of content.

Context 3 is that which is not expressed, not available, what we call *silent attention/presence*. Attention represents awareness and focus. Presence represents immediate proximity in terms of time or space. Recall the Post-Modernist query, does a tree really fall if no one is around to hear it? In Context 3, someone is there—present and aware—but no tree is falling. There is silence.

Presence without interaction objectifies, what has historically been defined (in a negative sense) as treating people like things. But even this objectification cannot be separated from language. In the presence of another, even in silence the perceiver is embedded in an unseen dialogue based on past and perceived future interactions. In fact, Hanks states that, "In the production of meaning, silence and the tacit dimension play as great a role as—if not an even greater role than—does articulate speech. (Hanks, 1996, p. 3) Silence can pull feelings and memories into conscious awareness.

Silence has language in terms of meaning, i.e., when somebody does *not* answer a question, they are communicating more than their non-words. Sometimes what is not said can have more meaning than what is said. For example, in solving the Mystery of Silver Blaze, Sherlock Holmes says,

> Before deciding that question I had grasped the significance of the silence of the dog, for one true inference invariably suggests others. The Simpson incident has shown me that a dog was kept in the stables, and yet, though some one had been in and had fetched out a horse, he had not barked enough to arouse the two lads in the loft. Obviously, the mid-night visitor was some one whom the dog knew well." (Doyle, 1994, p. 26)

Context 4 includes the non-verbal, non-voiced communication patterns that inevitably exist in conjunction with the content, whether (in our example) face-to-face interaction, hand written exchanges, or computer supported information. This is what could be termed associated information signals. In the convention used in nonverbal communication literature, this would be encoding (expression) from the source, and decoding (interpretation) of the perceiver. These are, of course, interdependent.

In our face-to-face example, this would include emphasis (stress) and tone as well as body expressions (facial, hand movements, eye activity, posture, etc.), physical appearance, and every way that attitude can be expressed non-verbally. Non-verbal gestures can provide a form of semantic representation in a visual mode. This can affect both integration and inference making (Nisbett & Ross, 1980). Visual cues such as nodding and eye and facial movements have been shown to improve comprehension (Rogers, 1978). In their recent work, Choi et al. (2004) explore non-verbals in terms of *unintended* communication and perception. They focus on the automaticity of communicating emotions, expectancies, social relations and personality from what they term the actor's (source) and perceiver's perspectives. They conclude that although people exert some control over social exchange, a great deal is accomplished automatically as they unknowingly and effortlessly express feelings, beliefs and desires through non-verbal means as they navigate their social worlds (Choi et al., 2004). In other words, a great deal of the context provided by the source in a face-to-face encounter through non-verbals is absorbed by the unconscious mind of the perceiver based on feelings, beliefs and desires. Thus, non-verbals are a form of expression, closely linked to context 6 below, which can be viewed as an unconscious expression of internal beliefs, values, feelings and expectations of the source in a face-to-face exchange.

This area of context also includes sensory inputs via smell and possibly taste. For example, if the content of the message (the information sent to the perceiver) dealt with a local fire or gas spill, the sense of smell would increase attention to—and understanding of—what is being communicated, resulting in knowledge (and action). The sense of taste is closely related to the sense of smell. These senses can also be cross-activated by seeing or touching. One out of every 200 people experience blending of the senses, a condition known as synesthesia. While the cause is not fully understood, it appears to be caused by cross-activation of different sensory-processing regions in the brain. For example, specific words and sounds might produce recognizable tastes. "One synesthete reports that the spoken Lord's Prayer 'tastes' mostly of bacon ... the name "Derek' tastes of earwax whereas the name 'Tracy' tastes like a flaky pastry." (Ramachandran & Hubbard, 2006, pp.79-80)

McLuhan judged participation in communication (engagement of the perceiver) by how the medium of communication *engaged our physical senses*. As Gordon explains, "When McLuhan speaks of the information that a medium transmits he does not refer to facts or knowledge but to how our physical senses respond to the medium." Media are generally broken down as high-definition (providing a high level of information with little for the receiver to do) or low-definition (providing a low level of information with the receiver having to work to fill in that which is missing). McLuhan referred to high-definition media as *hot* (examples would be radio, print, photographs, movies and lectures) and low-definition media as *cold* (examples would be the telephone, speech, cartoons, television, and seminars). (McLuhan, 1964) While chapter 2 of the reference is actually titled "Media Hot and Cold," in a later letter to Claude Bissell (National Archives of Canada, 28 January 1966) McLuhan used the term *cool*, defining it as a medium where the receiver shares in the creative process without merging in it. (Gordon, 1997, p.403) While McLuhan was researching what was then thought of as information transfer, his work was very much focused on the transfer of content in terms of understanding, what we know today as knowledge sharing. The combined activities included as part of Context 4 are in response to the medium and can be valued in terms of a continuum ranging from hot to cold (full participation to little participation).

Context 5 is focused on the system within which interaction takes place, the mutually-shared, common information and patterns with meaning *within the system*. The context of the system would include an understanding, either consciously or unconsciously, of the boundaries, elements, relationships and forces within the system.

This is the domain of shared context, generally including factors related to a mutual past or current environment, and potentially including culture, organizational structure, and former and current social relationships. While most of this resides in the unconscious, since it is continuously massaged by day-to-day experiences and thoughts, it is near the surface of the mind and readily accessible. For example, if the actors have a past relationship and know each other's personality, background, competency, and way of thinking, knowledge sharing may proceed easily and effectively. On the other hand, if the source is speaking to an audience of 200 conference attendees, unless they are all in the same profession or share some other common domain of interest and knowledge, the style, words and behavior need to be carefully planned to ensure widespread re-creation (sharing) of the speaker's knowledge.

Context 6 is the personal context which includes beliefs, values, experiences and feelings that emerge into conscious awareness. Personal context includes positions that we take that are locked into our conscious mind, unconscious patterns that are made conscious by the emerging content of the message (what might be termed implicit knowledge), and the core values and beliefs that rise to our awareness by virtue of "feelings." Contexts 6 and 7 work together, with context 6 being those aspects that surface in our thoughts and feelings and context 7 being those processes occurring of which we are not aware, i.e., in the unconscious.

When we hear information, we immediately compare it with what we already know and believe is true. We also interpret what we hear from our own frame of reference—our beliefs, values and objectives. We also connect what we hear with our recent memories and past experiences. Very quickly, a judgment or feeling about the received information is generated and this feeling, modulated by our personal feeling about the individual speaking and our reaction to the overall environment and interpersonal history will play a strong (often unconscious, which moves us into context 7) role in how we react to, interpret and accept what is said. In fact, we may reject and not hear something that the speaker is saying if it conflicts with our own beliefs. If our feelings are strong, we may quit listening entirely while we internally prepare our rebuttal. We hear what we want to hear in a threatening or uncomfortable environment.

Personal context could also include elements of proxemics, haptics and chronemics, which relate to the formality or informality of the exchange. In a face-to-face exchange, proxemics deals with the distance between the source and the perceiver, with formality increasing along with conversational distance (Aiello & Cooper, 1972; Sundstrom & Altman, 1976). Batchelor and Goethals (1972) found that people engaged in task interaction have closer interpersonal distances than people not working together. Haptics refers to the sense of touch, with the absence of touch common in formal settings and increased frequency of touch, denoting more informal and personal exchanges (Hall, 1974). Chronemics come into play in terms of timing and an emphasis on punctuality of response. "Adherence to schedules and a careful management of chronemic elements reflect formal situations, while a flexible and socially negotiated approach to chronemic elements reflects informality." (Burgoon et al., 1989, p. 207)

Context 7 is the impact of *unconscious processes*. These unconscious impacts can be thought of in terms of (1) the unconscious response to external stimuli (environment); (2) experiences and feelings (memories) not in conscious awareness; and (3) empathetic processes that can mirror behavior.

The unconscious response to external stimuli and experiences and feelings (memories) not in conscious awareness were discussed in depth in (Bennet & Bennet, 2006a). In that article, the authors forwarded that the selection, interpretation and meaning of incoming patterns are very much a function of pre-existing patterns in the brain. In other words, learning and understanding are created in the mind when patterns already in the mind combine with incoming patterns from the external world or current situation, in our example the source.

In fact, experimental evidence coming out of social psychology (Dijksterhuis & Bargh, 2001), cognitive psychology (Knuf et al., 2001) and neuro-psychology (Frith et al., 2000) have reached the same conclusion that there is a "disassociation between conscious awareness and the mental processes responsible for one's behavior ..." (Bargh, 2004, p. 38). This would purport that an individual's behavior (the behavior of the source in our face-to-face example) would not necessarily be driven by conscious awareness and intentions. Empathetic processes that mirror other's behavior indicate a positive, receptive attitude on the part of the perceiver. Such mimicking as arms folded while standing and conversing frequently occur without either participant's awareness. These are subliminal connections.

Context 8 is the overarching pattern context, higher levels of patterns of significance that emerge in the mind. These include: (1) the unconscious—and sometimes conscious—connecting of contexts 1 through 7 to develop a pattern of understanding or behavior; and (2) the development and recognition of patterns of patterns among different interactions (over time). The connecting of multiple contexts would include comparing, manipulating and combining patterns. While generally only a "feeling" or "knowing" will be available in the conscious mind, underneath any interaction or sequence of interactions our unconscious may be busy recognizing, storing and integrating the patterns emerging out of contexts 1 through 7.

As noted above, the development and recognition of higher-level patterns among multiple and different interactions occurs over time. While this generally forms in the conscious mind as a feeling or sense of knowing (intuition), it may also be accompanied by a mental remembering of an emotional response from previous interactions. In our face-to-face example, the thought, knowing or feeling that emerges as a result of different or multiple interactions provides a guide or pattern for our response, knowledge that can be applied to the current situation in terms of response to the source. By way of review, Figure 6-2 provides a brief description of the avenues.

PATTERNS IN TERMS OF CONTEXT

CONTEXT 1
CONTEXT 2
CONTEXT 3
CONTEXT 4:
CONTEXT 5
CONTEXT 6
CONTEXT 7
CONTEXT 8

--Information ... content (specific nouns and verbs selected, and the adjectives and adverbs used in the primary expression, and structure of sentence that supports content.
--Information ... the setting or situation surrounding the content of information.
--Silent attention/presence ... that of which we are aware but is not expressed, not available.
--Non-verbal, non-voiced communications patterns ... associated information signals (Emphasis and tone.) In face-to-face interactions this would include body expressions, attitude and physical appearance, as well as other sensory inputs.
--System of shared context. Mutually shared common information/patterns with meaning (culture, environment, history, etc.)
--Personal context. Internal beliefs, values, experiences and feelings that emerge into conscious awareness. (6 and 7 work together)
--Impact of unconscious processes, memories and feelings on context 3, 4, 5 and 6. Can be thought of inter terms of (1) the unconscious response to external stimuli (environment); (2) experiences and feelings (memories) not in conscious awareness; and (3) empathetic process that can mirror behavior.
--Overarching pattern context. Higher levels of patterns of significance that emerge in the mind.

Higher number of related (relevant) patterns equals greater resonance between the source and perceiver and the increased sharing of understanding.

Figure 6-2. *Descriptions of the avenues of context.*

There is significant power and opportunity offered by raising our awareness of patterns. For example, this overarching pattern context is what is so significant about best practices in an organization. Some consultants consider best practices as knowledge. In relatively stable environments with repetitive processes where best practices can be transferred successfully, they may significantly improve performance. However, best practices focus on rules of action and frequently omit the level of belief and understanding of how and why things actually work. Therefore, best practices themselves are often non-transferable or ineffective in *differing* situations and context. (Brown & Duguid, 2000) Building on the concepts introduced in Context 8, *another way of thinking about using best practices is by thinking in terms of best patterning, where a number of best practices are compared in similar situations and similarities and differences surfaced to develop patterns of transfer that could potentially drive effective actions in similar situations.* Conversely, different patterns could be developed by exploring similar practices in varied situations to develop general trends—a general or generic formula—of the *types* of things that might work in different situations to achieve specific desired outcomes or head an organization in a desired *direction* (Bennet & Bennet, 2004).

Whether promulgated by the conscious or unconscious mind, the higher the number of related patterns, the higher the possibility of resonance between the source and perceiver and the greater the level of shared understanding.

Contexts as Sources or Sinks?

Source as used repeatedly above refers to the individual who is promulgating the message (in our face-to-face example). The term "source" connotes the originator of the message and some context, as well as the protagonist of any interaction effects that are part of the contexts above. Shifting our perspective, in complexity sources are the centers of energy, power and influence. Adversely, sinks absorb energy, information and knowledge and do not broadcast it, *draining* power and influence. In deep-diving to understand context in a larger way, the question becomes: Are these contexts facilitating understanding or impeding understanding of the message? In other words, are they serving as sources or sinks relative to the process of shared understanding?

If we limit our consideration of these questions to the *conscious intent* of the source in our face-to-face example, then context may well be serving as a sink. For example, a past emotion-laden experience (context 6 and/or 7) between the source and the perceiver may well be waylaying the power and influence of the intended message. However, since we have discovered that our unconscious mind plays a major role in contributing contexts, the sharing of understanding becomes one based on every aspect of each individual (values, feelings, education, experience), their relationship (historic, present and perceived future), and the environment within which they share understanding. This means that the shared understanding that occurs in our face-to-face example is *exactly as it should be* based on both the *conscious and unconscious intent* of the source and the *conscious and unconscious perception* of the perceiver and the state of the surrounding environment. **To change the efficiency of the knowledge sharing situation, influential aspects within the eight context avenues can be changed.** This may quickly become a complex problem in that there are many factors that are interconnected and interweaved and therefore simple actions will often be non-productive (Bennet & Bennet, 2008b; 2013).

This discussion of intent and perception pushes us to question whether our conscious or unconscious mind is in control. While the influence of the unconscious has been the subject of much recent research, this influence is largely downplayed, driven by a concern over the implication of loss of control. In addressing the question of whether consciousness is in charge, Dijksterhuis et al. (2006) cite Jaynes (1976) in saying that conscious thought does not exist; that thought (defined as producing meaningful associative constructions) happens unconsciously. They conclude that without unconscious perception "we would not be able to accomplish much at all. If we assume … that it takes the processing of roughly 6.6 billion bits to decide to buy a house, consciousness alone would need 4 years to make such a decision." (p. 83)

Concluding Thoughts

In a 1942 semantics monograph titled *A Theory of Meaning Analyzed*, the Foreward points out that the papers included in the document "elucidate some of the fundamental difficulties in building any theories of 'meaning' which would be adequate to cover the range of human significant reaction …." John Gordon Spaulding, author of one of those papers, then goes on to present a documented critical analysis of the then current theory of meaning, citing the inadequacy of that theory based on "unconscious assumptions embedded in the Aristotelian system and structure of language." (Pollock & Spaulding, 1942, p. vii) While we have made much progress in understanding ourselves over the past 65 years and have built on and moved beyond this early work, *we still face fundamental difficulties in building theories of meaning in terms of shared knowledge*. It is still an enigma. Exploring context offers a significant contribution.

Clearly the sharing of understanding is a complex iterative process, an autopoietic, self-referential system that is continuously recreating its boundaries as the conscious and unconscious mind extract patterns from multiple contexts and sequences of information. Since a great deal of this system is influenced by the unconscious, there appears to be an internal capability and objective to self organize relevant brain patterns to create the understanding and meaning that provides the ability to anticipate the results of an action—in other words the creation of knowledge. Stonier puts it his way:

Understanding goes beyond meaning. Meaning, as stated above, involves the integration of a message into the internal information environment of the recipient. Such a process creates a new information unit: the combination of the external information complexed with the information provided by the internal information environment. This unit will be referred to from here on in as a 'semantic complex'. Such a semantic complex may be further information-processed as if it were a new message in its own right. By repeating this process, the original message becomes more and more meaningful as, at each recursive step, new semantic complexes are created. As these impinge on ever larger areas provided by the internal information environment, whole new and elaborative knowledge structures may be built up—a process which leads to understanding. (Stonier, 1997, p. 157)

Given this learning, how can our source create, mold or design information so that the perceiver has the highest chance of converting it to the knowledge that is the intent of the source? What can be done to encourage the resonance that can ensure shared understanding? As always, every exploration of knowledge and thought produces more questions. Alas, probing the answers to these questions will have to be another chapter … perhaps another book. What are your thoughts?

Section III
The Neuroscience of Knowledge

The term *Epistemology* has been historically used to describe how knowledge interacts with the mind of the observer. We contend that knowledge is created within the individual; it is information that is exchanged with enough context that the observer can create (or recreate) the knowledge that is being shared. As we moved into the Industrial Age, expanding our knowledge, as incomplete and imperfect as it was *it formed the basis for power*. "Every bureaucracy seeks to increase the superiority of the professionally informed by keeping their knowledge and intentions secret" (Gerth & Mills, 1946, p. 233). Thus the emergence of Max Weber's formal theory recognized today as the bureaucratic model (Bennet & Bennet, 2004).[1] Competition in and among organizations was based on Darwin's early conclusion of *survival of the fittest* (Darwin, 1964), becoming a meme that ignored Darwin's later findings that "Those communities which included the greatest number of the most sympathetic members would flourish best and rear the greatest number of offspring" (Darwin, 1998, p. 110).

With the emergence in the 1990's of knowledge management as an organizational construct in support of decision-making and innovation, there was recognition of the power of knowledge sharing[2] to facilitate creativity and expand knowledge resources. As knowledge became the product of choice, there was a relook of the perceived value of competition (which produced winners and losers) versus cooperation and collaboration (which produced expanded knowledge resources).

Enter an intense interest in neuroscience research spurred onward by the creation and sophistication of brain measurement instrumentation such as functional magnetic resonance imaging (fMRI), the electroencephalograph (EEG), and transcranial magnetic stimulation (TMS) (George, 2007; Kurzweil, 2005; Ward, 2006). For the first time we could see what was happening in the mind/brain as we process information and act on that information. Based on neuroscience findings since the turn of the century, we begin this section exploring the workings of the individual mind/brain and, specifically, its relationship with knowledge. We then join Cozolino (2006) in waking up to the realization that humans are social creatures, and look at the phenomenon of social knowledge. Finally, we entangle many of the thoughts introduced in this book to explore the fallacy of knowledge reuse.

Section III includes: The Magnificent Mind/Brain (Chapter 7); Social Knowledge (Chapter 8); and The Fallacy of Knowledge Reuse (Chapter 9).

Chapter 7
The Magnificent Mind/Brain[1]

Although there is much that is not understood about the mind/brain from a scientific viewpoint, the explosion of new measurement technology coupled with neuroscience research is providing significant insights into the operation of the mind/brain/body. When considering learning and knowledge, neuronal patterns offer a useful perspective (Stonier, 1997). Taking a multi-disciplined approach, we will move toward an understanding of tacit knowledge through the lens of neuroscience, evolutionary biology, psychology, competency theory and knowledge management. Each of these domains offers ideas, perspectives and insights that help build a holistic understanding of the nature, challenge and efficacy of knowledge concepts.

The brain stores information in the form of patterns of neurons, their connections (synapses), and the strength between those connections. These patterns represent thoughts, images, beliefs, theories, emotions, and so on. A single thought could be represented in the brain by a network of a million neurons, with each neuron connecting to anywhere from 1 to 10,000 other neurons (Ratey, 2001). Although the patterns themselves are nonphysical, their existence as represented by neuronal cells and their connections *are* physical, that is, composed of atoms, molecules and cells. If we consider the mind as the totality of neuronal patterns, then we can consider the mind and the brain to be connected in the sense that the patterns cannot exist without the brain (atoms, molecules, and neuronal cells), yet the brain would have no mind if it had no neuronal patterns.

It may be helpful to consider the following metaphor: the mind is to the brain as waves of the ocean are to the water in the ocean (Bennet and Bennet, 2008a). Even this is simplified because surrounding the neurons are continuous flows of blood, hormones and other chemicals which have complex interactions within the brain and the body (Church, 2006; Pert, 1997). The power of the metaphor derives from the relationship between the neuronal network patterns used to represent the external (and internal) world of concepts, thoughts, objects and their relationships, and the physical neurons and other material in the brain.

To get some idea of the density and intricacies of the brain, consider the following: "A piece of brain tissue the size of a grain of sand contains a hundred thousand neurons and one billion synapses, all talking to one another" (Amen, 2005, p. 20). A single thought might be represented in the brain by a network of a million neurons, with each neuron connected to 10,000 other neurons (Ratey, 2001). See Figure 7-1 below.

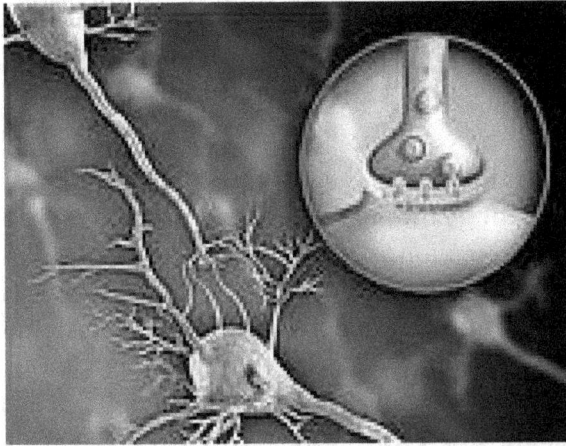

Figure 7-1: *Neurons in the mind/brain. The picture above shows a typical neuron and one of its synaptic connections to the neuron. It has been estimated that the average brain contains 10 billion neuron cells with each neuron connected to about 10,000 other neurons through synapses or small gaps through which neurotransmitters may flow. The pattern of neuron connections, the flow of small electrical impulses through the neuron axons and dendrites, together with the flow of molecules through the synaptic junctions, creates the patterns within the mind/brain.*

As another example, consider the following description of how the brain creates patterns of the mind. Antonio Damasio uses the term "movie" as a metaphor for the diverse sensory images and signals that create a show and flow we call mind. In the following quote Damasio also brings out a few of the large number of semi-independent systems in the brain that work together to make patterns that make sense of our external environment.

Further remarkable progress involving aspects of the movie-in-the-brain has led to increased insights related to mechanisms for learning and memory. In rapid succession, research has revealed that the brain uses discrete systems for different types of learning. The basal ganglia and cerebellum are critical for the acquisition of skills—for example, learning to ride a bicycle or play a musical instrument. The hippocampus is integral to the learning of facts pertaining to such entities as people, places or events. And once facts are learned, the long-term memory of those facts relies on multi-component brain systems, whose key parts are located in the vast brain expanses known as cerebral cortices. (Damasio, 2007, pp. 63-64)

We learn by changing incoming signals (images, sounds, smells, sensations of the body) into patterns (of the mind and within the brain) that we identify with specific external concepts, objects, or relationships. These incoming neuronal patterns have internal associations with other internal patterns that represent (to varying degrees of fidelity) the corresponding associations in the external world. Thus we re-present external reality through the creation and association of internal patterns of neuron firings and connections. Stonier (1997) refers to this process as semantic mixing or complexing.

Incoming external information (new information) is mixed, or associated, with internal information, creating new neuronal patterns that may represent understanding, meaning, and/or the anticipation of the consequences of actions, in other words, knowledge (Stonier, 1997). The term *associative patterning* describes this continuous process of learning by creating new patterns in the mind and stored in the brain (Bennet & Bennet, 2006a, 2008f). See Figure 7-2. From the viewpoint of the mind/brain, any knowledge that is being "re-used" is actually being "re-created" (see Chapter 9) and, in an area of continuing interest, most likely complexed over and over again as incoming information is associated with internal information (Stonier, 1997). During reflection, the mind/brain is thinking about the incoming concepts, ideas, objects, and their relationships by associating them with various internal neuron patterns.

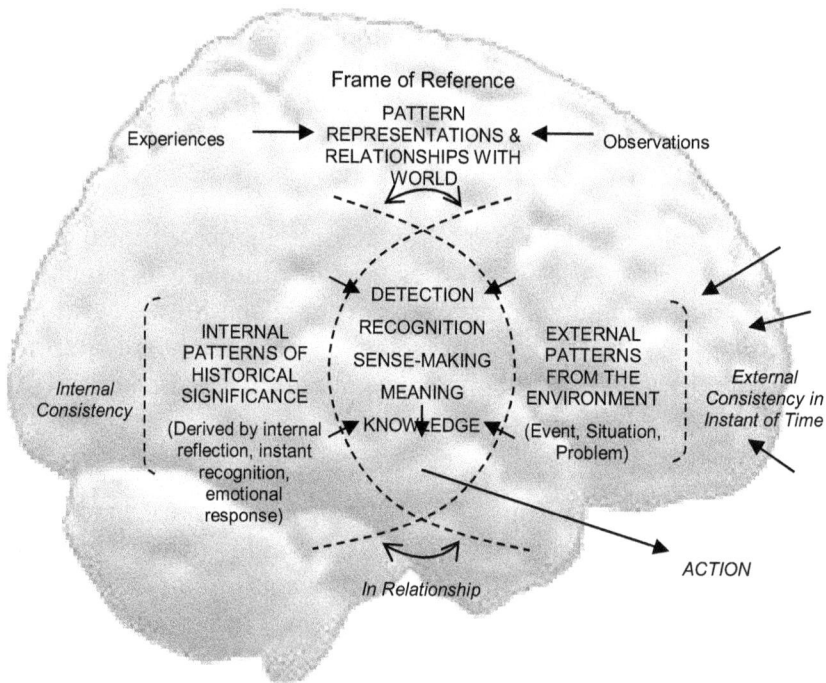

Figure 7-2. *Associative Patterning. The intermixing of the external patterns with internal patterns creates recognition, sense-making, meaning, and ultimately knowledge.*

The mind/brain is essentially a self-organizing, cybernetic, highly complex adaptive learning system that survives by converting incoming information from its environment into knowledge (the capacity to take effective action) and then using that knowledge. The mind, brain and body are replete with feedback loops, control systems, sensors, memories, and meaning-making systems made up of about 100 billion neurons and about 10^{15} interconnections. It is self-organizing because there is no central subsystem that "controls" the mind, brain or body.

Anticipating the Outcome of Actions

The process of storing sequences of patterns or memories is one way the mind/brain anticipates the outcome of actions. In 1949 the Canadian psychologist Donald Hebb explained learning and memory as a result of the strengthening of synapses (connections) between neurons in the brain. In other words, when connected neurons *fire simultaneously*, their synaptic connections become stronger (Begley, 2007). This has become known as Hebb's rule: learning takes place when pairs of neurons fire in coincidence. Although an oversimplification, the colloquial version is *neurons that fire together wire together*. One implication of Hebb's rule is the ease with which we can remember sequences of information. As Begley describes this process, "... traveling the same dirt road over and over leaves ruts that make it easier to stay in the track on subsequent trips" (Begley, 2007, p. 30). For example, we remember songs or stories (especially ones we sing or hear over and over again) much better than isolated or disconnected facts. This is also why memory of information can be improved by repeating the information over and over. In other words, the more often we recall what we have learned the better we will recall it in the future.

From another perspective, the rule is, "use it, or lose it" (Christos, 2003, p. 95). While the pattern may stay in memory if it is not repeated (used), it could prove very difficult to retrieve. Freud suggested that there are separate sets of neurons for perception and memory. The neural networks concerned with perception create fixed synaptic connections and by doing so ensure the accuracy of our perceptual capability. On the other hand, neuronal networks concerned with memory make connections that change in strength as we learn. This is the basis of memory and of higher cognitive functioning (Kandel, 2006a, 2006b).

We never see the same world twice; the brain (as distinct from a computer) does *not* store exact replicas of past events or memories. Rather, it stores invariant *representations*. These forms represent the basic source of recognition and meaning of the broader patterns (Hawkins & Blakeslee, 2004). In an email titled "Very Interesting Stuff" that made its way across the Internet, there is an anonymous entry that begins: "Don't delete this just because it looks weird. Believe it or not, you can read it." Reading the following text (from an anonymous source) begins to demonstrate the power of patterns stored as invariant forms.

I cdnuolt blveiee that I cluod aulaclty uesdnatnrd what I was rdanieg. The phaonmneal pweor of the hmuan mnid Aoccdrnig to rscheearch at Cmabrigde Uinervtisy, it deosn't mttaer in what oredr the ltteers in a word are, the olny iprmoatnt tihng is that the first and last ltteer be in the rghit pclae. The rset can be a taotl mses and you can still raed it wouthit a porbelm. This is bcuseae the huamn mnid deos not raed ervey lteter by istlef, but the word as a wlohe. Amzanig huh?

According to Hawkins, "...the problem of understanding *how* your cortex (a small part of your brain) forms invariant representations remains one of the biggest mysteries in all of science" (Hawkins, 2004, p. 78). This isn't for lack of trying; "no one, not even using the most powerful computers in the world, are able to solve it" (Hawkins, 2004, p. 78). Nobel laureate Eric Kandel describes this process:

> By storing memories in invariant forms, individuals are able to apply memories to situations that are similar but not identical to previous experiences. Cognitive psychologists would describe this as developing an internal representation of the external world, a cognitive map that generates a meaningful image or interpretation of our experience. (Kandel, 2006b, p. 298)

In summary, the ability to anticipate the future stems from the brain remembering the patterns associated with past experiences and their outcomes. When a new experience or situation is encountered, the brain tries to match it with past experiences and then identifies the probable outcome based on those prior experiences. A series of these similar experience-outcome events generates a belief, frame of reference, or mind-set that is likely to drive an individual's choice of what action(s) to take. The brain also may try to put these past experiences together, coupled with new possibilities based on current data and the creation of new possibilities, to *generate possible new scenarios for the future.*

While this system is robust with a high level of trustworthiness, it is not perfect. Because of the uniqueness of context and content of a situation coupled with the complexity of a situation, there is always the danger of oversimplifying and relying on largely unconscious beliefs learned from past—no longer applicable—experiences. Complexity creates many unique states, each of which may have to be independently explored from an individual's perspective. This foreshadows the need for each individual to consciously create and apply a set of theories that respond to their personal decision space; since this is going to happen whether or not an individual has awareness of it, conscious participation in the process can prove a powerful learning tool.

The Cortex

There are six layers of hierarchical patterns in the architecture of the cortex. For a deeper discussion of these levels we draw on the extensive work of Hawkins (2004). Using what he describes as the memory-prediction model of the cortex, Hawkins has developed a framework for understanding intelligence. The cortex's core function is to make predictions. A comparison of what is happening and what was expected to happen is part of the prediction process. In order to do this, there are not only avenues of incoming patterns but feedback paths, that is, information flowing from the processing area of the brain (the highest levels of the hierarchy) back to the lowest levels of the hierarchy that first received the input from the external world.

While only documented for the sense of vision, it appears that the patterns at the lowest level of the cortex are fast changing and spatially specific (highly situation dependent and context sensitive) while the patterns at the highest level are slow changing and spatially invariant. For example, since the light receptors in the retina are unevenly distributed and the cells in the cortex are evenly distributed, the retinal image relayed to the primary visual area of the cortex is highly distorted. Through the use of probes, it has been discovered that at the lowest level of the cortex any particular cell responds only to a tiny part of the visual input coming into the retina. Each neuron at this level has a "so-called receptive field that is highly specific to a minute part of your total field of vision" (Hawkins, 2004, p. 112). Further, each cell at this level also appears to be fine-tuned to specific kinds of input patterns which change with every fixation. A fixation occurs approximately three times a second as the eyes make a small, quick movement (a saccade) and then stop.

In contrast, when probes are used at the higher fourth level of the cortex, some cells that become active *stay active*. As Hawkins (2004, p. 113) explains,

> … we might find a cell that fires robustly whenever a face is visible. This cell stays active as long as your eyes are looking at a face anywhere in your field of vision. It doesn't switch on and off with each saccade … cells have changed from being rapidly changing, spatially specific, tiny-feature recognition cells, to being constantly firing, spatially nonspecific, object recognition cells.

What this conveys is the presence of higher-order patterns as incoming sensory information flows up from the lowest level to the highest level of the cortex, and then back down in a continuous feedback loop. Further, our example represents only the visual sense, yet *all* the senses (visual, auditory, somatic, etc.) are interconnected, acting as one associated whole, part of a "single multi-branched hierarchy" (Hawkins, 2004, p. 119). This affirms that an individual's ability to anticipate expected outcomes is based on the patterns of their experience, that is, incoming sensory information is integrated with stored information in invariant form as it moves up through the hierarchical structure of the cortex, with each level a representation of the information patterns beneath it. Now, add the presence of feedback loops from the higher-order patterns to the lower-order patterns and you have a continuously self-organizing system that relies heavily on its invariant forms that do not change easily.

Let us look at this process from the viewpoint of the four modes of Kolb's experiential learning model (concrete experience, reflective observation, abstract conceptualization and active experimentation) (Kolb, 1984). You have a situation. You experience the situation. Out of that experience you have a set of information (the first and lowest level pattern in the pre-frontal cortex), and all the details (in the form of information) that have come into your mind/brain. Then you reflect on the situation, and that reflection process is one of assembling and integrating all of the incoming information (thus creating second-level patterns). The third level of patterns is created in the comprehension phase, where not just understanding and meaning (started in the reflection process) are generated, but also insight, creative ideas, judgment and anticipating the outcome of various actions.

In your mind, you already have certain invariant patterns which represent past beliefs, experience, values and other previous assumptions that exist in the top level of the hierarchy in your cortex. Those patterns that already exist are matched with the patterns created at levels 1, 2 and 3, and through that learning process create high-level invariant forms. You've thrown away all of the excess information and are looking at the core meaning of the incoming information from the situation at hand. You have now generated neuro-knowledge that presents avenues for taking action to achieve the desired situation. *Here is where the highest level of invariant forms—theories, beliefs and assumptions—are used to select the best action to take.* This information is passed back down the hierarchical levels which then supplies the details of the solution that drive the actions that are anticipated to change the situation.

Learning from Ourselves

In storing experiences and thoughts in invariant form, the mind/brain has already completed a selection process, that is, storing that which is "most important" to you and which will provide the best accessibility to thought when it is needed. A parallel practice in information systems storage is to provide various levels of summaries and key words, easily searchable, all with connections to related information for depth and context as needed for the situation at hand.

In the mind/brain these invariant forms are weighted in terms of value. The more important a thought is to you and what you think and do, the more connections a thought has and the higher it is stored (in invariant form) in the frontal cortex. Thoughts and feelings that are repeated over and over again through a variety of experiences affect your core beliefs and values, or can become a core belief or value. As the individual moves through the myriad of information associated with each situation, opportunity or problem that emerges in life, that information is weighted in importance based on both external and internal criteria. External criteria would include relationship to, and potential impact on, the opportunity or issue in terms of input and output variables, sinks and sources, feedback loops, etc. Internal criteria would include the individual's memory, knowledge about the system, rational judgment capability, and feelings—all of which are affected by the individual's past experiences and associations and objectives. Taking a multi-disciplined approach, we now expand our focus to explore the phenomena of social knowledge from the mind/brain perspective.

Chapter 8
Social Knowledge[1]

Humans are social creatures. From a biological perspective, Cozolino believes that we are just waking up to this realization.

> As a species, we are just waking up to the complexity of our own brains, to say nothing of how brains are linked together. We are just beginning to understand that we have evolved as social creatures and that all of our biologies are interwoven. (Cozolino, 2006, p. 3)

Recall that learning is considered the process of creating knowledge (the capacity to take effective action). From an evolutionary perspective, those individuals who could observe, experience and take the best actions—whether it was to take flight, attack, or hide—had the best chance of survival. This capability to understand and see the meaning of a situation, and then figure out what to do and do it, we call knowledge. As the mind/brain evolved over thousands of years, it expanded the capacity to learn and act on what it learned. The advent of brain imaging in the late 1990's allows us to watch the neurophysiology of learning unfold. "Not only can we trace the pathways of the brain involved in various learning tasks, but we can also infer which learning environments are most likely to be effective" (Johnson & Taylor, 2006, p. 1).

While there are many ways to learn—self-reflection, observing others, our own instincts, etc.—as the value of knowledge sharing has been proven, the art of social communication and interactions has become an essential aspect of our organizations and communities. Global connectivity has assured the availability of massive amounts of information and a wide diversity of thought and opinion on every subject imaginable. This shift has prompted an exponential growth in learning from each other, without the potential penalty of mistakes made when we first attempt something new.

Let's take a closer look at the phenomena of shallow social knowledge.

Social Interaction and the Mind/Brain

When two people meet there may be a large amount of information (and only information) exchanged between them. Visibly, when they first see each other, light waves (or photons) travel between them, communicating patterns of movement, colors, pictures such as facial expressions, and sound waves as they speak or walk. Each person automatically creates in their own mind images, thoughts, feelings and an overall "sense" regarding the entire situation, including the surrounding environment. Much of this information is automatically processed by our unconscious, sometimes influencing our behavior and feelings before we become conscious of them.

All of this is primarily information (ordered patterns) or, at best, what could be called surface knowledge. It is not shallow or deep knowledge, these latter knowledges can only be created by each person within their own minds by thinking about the information coming in through the senses. Since we each have unique autobiographies, different belief systems and personal goals, to create knowledge (that is, understanding, meaning, insight, etc.) we must mix the incoming information with our own internal thought patterns as discussed above. This mixing process is most effective if there is a dialogue or affirmative inquiry process between two people.

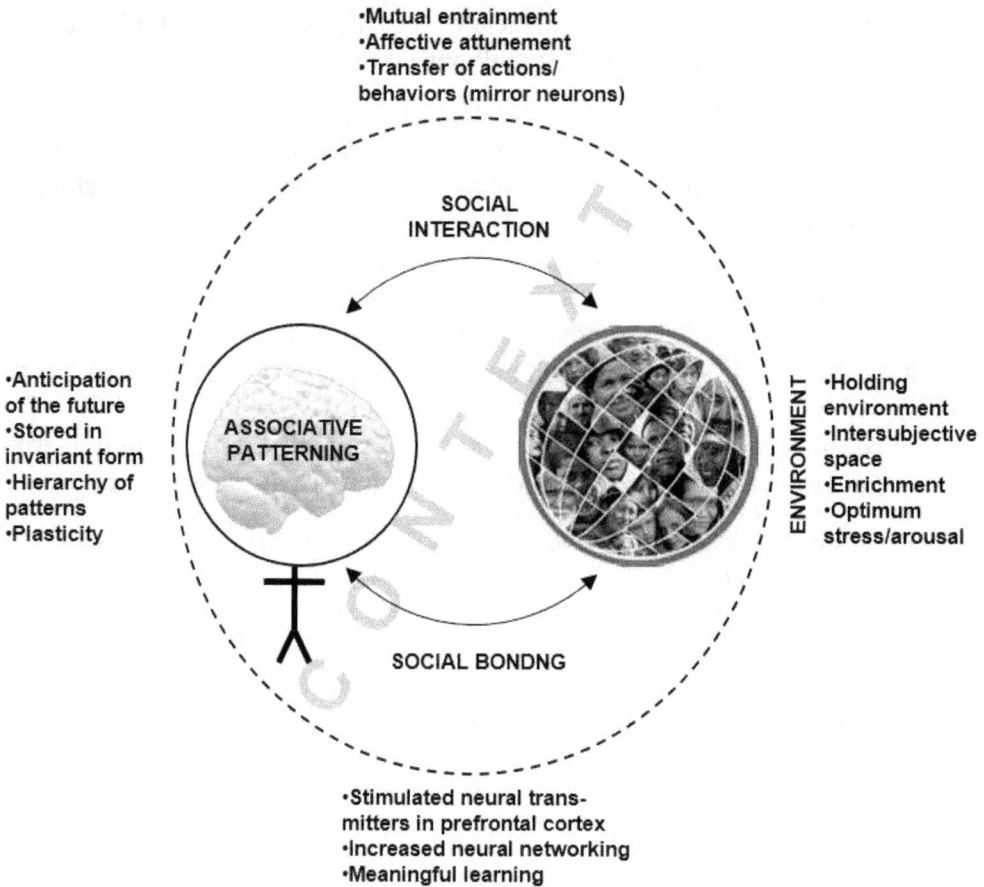

Figure 8-1. *The Social Creation of Knowledge*

Amen (2005) says that physical exercise, mental exercise and **social bonding** are the best sources of stimulation of the brain. Social neuroscience is the aspect of neuroscience dealing with the brain mechanisms of social interaction.

People are in continuous, two-way interaction with those around them, and the brain is continuously changing in response. As Cozolino and Sprokay explain,

It is becoming more evident that through emotional facial expressions, physical contact, and eye gaze—even through pupil dilation and blushing—people are in constant, if often unconscious, two-way communication with those around them.

It is in the matrix of this contact that brains are sculpted, balanced and made healthy. (Cozolino & Sprokay, 2006, p. 13)

Through these interactions, the genes are operating options "that are tested as an environment provides input that results in behavior" (Bownds, 1999, p. 169). Which supporting neuronal pathways become permanent depend on the usefulness of the behavior in enhancing survival and reproduction (Bownds, 1999). During this process, social preferences are also being developed. Tallis (2002) says that people's day-to-day social preferences are most likely influenced by unconscious learning. As he describes,

Human beings are constantly forming positive or negative opinions of others, and often after minimal social contact. If challenged, opinions can be justified, but such justifications frequently take the form of post-hoc rationalization. Some, of course, are laughably transparent. (Tallis, 2002, p. 129)

The literature suggests that there are specific changes within the brain that occur through **enriched environments**, that is, when the surrounding environment contains many interesting and thought-provoking ideas, pictures, books, statues, etc. Specifically, thicker cortices are created, there are larger cell bodies, and dendritic branching in the brain is more extensive. These are physiological changes in response to the environment, the feelings, and the learning of the participants. These changes have been directly connected to higher levels of intelligence and performance (Begley, 2007; Byrnes, 2001; Jensen, 1998). Byrnes sees the results of research on the effects of enriched environments on brain structure as both credible and well-established (Byrnes, 2001).

For example, Skoyles and Sagan presented the results of research on adolescent monkeys that suggested prefrontal cortices (considered the executive part of the human brain) respond better than other parts of the brain to an enriched learning environment. After a month of exposure to enriched environments the monkey's "prefrontal cortices had increased their activity by some 35 percent, while those of animals not exposed to an enriched environment had slightly decreased their activity" (Skoyles & Sagan, 2002, p. 76). These researchers go on to say that, "As the most neurally plastic species, we can choose to put ourselves in stimulus-rich environments that will increase our intelligence" (Skoyles & Sagan, 2002, p. 76).

Social forces clearly affect every aspect of our lives. As Rose (2005) describes,

The ways in which we conduct our observations and experiments on the world outside, the basis for what we regard as proof, the theoretical frameworks within which we embed these observations, experiments and proofs, have been shaped by the history of our subject, by the power and limits of available technology, and by the social forces that have formed and continue to form that history. (Rose, 2005, p. 9)

Studies in social neuroscience have affirmed that over the course of evolution physical mechanisms have developed in our brains to enable us to **learn through social interactions**. Johnson says that "these physical mechanisms have evolved to enable us to get the knowledge we need in order to keep emotionally and physically safe" (Johnson, 2006, p. 65). She also suggests that these mechanisms enable us to:

(1) Engage in affective attunement or empathic interaction and language,

(2) Consider the intentions of the other,

(3) Try to understand what another mind is thinking, and

(4) Think about how we want to interact. (Johnson, 2006, p. 65)

Mirror neurons provide a physical mechanism for this capability. Mirror neurons aid in stimulating other peoples states of mind. As Stern (2004) proposes, "This 'participation' in another's mental life creates a sense of feeling/sharing with/understanding the person's intentions and feelings" (p. 79). Blakemore and Frith describe the phenomenon called mirror neurons as,

> Simply observing someone moving activates similar brain areas to those activated by producing movements oneself. The brain's motor regions become active by the mere observation of movements even if the observer remains completely still. (Blakemore & Frith, 2005, pp. 160-161)

Further, Dobbs explains,

> These neurons are scattered throughout key parts of the brain—the premotor cortex and centers for language, empathy and pain—and fire not only as we perform a certain action, but also when we watch someone else perform that action. (Dobbs, 2007, p. 22)

Zull (2002) suggests that mirror neurons are a form of cognitive mimicry that transfers actions, behaviors and most likely other cultural norms. Thus when we *see* something being enacted, our mind creates the same patterns that we would use to enact that "something" ourselves. While mirror neurons are a subject of current research, it would appear that they represent a neuroscientific mechanism for the transfer of tacit knowledge between individuals, or throughout a culture. Siegel suggests that mirror neurons are the way in which our social brain processes and precedes the intentional or goal-directed action of others. Thus mirror neurons link our perception to the priming of the motor systems that engage the same action. In other words, "what we see, we become ready to do, to mirror other's actions and our own behaviors" (Siegel, 2007, p. 347).

The effects of social forces, of course, are often not in conscious awareness. The role of the conscious is to connect it all together. LeDoux (1996) says that the present social situation and physical environment are part of what is connected. Following extensive research, LeDoux (1996) concluded that,

People normally do all sorts of things for reasons they are not consciously aware of (because the behavior is produced by brain systems that operate unconsciously) and that one of the main jobs of consciousness is to keep our life tied together into a coherent story, a self-concept. It does this by generating explanations of behavior on the basis of our self-image, memories of the past, expectations of the future, the present social situation and the physical environment in which the behavior is produced. (LeDoux, 1996, p. 33).

Stonier agrees that when people are engaging in heavy duty thinking "it is not generally in terms of unlabelled images, sounds, smells, tastes or tactile experiences" (Stonier, 1997, p. 151). Stonier posits that thinking is actually talking to oneself, and that,

> This ability to talk to oneself is so basic a part of our human internal information environment that it tends to shape all our thought processes. It is this fact that allows us to be so influenced by our social and cultural surroundings. (Stonier, 1997, p. 151)

Building on our earlier discussion, knowledge (understanding, meaning, insight, etc.) can be thought of as theories, beliefs, practices and experiences coupled with a whole neighborhood of associated concepts, facts, and processes that together create the understanding, meaning and insight (to take effective action) we consider knowledge. If the individual receiving information from a knowledgeable person cannot recreate the invariant forms and neighborhood, or modulate his own invariant forms and neighborhood, then little or no learning will occur. Knowledge will not be shared, that is, the receiver has not recreated the sender's knowledge, nor is she likely to create her own comparable knowledge.

Further, knowledge is dependent on context. In fact, it represents an understanding of situations *in context*. This includes insights into the relationships within a system, and the ability to identify leverage points and weaknesses to recognize meaning in a specific situation and to anticipate future implications of actions taken to resolve problems. Shared understanding is taken to mean the movement of knowledge from one person to the other, recognizing that what passes in the air when two people are having a conversation is information in the form of changes in air pressure. These patterns of change may be understood by the perceiver (if they know the language and its nuances), but the changes in air pressure do not represent understanding, meaning or the capacity to anticipate the consequences of actions. The perceiver must be able to take these patterns (information) and—interpreting them through context—re-create the knowledge that the source intended. In other words, under perfect circumstances, *the content and context (information) originating at the source resonate with the perceiver such that the intended knowledge can be re-created by the perceiver.*

The innate ability to evoke meaning through understanding—to evaluate, judge and decide—is what distinguishes the human mind from other life forms. This ability enables people to discriminate and discern—to see similarities and differences, form patterns from particulars, and create and store knowledge purposefully. In this human process to create meaning and understanding from external stimuli, *context shapes content*. Context was discussed in depth in Chapter 6, where eight primary avenues of context patterns were introduced that may directly impact the content of a message: the content, setting or situation, silent attention/presence, non-voiced communications patterns, the system, personal context, unconscious processes and the overarching pattern context. These contexts are present and influential to various degrees depending on the specific social situation. Their influence on knowledge sharing may be through the participant's unconscious, but they are there. The higher the number of related (relevant) patterns (the greater the context), the greater the resonance between the source and receiver and the increased sharing of understanding. Cozolino (2002) says that along with language, **significant social relationships** stimulate learning and knowledge creation and shape the brain. He offers that the two powerful processes of social interaction and affective attunement, when involving a trusted other, contribute to "both the evolution and sculpting of the brain ... [since they] stimulate the brain to grow, organize and integrate" (Cozolino, 2002, p. 213).

Following a study of unconscious communications which supported the fact that people are in constant interaction with those around them (often unconsciously), Cozolino and Sprokay say that one possible implication of this finding of specific interest is the fact that "the attention of a caring, aware mentor may support the plasticity that leads to better, more meaningful learning" (Cozolino & Sprokay, 2006, p. 13). Plasticity refers to the fact that new ideas change the patterns in the mind which changes the physiology of the brain. Also, changes in the physical brain can change the patterns of neurons and thereby thoughts of the mind. As we live, learn and change through experience, our mind/brain also changes both physically and pattern-wise. Thus the mind/brain is said to have a great deal of "plasticity." Similarly, referring to recent discoveries in cognitive neuroscience and social cognitive neuroscience, Johnson (2006) says that educators and mentors of adults recognize "the neurological effects and importance of creating a trusting relationship, a holding environment, and an intersubjective space" (p. 68) where such things as reflection and abstract thinking can occur.

Social bonding reduces individual fears, creates trust, and makes the mind/brain much more open to incoming information, creating a desire to understand (and thereby re-create) the knowledge of the sender. In Sousa (2006) social bonding carries with it a positive, trusting relationship that allows the learner to take risks and not be concerned with mistakes made during learning. It also encourages an open mind and willingness to listen and learn from a trusted other.

Fear has been identified as an impediment to learning and knowledge sharing throughout the field of adult learning (Brookfield, 1987; Daloz, 1986, 1999; Mezirow, 1991; Perry, 1970/1988). The limbic system, the primitive part of the human brain, and in particular its amygdala, is the origin of survival and fear responses.

The literature is extensive on the need for a safe and empathic relationship to facilitate learning and knowledge sharing. Cozolino says that for complex levels of self-awareness, that is those that involve higher brain functions and potential changes in neural networks, learning cannot be accomplished when an individual feels anxious and defensive (Cozolino, 2002). Specifically, he says that a safe and empathic relationship can establish an emotional and neurobiological context that is conducive to neural reorganization. "It serves as a buffer and scaffolding within which [an adult] can better tolerate the stress required for neural reorganization" (Cozolino, 2002, p. 291). Taylor explains that,

> Adults who would create (or recreate) neural networks associated with development of a more complex epistemology need emotional support for the discomfort that will also certainly be part of that process. (Taylor, 2006, p. 82).

From a neuroscience perspective, trust in a relationship enhances the sharing of knowledge, especially regarding shallow and deep knowledge. When a secure, bonding relationship in which trust has been established occurs, the learner's neurotransmitters in the prefrontal cortex (dopamine, serotonin, and norepinephrine) are stimulated and lead to increased neuronal networking and meaningful learning (Cozolino, 2002). Schore describes this as "a cascade of biochemical processes, stimulating and enhancing the growth and connectivity of neural networks throughout the brain" (Schore, 1994, as cited in Cozolino, 2002, p. 191). **Thus, a caring, affirming relationship promotes neural growth and knowledge creation.** Such physiological changes can quickly influence the attitude and expectations of people involved in social knowledge sharing and learning.

Without such trust and bonding, a listener tends to defend his or her own pre-established beliefs, theories, frames of reference, and self-image. Under normal situations, we tend to defend our beliefs and how we see the world. This defense may accept some incoming information, reject other, and change some. When these distortions occur, the incoming information can no longer represent the knowledge of the sender and therefore it is not shared. New knowledge that challenges or contradicts what we already know also tends to threaten our concept of Self, and thereby creates defensive reactions that minimize or negate learning. Our mind concentrates on "defending itself" and does not have time for listening or taking the other person's view and understanding.

On the other hand, if a trusting, nurturing relationship exists between two people, a safe environment can be created that eliminates or minimizes potential threats to the learner. Daloz (1986) refers to such a situation as a holding environment (in Johnson, 2006, p. 64). When such a relationship is created, the receiver can build a new sense of Self while building the sender's knowledge out of the information that moves from the sender to the receiver. Such knowledge may not be identical to the sender's knowledge because the mind/ brain of each participant is different. However, when the knowledge sharing is successful, the knowledge in each person may be equally capable of taking effective action even though their understanding, meaning and insight may differ in some ways.

Andreasen cites mentoring as one of the elements that helps create a cultural environment to nurture creativity. From a broader perspective, the five circumstances that create what she calls a "cradle of creativity" include an atmosphere of intellectual freedom and excitement; a critical mass of creative minds; free and fair competition, mentors, and patrons, and at least some economic prosperity. As she concludes, "If we seek to find social and cultural environmental factors that help to create the creative brain, these must be considered to be important ones" (Andreasen, 2005, p. 131).

Cozolino (2002) says that the efficacy of the mentoring relationship—a balance of support and challenge—is supported by the literature on brain function. "We appear to experience optimal development and integration in a context of a balance of nurturance and optimal stress" (p. 62). Considering stress, Akil et al. state,

> The stress system is an active monitoring system that constantly compares current events to past experience, interprets the relevance (salience) of the events to the survival of the organisms ability to cope. (Akil et al., 1999, p. 1146)

If the emotional content of incoming information from a conversation is one of strong fear or uncertainty to the individual, stress is created and can significantly limit any learning involved. However, if there is too little arousal/stress involved then there may be no desire for listening. Thus, **for each individual there exists at any given time some optimal level of arousal/stress** (Zull, 2002). Note that low levels of stress are often referred to as arousal.

Plotting knowledge creation rate on the vertical axis and arousal/stress level along the horizontal axis, we get an inverted U. See Figure 8-2. The optimum arousal level shown just to the left of the center of the inverted U challenges the listener but does not make them fearful of failure or embarrassment (Akil et al., 1999). This optimal level of learning and knowledge creation is context sensitive and content dependent and is also influenced by the individual's history. The learner's personal beliefs and feelings about the content of the materials can also play a role in determining his or her stress level. To optimize learning in a given situation, individuals need to understand their own arousal/stress level that challenges them to create knowledge from what they hear, but does not reduce this capacity because of fear. It is possible for individuals to control their perception of stress by recognizing its existence and understanding that stress is created *inside* the body and can therefore be understood and managed (Begley, 2007).

The notion of affective attunement is connected to Dewey's observations that an educator needs to "have that sympathetic understanding of individuals as individuals which gives him an idea of what is actually going on in the minds of those who are learning" (Dewey, [1938] 1997, p. 39). As Johnson (2006) explains, "According to social cognitive neuroscience, the brain actually needs to seek out an affectively attuned other if it is to learn. Affective attunement alleviates fear," (p. 65) a significant impediment to learning. These mechanisms support learning situations by enhancing understanding, meaning, truth and how things work, and anticipating the results of actions.

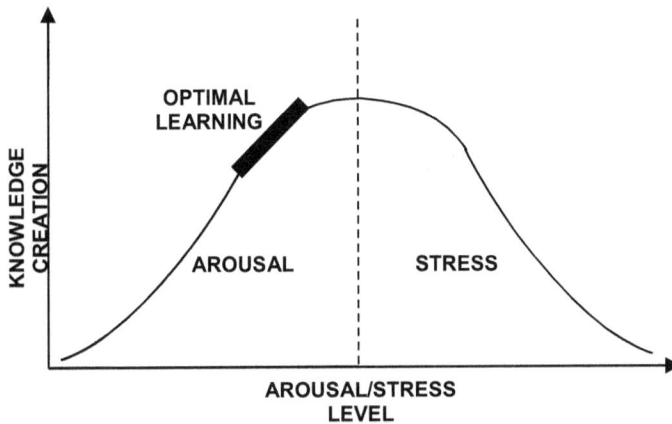

Figure 8-2: *Representation of the relationship between knowledge creation and arousal/stress*

One example of affective attunement that stimulates the orbitofrontal cortex is eye contact because "specific cells are particularly responsive to facial expression and eye gaze" (Schore, 1994, p. 67). As Johnson explains, literally "looking into the eyes of the affectively attuned other is another significant form of social interaction that can assist in promoting development" (Johnson, 2006, p. 67). This reflects the earlier discussion on the importance and natures of context. Similarly, Frith and Wolpert (2003) forward that an infant and caregiver enter into an intersubjective space. This space may be created around the infant and caregiver through the process of emotional resonance or affective attunement (Johnson, 2006).

Introducing Collaborative Entanglement

Biological systems are remarkably smarter in their support of the body than we are in sustaining our work places and communities. Fortunately, we can and are learning from ourselves in this sense, and whether we reflect on this learning in the form of a reality or as an analogy is insignificant as long as we keep learning and creating knowledge (Bennet and Bennet, 2008c).

In a social setting new thoughts and behaviors proposed through research or personal reflection (based on earlier learning) emerge and then build on other's thoughts and behaviors and then become mixed with yet another set of thoughts and behaviors from the community, and so on. We call this mixing, entwining and creation of unpredictable associations the process of *entanglement*. In other words, the knowledge creation process in a group or community works very much as does the human mind/brain.

Collaborative entanglement as a social phenomenon can be analogous to the natural activities of the brain, with the brain representing the researcher (in our example) and the stakeholder community representing the knowledge beneficiary. All the living and learning of the host human is recorded in the brain, stored among some hundred billion neurons that are continuously moving between firing and idling, creating and re-creating patterns. Information is coming into the individual through the senses which, assuming for the sake of our analogy, resonates with internal patterns that have strong synaptic connections. When resonance occurs, the incoming information is consistent with the individual's frame of reference and belief systems. As this incoming information is complexed (the associative patterning process) it may connect with (and to some degree may bring into conscious awareness) deep knowledge. The unconscious continues this process (24/7), with new knowledge stored in the unconscious and perhaps emerging at the conscious level.

The collaborative entanglement model is discussed in more depth in Chapter 9. Also, see Bennet and Bennet (2007b).

An Extrapolation

With the new century emerged new ideas on every front, one of which was expansion of the global brain concept. The term originally emerged in print in 1983 with the publication of Peter Russell's book by that name. Grounding his work on historic observations of new levels of organization occurring based on the tight-but-flexible coupling of 10 billion units in a system, Russell described an interconnected network of humans as becoming a Global Brain (Russell, 1982). In 1995 Gottfried Mayer-Kress and Cathleen Barczys proposed that "a globally and tightly connected network of computer workstations such as the Internet can lead to the emergence of a globally self-organized structure that could be called the Global Brain" (Mayer-Kress & Barczys, 1995, p.1). In 2000 Howard Bloom's treatment described the network of life on Earth as a complex adaptive system. He shows how animals and plants have evolved together as components of a worldwide learning machine, with humans playing conscious and unconscious roles, with development of the World Wide Web as part of this learning. And so forth.

We choose to explore the concept of Global Brain from the viewpoint of the mind/brain—perhaps moving towards the higher level of evolution introduced by Pierre Teilhard de Chardin's *noosphere*, a network of thoughts ushering in a new level of consciousness. Recognizing that the mind/brain supports survival and sustainability in a complex and unpredictable world, we now consider, somewhat metaphorically, the potential of learning from the totality of ourselves to further explore the emergence of social knowledge. Perhaps the simplest way to extrapolate our model of the individual mind/brain to the societal level is through story. Enjoy!

* * * * *

As SETH streamed into unknown territory, he was further excited by the feelings of familiarity and resonance emerging within. SETH represented Self-Evolved Thinking Humans, a pattern of men and women exalting diversity, crossing cultural, ethnic, religious, age and gender boundaries in pursuit of ultimate knowledge. SETH's capacity to anticipate was high, honed by the association of a wide range of experiences and a highly tuned emotional guidance system. Still, with all her historic success in anticipating and dealing with the future in her area of expertise, this landscape was different ... was that a tinge of fear in her side tagging along for the ride?

SETH was responding to a strong message received from this distant realm, a message associated with survival, no doubt one of those learnings worthy of a new category of The Nobel Prize, a grand new way of thinking and being. He now stood on the high ground above that distant realm, a hundred thousand homes stretched out as far as he could see, lights twinkling through the windows and pulsing along the billion connecting three-dimensional highways, roads and paths that made the community One.

Some spots were brighter than others: flitting patterns from a movie theatre playing reruns; flashing sparks from a loudly-buzzing generator; colorful streams from an observatory at the far edge of the city sporting a large, upward-focused telescope. And near the center of this hub of activity, to the left, where connecting paths intertwined with incessant beams of entangled reds and blues and yellows, the brightest light moved in and out of the central library. SETH understood the power of record-keeping at its best, a living, vibrant field of growing and expanding patterns evolving from instant to instant.

SETH moved toward that light, carefully navigating the busyness of the intersections, pulled this way and that by the excitement, but **committed to staying the course**. He had come to learn from the Master, to discover that single thought that guided all the others. He paused to reflect on this singular yearning for the discovery of something more that had emerged since his first feeling of the message.

Then he arrived at his destination, startled by the peace within the hub of excitement but gently perceiving the silence and fullness that comes with knowing. What might be described as an inner council of sorts welcomed him, each member of the council a different aspect of the One. Eager to discover answers to his questions, he moved quickly through the formalities of introductions, conveying greetings from mutual distant relatives, sharing the urgency of his mission, and expressing gratitude for a warm reception.

"*The environment is rapidly changing,*" the leader began, "*and though you journeyed quickly following the first conscious flash, much new information is coming in through our sensors and emerging from our internal sources that is shifting our direction. There are new choices to make. Let us see how you fit, what you contribute ...*"

"*And what **we** can learn from you,*" SETH interrupted.

"*Yes,*" the leader confirmed, "*that is also a possibility.*"

"*Possibility?*" SETH questioned. "*But this sounded like the answer we have been seeking; finally, absolute knowledge. It resonates with our beliefs, with our preferred frames of reference, with our values ...*"

"*Ah,*" responded the leader, "*but beliefs and frames of reference and values also change. They are tools for us to act effectively in an uncertain and changing environment.*"

SETH was puzzled, confused even. "*No. Our community is also one hundred thousand strong, although many of those connections are outliers, at a distance, only a few reside in the center of town. Still, we have held onto those early values embedded during the beginning of time, and have picked up incoming information throughout our history that has reinforced those values, and we have sent continuous messages beyond our boundaries to guide those who are on misdirected paths ...*"

"*So that was you,*" the leader sighed. "*Those historic values were holding all of us back for a while.*" There was a short pause, accented by rhythms of soft bursts of light. The leader continued, "*And yet you are here. You were able to sense something new and different with the potential of evolving our connections and firings to another level.*"

"*Yes ... it was magical!*" responded SETH. "*There was an explosion right in the center of town—at our Central Library—that coincided with the explosion here, which was visible and felt even across such great distances. A high vibration so strong that it pulled me here. Where did it come from? What exactly is it? Tell me what it is. Give me the words, the pattern, the context, to understand and learn and connect and share.*"

The leader smiled and silently moved away from SETH even as another form approached and continued the interaction. "*YOU are part of the answer to your questions! It is at the core of who you are and now you are more or you are more strongly connected to us through this journey, and, in turn to all those with whom we interact. We welcome your contribution.*"

SETH was beginning to tire of these circular responses. "*But I'm here to discover the grand new way of doing and being, the answer!*"

A third form was now moving toward SETH, hand out-stretched, eyes sparkling with amusement. "*There is no such thing; and simultaneously all you know is part of such a thing!*"

"*We are part of such a thing that does not exist?*" SETH blurted out.

The third informer gently motioned to the shelves and shelves of books and movies surrounding them in a hazy glow. "*We store here only a small amount of what we observe, what we reflect, what we discover, and it is always reforming and reconnecting in new ways to create the wonderful flash which brought you here.*" She gestured a full circle, gliding around with the gesture, a lightness and happiness in the movement. "*Perhaps you had forgotten? This is the process of birth and regeneration, the way of knowledge, the capacity to take effective action, a human gift to navigate the rapids of change, uncertainty and complexity.*"

"*I don't understand,*" SETH sorrowed. "*How can I anticipate those rapids?*"

"*You've started that journey already,*" came the slow response. "*You are here with us, interacting, each of us learning from the other. Our thoughts are no longer distant to you. We are moving toward intelligent activity.*" The third informer paused, pulsing with soft light that reached toward SETH.

"*My friend, our future is neither predetermined nor knowable. We are co-creators of that future, and it rests with the dynamics of an almost infinite number of quasi-independent biological thinking subsystems that are entangled and deeply interconnected, with each trying to comprehend the whole while acting to the benefit of the individual. There is no 'answer' or ultimate action; there is learning, thinking and acting, the role of each biological subsystem which, in turn, affects the learning, thinking and acting of the whole in completely unpredictable ways.*"

SETH reflected. Patterns in a never-ending journey in which SETH was fully participating?

As SETH turned her energy towards home, she reflected on re-connecting with her trusted network, sharing new patterns, expanding their thoughts through exchange and dialogue, and **continuously re-creating themselves to co-evolve with a changing Universe** ...

Final Thoughts

Experiential learning is not just a function of the incoming information. It becomes clear that the nature of the social interaction plays an important role in determining knowledge creation and sharing. The overall environment, a trusted other, and the conscious and unconscious state of the learner all have a role in the final efficiency and effectiveness of learning that occurs. [For a new treatment of experiential learning see: Bennet, D. & Bennet, A. (2015), *Expanding the Self: The Intelligent Complex Adaptive Learning System,* MQI Press, Frost, WV.]

Further, the specific social interaction that influences the neural structure, and the perceived stress level of the individual, will affect the nature and amount of knowledge that is created and shared. By being aware of these factors, learners may be able to change the local physical environment, improve communication with others, or perhaps position and adjust their own internal feelings and perspectives to maximize learning.

Here are a few summary highlights of this chapter in terms of recent neuroscience findings:

There is an optimum level of stress for learning (the inverted "U"). This level is somewhere between a positive attitude and a strong motivation to learn (arousal), and some level of fear of learning or the learning situation.

Physical mechanisms have developed in our brain to enable us to learn through social interactions. These mechanisms support affective attunement, help us consider the intentions of others and what others are thinking, and help us think about how we want to interact (Johnson, 2006).

The brain actually needs to seek out an affectively attuned other for learning. As Johnson explains, effective attunement reduces fear, and creates a positive environment and motivation to learn (Johnson, 2006).

Physical and mental exercise and social bonding are significant sources of stimulation of the brain. Studies in social neuroscience have affirmed that over the course of evolution physical mechanisms have developed in our brains to enable us to learn through social interactions (Amen, 2005).

Language and social relationships build and shape the brain. This significantly impacts the sensing aspect of concrete experience and the concepts, ideas, and logic of abstract conceptualization. Good social relationships enhance learning through a reduction of stress, a shared language, and the use and understanding of concepts, metaphors, anecdotes, and stories.

Adults develop complex neural patterns need emotional support to offset discomfort of this process. Taylor (2006) suggests that this support is needed by individuals developing complex knowledge. Such emotional support will enhance the feelings of an individual during concrete experience, and also aid in the creation and understanding of concepts and ideas during abstract conceptualization.

Affective attunement contributes to the evolution and sculpting of the brain. Affective attunement involves a mentor, coach, or another significant individual who is trusted and capable of resonance with the learner. When this happens, a dialogue with such an individual can greatly help the learner in understanding, developing meaning, anticipating the future with respect to actions, and receiving sensory feedback. As these new patterns are created in the mind, they in turn impact and change the structure of the brain.

An enriched environment increases the formation and survival of new neurons. Such an enriched environment can influence both the nature of the experience of the learner and his or her learning efficacy. As Begley (2007) describes, "exposure to an enriched environment leads to a striking increase in new neurons, along with a substantial improvement in behavioral performance" (p. 58).

Collaborative entanglement represents the continuous interaction, movement of information, and sharing and learning of knowledge resulting in a community movement toward a higher level of awareness, understanding and meaning. Such a process builds both explicit and implicit knowledge and creates a learning, trust and bonding that may energize and accelerate community progress.

While we have addressed information, knowledge, learning and the factors and conditions which influence the social creation and/or sharing of knowledge, it must not be forgotten that every individual learns (creates their own knowledge) from a baseline of past experiences, theories, biases, motivations and perceptions of their Self (Bennet & Bennet, 2009a). It is concepts and their associated internal patterns that can be mixed with incoming information. Thus we can only create new knowledge from our personal autobiography—and information coming to us in the future will be complexed with what we are learning today. Then again, our personal autobiography is rich with social interactions, social bonding experiences, and reflection—a richness to which we contribute every day of our lives.

Chapter 9
The Fallacy of Knowledge Reuse[1]

In a little over 30 years, Singapore raised its annual per capita income from $1,000 to $30,000 (Yew, 2000), and by 2007 Singapore was recognized as having the second highest per capita income in the world. In October of 2007 Singapore was named The Most Admired Knowledge City (The World Capital Institute & Teleos, 2007). Singapore was perceived by a panel of experts as the world winner based on their identity, intelligence and financial capital, all largely built on Singapore's ability to identify, transfer and apply the best knowledge from around the world. In just two years, the number of annual U.S. tax returns prepared in India jumped from 100,000 to 400,000 (Friedman, 2005), serving as an example of the international flavor of knowledge work making its way around the world from the U.S. into the economic life of India. Over the last eight years, the number of Americans using their knowledge to work from home has doubled to represent 16 percent of the U.S. workforce (Friedman, 2005). **In the midst of what might be called a knowledge millennium, organizations, communities, cities and nations are hungry for knowledge and the potential advantages it offers towards sustainability and a higher quality of life.**

No matter what the venue, there are two approaches to increasing knowledge capacity and capability: either bring it in from the outside or grow it from the inside. Bringing it in from the outside might include buying information, hiring experts, partnering, benchmarking and/or adopting and adapting best practices. When efficiency was the defining factor of success in the 20th century, the attempted transfer of best practices flourished. As long as a best practice was relatively simple and dealt with a repetitive process—and the environments of the organizations or communities involved were similar and fairly stable—a successful transfer *was possible*. However, since best practices focus on actions and often neglect the level of understanding and insight into the *how* and *why* things actually work, they were often ineffective in *differing* situations and contexts (Brown & Duguid, 2000).

As we enter the 21st century, the explosion of information coupled with global connectivity is creating a future filled with change, uncertainty and increasing complexity[2], a future that is best understood as accelerating towards us (Bennet and Bennet, 2004). While best practices may be indicators of past needs and capabilities that worked in specific situations, best practices are typically not robust or adaptable. Since we (1) are all facing *new* challenges, (2) cannot do things the way we've done them in the past, and (3) may not be able to use best practices from others, where *will* we get the new knowledge necessary for success?

As introduced in the best practices example above, all too often we look to the past for answers. This chapter explores the concept of knowledge reuse through (1) providing a new model of information and knowledge consistent with neuroscience and the demands of a changing, uncertain and complex environment, (2) using that model as an analogy to explore the social context of knowledge mobilization with its process of collaborative entanglement, and (3) looking at the concepts of knowledge robustness and sustainability from the viewpoints of individuals and the community.

The Fallacy of Reuse

The fallacy of knowledge reuse is addressed from several viewpoints. First, in terms of knowledge as context-sensitive and situation dependent. Second, as explicated in Chapters 7 and 8, in terms of how information is stored in and re-created by the brain. Note that the explosion mentioned in the opening paragraphs of this chapter was a reference to *information*, which may or may not have been used in a specific situation or context as a part of knowledge (as knowledge artifacts). Recall that knowledge is differentiated from information in that knowledge contains information that supports the capacity to take effective action. Thus knowledge relates not only to its information content, Knowledge (Informing), but also to the efficacy of that information content *in terms of the situation at hand*, Knowledge (Proceeding).

Today we recognize that all knowledge, to varying degrees, is context-sensitive and situation dependent (there are no impenetrable boundaries). (See Chapter 6 for discussion of context.) This means that while the content may be constant, when you change the context the meaning of the content in that new context may be entirely different. The greater the complexity of a situation, the greater the potential number of patterns and relationships of patterns that make knowledge relevant to that situation, and the less likely that knowledge would apply to different situations.

Pragmatic knowledge (introduced as Kpraxis in Chapter 3) draws directly on the lessons of past hands-on experiences *within specific circumstances* to determine how things actually work. Pragmatic knowledge is knowledge focused toward action because it is *continuously customized and improved* by close observation of the effectiveness of those actions in meeting expected results. This is earned knowledge, a "knowing" that individuals—and by extension the organizations with which they are associated—have built through experience, reflection and comprehension of how to interpret situations and what actions to take to achieve desired outcomes. Note that pragmatic knowledge is not directly linked to surface, shallow or deep knowledge, although it may be any one of these, or any combination of these. This pragmatic way of knowing helps interpret relationships difficult to recognize, that is, those that exist between *how* we see a situation (our frame of reference) and *what rules we use* to determine our actions. Pragmatic knowledge can be closely linked to the capacity of community members to learn from their own experiences. From this perspective, knowledge arises through interacting individuals as they reflect, experiment, and identify new ways of doing things in their communities. *Pragmatic knowledge creation*

*is then primarily a matter of learning through actions, feedback and day-to-day
conversations with others, and secondarily through internal discovery and inquiry.*

The Representation of Thought in the Brain

As detailed in Chapter 7, in the brain thoughts are represented by patterns of neuronal
firings, their synaptic connections and the strengths between the synaptic spaces. For
example, a single thought could be represented in the brain by a network of a million
neurons, with each neuron connecting to 5,000 other neurons. Incoming external
information (new information) is mixed, or semantically complexed, with internal
information, creating new neuronal patterns that may represent understanding,
meaning, and/or the anticipation of the consequences of actions, in other words,
knowledge. We introduced the term *associative patterning* to describe this continuous
process of learning.

Thus, from the viewpoint of the mind/brain, any knowledge that is being "re-used"
is actually being "re-created", and, in an area of continuing interest, most likely
complexed over and over again as incoming information is associated with internal
information. Further, if Knowledge (Informing) is different, there is a good chance that
Knowledge (Proceeding) will be different, that is, the *process* of pulling up and
sequencing associated Knowledge (Informing) and semantically complexing it with
incoming information to make it comprehensible is going to vary. In essence, every
time we apply knowledge whether Informing or Proceeding, it is to some extent new
knowledge because the human mind—unlike an information management system—
unconsciously tailors what is emerging as knowledge to the situation at hand! This is
the art of Knowledge (Proceeding). See Edelman (2000) for an enlightening discussion
on the non-repeatability of memory recall.

Further, when you see a picture only about 20 percent of what you are seeing is
represented in the image in your brain; the other 80 percent of that image comes from
information, ideas and feelings already in your brain (Marchese, 1998). While this
statement may appear a bit strong, the point that is made is that the mind doesn't store
memories like a computer, that is, storing everything that comes in. The mind stores
the *core* of the picture, what Hawkins calls an invariant (Hawkins & Blakeslee, 2004).
This particular phenomenon of relating external and internal forms of experience is
called appresentation (Marton & Booth, 1997). As Moon explains,

> Appresentation is the manner in which a part of something that is perceived as an
> external experience can stimulate a much more complete or richer internal
> experience of the 'whole' of that thing to be conjured up (Moon, 2004, p. 23).

For example, if you see your friend from the side or back you can usually recognize
who they are since your mind has stored a core basic memory that includes major
features of that person. When you see your friend, your mind is filling in the blanks
and you recognize the incoming picture as your friend. There is efficiency in this

process. Simultaneously, there is robustness in the way the brain *stores* core memories. If it takes a million neurons to create a specific pattern (the core part of incoming information), the brain may set aside 1.4 million neurons with their connections as space for that pattern, providing a looseness to account for future associative changes (or perhaps for dying cells). Thus, for this particular pattern you could lose tens of thousands of brain cells and still have significant aspects of the core memory available for future retrieval via re-creation. While this may not appear efficient in terms of energy utilization, from an effectiveness viewpoint it is extremely well-designed. Similarly, network theory espouses the development of repetitive nodes built on a distributed information model, thereby creating redundancy. Similar to neuron signals, the flow *among* nodes becomes essential for success. An example of this is expressed in the network centric warfare which is *more about networking than networks* (DONCIO, 1998).

Knowledge reuse contains the same dangers as those recently recognized by the legal system concerning eye witness testimony. Witness testimony assumes memory recall is stable, accurate and reliable. As introduced above, findings in Neuroscience have indicated that this is not true (Edelman, 2000). Since every time you re-member something you regenerate it, and since you don't store 100 percent of a memory, you can rarely pull anything up exactly as you did previously. The significance of these findings to the legal system is staggering. Moenssens et al. (1995) state that more than 4,250 Americans every year are wrongfully convicted due to inaccurate eyewitness testimony.

The physical aspects of an event are obviously compromised by the selective nature of the acquisition stage of memory. However, matters are further complicated by the fact that acquisition also involves a social component. Thus, a witness' ability to perceive accurately is affected by both event factors—those inherent to the event itself—and witness factors—those inherent to the witness (Moenssens et al., 1995, p. 1171).

While our earlier examples dealt with relatively simple situations, as Moenssens et al., point out, life is not simple. At the same time you catch sight of your friend and are smiling, getting ready to call out and wave, you may be swatting gnats away from your eyes, shivering from a soft breeze, smelling burning rubber from a car that just sped by, registering the dark clouds moving in from the west, feeling hunger pains in your stomach, and sensing a soreness in your little toe due to tight shoes. Etcetera. *The brain is multidimensional,* simultaneously processing visual, aural, olfactory and kinesthetic sensory inputs and, as discussed above, combining them with mental thoughts and emotional feelings (internal patterns) to create an internal perception and feeling of external awareness (Bennet and Bennet, 2006a). As discussed above, the brain is simultaneously identifying and storing core patterns from incoming information; in other words, there is a hierarchy of knowledge where hierarchy represents "an order of some complexity, in which the elements are distributed along the gradient of importance" (Kuntz, 1968, p. 162). The core pattern stored in the brain could be described as a pattern of patterns with possibly both hierarchical and associative relationships to other patterns.

Hierarchical relationships affect the robustness and sustainability of knowledge. Recall the story of the two watchmakers, Hora and Tempus (Simon, 1969). Tempus constructed his watches such that his work fell to pieces every time he was interrupted. Hora designed his watches so that he could put together subassemblies so that when he was interrupted only a portion of his work was lost. Simon calls this a hierarchy of potential stable subassemblies, "Nothing more than survival of the fittest—that is, of the stable" (Simon, 1969, p. 93).

The idea underlying this description is that some semi-independent subcomponents within a complex system will perform specific sub-functions that contribute to the overall functioning of the system (Simon, 1969). Complex adaptive systems are partially ordered systems that unfold and evolve through time and are often constructed in a hierarchy of levels (Bennet & Bennet, 2004; 2006b). Considering the brain as a semi-independent subcomponent of the body that contains a hierarchy of patterns associated with other patterns, the higher level (core) patterns would retain their associations (in terms of meaning, understanding and anticipation of the future) even as the lower level patterns (internal information that is situation dependent) are re-created in response to new incoming information. A recent study of chess players showed that experts examined the chessboard patterns (not the pieces) over and over again, looking at nuances, generally "playing with" and studying these *patterns* (Ross, 2006). Similarly, an expert in a bounded domain who has developed higher level patterns through years of trial and error in varied situations *would most likely use pattern recognition and chunking rather than logic and lower-level relationships* as a means of understanding and decision-making.

The above discussion brings home the fact that **the mind/brain develops robustness and deep understanding derived from its capacity to use past learning and memories to complete incoming information instead of storing all the details**. This provides the ability to create and store higher level patterns while simultaneously semantically complexing incoming information with internal memories, adapting those memories to the situation at hand. Through these processes—and many more that we do not yet understand—the brain supports survival and sustainability in a complex and unpredictable world.

Learning to Mobilize Knowledge in Communities

Biological systems are remarkably smarter in their support of the body than we are in sustaining our work places and communities. Fortunately, we can and are learning from ourselves in this sense, and whether we reflect on this learning in the form of a reality or as an analogy is insignificant as long as we keep learning. For example, consider the social process of knowledge mobilization, with specific focus on the application of university or research findings to the community stakeholder group where they can make a difference for the citizen. For purposes of this discussion, *knowledge mobilization* (KMb) is the process of generating value or a value stream through the creation, assimilation, leveraging, sharing and application of focused knowledge to a bounded community (Bennet & Bennet, 2007b). In communities and cities this concerns the creating, moving and tailoring of knowledge from its source in universities and individual experts to practitioners, community leaders and larger stakeholder groups such that consequent actions are effective and sustainable.

KMb is a process—or a program comprised of a number of specific processes. The KMb approach taken depends on the timing, application, situation and needs of the community and stakeholders it touches. For a simple problem, the KMb process may end when the problem is solved, but for a more complex problem the process may continue as long as the action sequence is needed to achieve the objective. In a social setting new thoughts and behaviors proposed through research emerge and then build on other thoughts and behaviors from practitioners and then become mixed with yet another set of thoughts and behaviors from the community, and so on. We call this mixing, entwining and set of unpredictable associations the process of *entanglement*. In other words, the knowledge mobilization process in a community—moving bounded theoretical knowledge into the community—works very much as does the human mind.

As introduced in Chapter 8, collaborative entanglement consistently develops and supports approaches and processes that combine the sources of knowledge and the beneficiaries of that knowledge to interactively move toward a common direction such as meeting an identified community need. Beyond decision-making, collaborative entanglement includes the execution and actions that build value for all stakeholders, engaging social responsibility and providing a platform for knowledge mobilization. The collaborative entanglement model is highly participative, with permeable and porous (unclear and continuously reshaping) boundaries between the knowledge researcher and knowledge beneficiary as well as between the research and application of the research. In other words, the research itself becomes part of the process of implementing research results (Bennet & Bennet, 2007b). Lee and Garvin (2003) contend that to be effective, knowledge exchange depends on multi-directional, participatory communication among stakeholders. *The collaborative entanglement model moves beyond knowledge exchange to the creation of shared understanding resulting in collaborative advantage and value results.* While an in-depth treatment of approaches to collaborative entanglement is not the focus of this book, these include appreciative inquiry, social marketing, community service-learning, participative inquiry, action research and action learning, as well as other experiential learning techniques (Bennet & Bennet, 2007b).

Analogous to the natural activities of the brain, in the collaborative entanglement model individuals and groups are continuously interacting as new information comes through their sensors: (1) they recognize a problem or issue and/or solution, (2) they see new indicators that bode well or poorly for the community, or (3) new events occur that affect an on-going project or community effort. From these interactions and others—often related to strong emotional feelings which increase the importance and strength of their meaning—new knowledge emerges. When researchers and practitioners are engaged in this interactive, emergent process with other stakeholders, the new knowledge that emerges is *informed* by their learned expertise. As new knowledge is applied and this iterative loop of collective learning continues, a large amount of tacit knowledge (embodied, affective and intuitive) is created beyond that which visibly affects the community. This tacit knowledge then forms the grounding (state-of-the-art thinking) for future incoming information that will be associated with these patterns. In other words, the process of collaborative entanglement among experts and stakeholders not only helps provide a specific solution to a current issue, but seeds the ground for continuous community improvement, collaboration, and sustainability.

A Closer Look at Knowledge Sustainability and Robustness

Knowledge as we have defined it has meaning and is in reference to some domain of action. By domain is meant an area with reasonable boundaries, a sphere of activity or field of concern. For example, for a firefighter the domain is fire and the expertise is putting fires out (perhaps specializing in specific types such as forest fires). Over time a domain of action can be stable, variable (slow or fast), or unpredictable and uncertain. For knowledge to be sustainable, it must maintain its capacity to take effective action even when the nature of the domain changes. For example, if the domain becomes highly dynamic, there is less time to make decisions and the application of knowledge must occur much faster. This means that the best knowledge will consist of immediately available information with the appropriate actions already developed. Previously developed scenario knowledge (an approach used in warfare) might be the only way to survive. On the other hand, if the domain becomes increasingly complex, but slower to change, knowledge of seeding, modeling, pattern detection or sense and response techniques may produce the most effective results (Bennet & Bennet, 2008b; 2013).

For a community, a particular domain can be characterized by major factors or characteristics such as: growth rate, nature of culture, economic system, educational level or political structure. If you looked at a small town in West Virginia or the Alps that had not changed much in the last 100 years, you'd have a very stable domain for a decision-maker who had an expertise related to similar environments. A small town water problem could be vastly different than a large city's problems; in fact, the differences may be so great that they could easily fall into different domains. So, in addition to deep knowledge pertinent to a specific domain, an expert would need *specialized* knowledge and experience, much of which could be highly context-sensitive and situation-dependent.

For a more complex and publically visible environment, an expert would need a higher level of awareness and a good understanding of issues *and* politics, that is, a more robust knowledge base. At any point in time, an expert's knowledge would be effective over a certain range of variability within a domain of action. The robustness of that knowledge would involve its strength (quality and depth) and hardiness (breadth and relevance over time). For example, when you first start teaching your daughter to drive a car, you explain the basics to her and take her to an empty parking lot to try it out. As she demonstrates competency, you expand the areas in which she practices driving. Over time her driving ability becomes more robust. She can effectively deal with a broader range of environments and emerging requirements, and a large amount of the knowledge she is building becomes tacit. Even as she is learning "the rules of the road" that you are repeating over and over again in her ear, she is embodying physical knowledge of how to successfully navigate the car in and out of tight situations. Embodied tacit knowledge is built up in all of us as we repeat physical manipulations and/or use our other senses to make judgments and decisions.

As another example, think of an expert golfer whose knowledge is strongly intuitive, embodied and affective but at the same time has to be robust enough to play all the major golf courses in varied weather (temperature, rain, wind, etc.). Compare his knowledge to that of a football quarterback who must play not only in varied weather but with different teammates and against different teams with different plays, all unique. The quarterback's tacit knowledge would have to be considerably more robust than that of a golfer. Both would include elements of spiritual tacit knowledge; the golfer in connecting with the larger aspects of nature, the football player in connecting with his teammates.

People who repeatedly make effective decisions are said to have good knowledge, howbeit that knowledge may only be effective in a specific type of situation. However, higher order patterns help determine the probability of success. An expert who has robust knowledge will be more successful in a dynamic environment than one whose expertise only applies to a narrow band of situations. The higher order patterns discussed earlier, i.e., patterns of patterns that apply to a wide range of situations, provide robust knowledge (Bennet and Bennet, 2006a). These patterns, when they exist, may be recognized by the unconscious mind without any conscious awareness on the part of the expert. This is why highly competent people often cannot explain how or why they know what to do, they just know what needs to be done and how to go about doing it. They consistently demonstrate high quality knowledge. Note that the quality of knowledge is an indicator of the probability of its action yielding the intended effectiveness. While every decision is to some extent a guess about the future (Bennet and Bennet, 2004), conceptually there is some degree of probability of success, or quality of knowledge (the capacity to take effective action).

Several dangers come into play for community experts in a specific domain of action. If the domain changes and the expert does not recognize it, then the application of his/her knowledge can fail. On the other hand, the expert may recognize that a situation is different but think that the current knowledge will work when, in fact, it will not. Another issue enters at this point. Since individuals typically find what they are looking for, or see what they expect to see, there is a bias to interpret a problem from an historical, proven, and comfortable frame of reference, one that may not recognize the complexities of the current problem. *This produces a bias toward knowledge reuse.* At any single point in time no one can see beyond their threshold of perception (based on a lifetime of living and learning). Another bias toward knowledge reuse arises because of the perception of a "blessed history". The ramifications or loss of face when "tried and true solutions" fail may be considerably less than when new, creative solutions fail. An advantage in looking to the human brain for answers rather than to an information system is that the human brain is more likely to take into account the uniqueness of each situation. Unfortunately, our brains also carry baggage from the past in terms of prejudice; technology has no prejudices, but it never forgets.

The value of the robustness and sustainability of knowledge lies far beyond its impact through experts. If learning comes primarily from the internal complexing of individual lived experience, then most of our knowledge is connected to our experience. If reusing this knowledge is dangerous, how are we to survive in the world? The answer is at once complex and simple. Considering the simple side of the answer, sustainability is not a constant, but rather comes from continuous learning and re-learning—creating, re-creating and adapting knowledge—as we co-evolve with our environment. For our communities and cities, as well as each of us as individuals, the objective is no longer a stable, secure environment. **Sustainable communities and cities are those engaged in the continuous process of collaborative entanglement** (complexing and associative patterning) and mutual adaptation from which we can learn, grow and thrive.

Answering from the complex perspective, is there a set of actions that can improve the sustainability of knowledge? *Perhaps the best way to create a capability for robust knowledge is for a city or community to spawn, foster and encourage diversity, dialogue, open-minded thinking and honest opinion.* This allows all major decisions to use—and create—up-to-date, relevant and appropriate knowledge for the long-term effectiveness of actions. Given this approach, key community groups could develop the capacity for efficient, rapid and effective dialogues, problem-solving and decision-making, processes that are particularly appropriate for emergency situations or rapidly changing events within a community. This would include addressing the significant challenge of communicating to citizens (in terms of shared understanding) the need for redirection or changes through knowledge mobilization. For example, if a community has been successfully doing something one way through a local political group and there is a significant political shift at the national level, there will undoubtedly be changes at the state and community levels. The local governing board would not only be responsible for deciding what the right decision is from a knowledge perspective, but would have to also address the social and political issues involved in terms of the larger stakeholder group.

Communities, cities and nations can only be as effective as their constituents. Every decision-maker—which at some level includes every individual in the community—has the responsibility to pursue sustainability in the domains of knowledge they influence or that influence them. This process starts with the active involvement of all community members in knowledge mobilization processes, connecting through the ways each individual best learns and can best contribute, whether that means involvement in formal learning processes or spending time reading, reflecting, and engaging in community dialogues and events. Some specific thoughts regarding sustainable knowledge are detailed below:

(1) **Practice action learning**. Every time you apply knowledge, even when it is successful, question the results, the domain, the key factors, etc. *Ask:* If this or that variable or critical factor had been different, would this action have worked? From this response you can (1) get a sense of the robustness of your knowledge, and (2) modify or expand your knowledge as needed. *Ask*: While my action worked, did it work exactly as I thought it would? Why or why not? While knowledge may work in the cone of acceptability, if the results were not exactly as planned or anticipated, then there is something in that domain or situation that has been missed.

(2) **Absolute knowledge does not exist**; therefore, all knowledge should be questioned by associating what you know and believe with new ideas, then questioning your own knowledge. Never take your knowledge for granted, that is, never let knowledge decay to a set of rules, habits, or routines. When this happens, knowledge is transformed into cold, lifeless information, perhaps even dangerous information because you may use it as knowledge!

(3) **Always recognize the difference between information and knowledge**. Information will tell you what is, knowledge will tell you *why* it is and what to do about it (under what conditions, critical variables, key relationships, what is and is not important, etc.). Information that tells you what to do without being accompanied by knowledge may be dangerous.

(4) **Your frame of reference determines what you see and know**, and your past success with knowledge influences your frame of reference and cone of perception. This could become a dangerous bias in new situations. A first step in softening this bias is to understand your frame of reference. A second step is developing the ability to look at a situation from different perspectives, through different frames of reference. *One technique* for doing this is to take an individual you know well and respect, but who thinks differently than you, and try to look at the situation from that individual's point of view. *Another useful tactic* when problem solving or making a decision is to write down a list of all individuals or parties that would be affected by the problem solution or decision. Then ask yourself how each of them would view the problem or

the decision. This shifts your own frame of reference and helps understand issues and consequences from multiple perspectives. The resulting insights from these and similar techniques frequently give rise to more robust and effective knowledge and problem solutions.

(5) **Consider group knowledge and the danger of group knowledge reuse**; for example, groupthink, assumed expertise, a limited frame of reference, and third-order knowledge. Third-order knowledge assumes loss or gain in translation. The signal to noise ratio goes down or up in any transfer of knowledge, either decaying or improving for the specific situation at hand (Bennet and Bennet, 2007a). (NOTE: What is transferred is "knowledge re-created", not the *same* knowledge.)

Final Thoughts

From a neuroscience viewpoint, we quite literally live in an infinite sequence of continuous "now's", and everything else is memory. Yet a significant part of the knowledge in our now's is anticipation of the future. Any futurist will admit that the goal of forecasting is not prediction but is figuring out what you need to know about the future in order to take effective action today (Saffo, 2007). From a high level perspective, we must ask, *what is the sustainable knowledge that best ensures survival and the desired quality of life for our society?* From an individual and community perspective, we must ask, what do I need to know next week, next month? What sustainable knowledge can I begin to build that will help me in tomorrow's now's

As we are discovering from our unfolding understanding of how the brain works, sustainable knowledge is clearly the process of continuous learning through associative patterning—the semantic complexing of incoming information with that which is stored from our lived experience—taking the form of both Knowledge (Informing) and Knowledge (Proceeding). In other words, for sustainability in our communities we must be able to find or have available robust sources of information through (1) facilitating the continuous flow of information needed for improvement and (2) developing the processes to assimilate, integrate and apply the knowledge we need. In a nutshell, this is the rich process of knowledge mobilization.

Section IV
Values, Wisdom and Knowing

We are so much more than our knowledge. In this section we begin to explore that "more" in terms of values, wisdom, knowing and the sub-personalities we create to navigate through life. Looking at wisdom and knowing through the lens of knowledge, it is clear that there is much more at play than knowledge.

When exploring the unique relationship knowledge has with these larger concepts, we have left out the concept of truth, although (truth be told) it is mentioned in the Chapter 10 on knowledge and values. Truth (with a small "t", although it is capped here as the beginning of a sentence), like knowledge and values, is context sensitive and situation dependent, although it may, also like knowledge and values, potentially apply across a spectrum of contexts and situations. However, like values, truth is of a higher order than knowledge, directly tied to the perceived reality of a situation. *The truth of today is certainly not the truth of a distant tomorrow* (MacFlouer, 2011). When sharing knowledge, the concept of truth can be used as a value marker. The more truthful the knowledge that is shared—that is, the truth according to a mutually-perceived reality—the closer that knowledge moves to representing intelligent activity.

Our treatment of knowing gets down to the nitty-gritty, with specific ideas of how to expand our sensory capabilities and perhaps connect to our internal resources. Knowing is poetically described as **seeing beyond images, hearing beyond words, sensing beyond appearances, and feeling beyond emotions**. Building on our development of tacit knowledge, we look at how this supports the capacity of knowledge (potential and action) and the sense of knowing (moving through the subconscious and the superconscious).

In exploring sub-personalities as knowledge, we begin to realize that not only is knowledge context sensitive and situation dependent, but WE become what the situation demands! We quite literally chunk knowledge that is appropriate for specific situations and develop sub-personalities that are very fluid processes, each existing as an unconscious "I". As we move through life these sub-personalities navigate the rough spots, emerging in response to challenges, bringing us through those challenges to a state of interdependency and comfort, and finally reaching a state of *fulfillment*, the ability to function adequately in our environment.

This section includes Knowledge as Values (Chapter 10); Knowledge to Wisdom (Chapter 11); Knowledge and Knowing (Chapter 12); and Sub-personalities as Knowledge (Chapter 13).

Chapter 10
Knowledge and Values[1]

As a noun, **values** have two dimensions (1) that which is highly regarded, and (2) that which is perceived as worthy or desirable. As with all knowledge, values are relative, that is, *context-sensitive and situation-dependent* (Bennet and Bennet, 2007b). (See Chapter 6 for an in-depth treatment of context). Thus, values can be considered as a preference, that is, "A value can be described as a preference, multiplied by its priority" (Henderson and Thompson, 2003, p. 15). Values provide guidelines around what is important and not important, and how to get things done to meet performance objectives and cope with the environment. Truth, when defined as "that which is correspondent to reality or fact" (Encarta World English Dictionary, p. 1912), shares the same four qualities as values: context sensitive and situation dependent, culturally colored, and geographically influenced. Both shift and change over time as the perception of reality changes and facts are revisited.

Shared values mean that the personal values of a group of individuals are congruent with each other and, in an organizational setting, consistent with their organization's values. Shared values provide a common context for understanding and interpreting the rapid proliferation of information from the environment and using that information to create knowledge that leads to quality decisions and the capacity to take effective action.

Values and Knowledge

Consistent with Knowledge (Informing) and Knowledge (Proceeding), there is both an *information* (or content) part of values, and a *process* or *action* part of values, that is, Values (Informing) and Values (Proceeding). Values (Informing) is that which is highly regarded, perceived as worthy or desirable, and Values (Proceeding) is the way values are put together and acted upon in a specific situation or context.

Values may begin as principles, a rule or standard considered good behavior (American Heritage Dictionary, 2000). As these principles are repeatedly expressed (acted upon) by an individual or across an organization, they become embedded behaviors, both considered the norm and expected. For example, the principles of freedom, equality, human dignity, tolerance, and the celebration of diversity have a long and storied history in the United States (Lakoff, 2006). Although today these are recognized as values core to a democracy, i.e., Knowledge (Informing), there is still disagreement among the political infrastructure when translating them into action, Knowledge (Proceeding). Knowledge (Informing) appears to be the higher-order pattern, that is, less susceptible to change.

A recent example that sets forth principles, destined to become values as the world evolves, is the Open Government Directive issued in December 2009 which supports the U.S. President's Memorandum. The Directive sets forth three principles for government: transparency, participation, and collaboration. Government organizations—and by extension the private, educational and nonprofit sectors that support those government organizations—are provided general and specific directions for achieving behavior changes in support of these principles. Per the Directive, a starting place is expanded access to information by making it available online in open formats, and developing a policy framework supporting the use of emerging technologies. Concurrent with this Directive, the U.S. Attorney General issued new guidelines under the Freedom of Information Act (FOIA) reinforcing the principle that openness is the Federal Government's default position. As these directives and guidelines ripple down through the U.S. Federal sector, each government organization develops and puts into action an implementation plan (including their own directives and guidelines) consistent with the higher-level direction, and so on down through the hierarchy that comprises government organizations. Dependent on the strength of these various directives, individual behaviors begin to change which, over time, become part of the way work is done. For those individuals in resonance with these principles, as actions consistent with these principles are repeated over and over, they not only become organizational values, they may become personal values, if they are not already.

Values (Informing) provide a central core of meanings and feelings which influence what people see, think, and feel, providing the meanings they subscribe to what they see and feel, and guiding how they evaluate alternatives, make decisions, and take actions, Values (Proceeding). Values (Informing) also influence how people see, think, feel about and interact with dimensions such as time, change, activity, human nature, and relationships, and artifacts and tools such as technology.

As knowledge, values can also be thought of in terms of surface, shallow and deep. At the surface level, where the routine decisions in our daily lives occur, values would be involved in simple situations and decisions. There is a conscious awareness and understanding of what is "right" or "best" in terms of personal or organizational values, and, most often, this understanding can easily be communicated and acted upon. At the shallow level, situations become more complicated, although a cause and effect relationship can often be determined through developing an understanding of the context of a situation or decision at hand. Because knowledge (including values) is context sensitive and situation dependent, the application of values may become more confusing at this level, requiring more social interaction to help understand the context in which they are being applied, and the anticipated results of decisions and actions. At the deep level, values have to be sensed or intuited as well as understood as they are applied to complex situations and decisions, and anticipated results of decisions and actions are most likely part of a larger decision journey rather than a single decision (Bennet and Bennet, 2008b).

Noting that all models are artificial constructs, reflecting on the surface, shallow and deep levels of values provides a framework for exploring the relationships among different types of values, and looking at the gaps between behaviors at the surface and deep levels. Values which truly drive behavior may be conscious or unconscious, explicit or tacit. For example, leaders and knowledge workers may espouse personal and/or organizational values (surface values) which are not the authentic values (shallow or deep values) which they demonstrate through their strategic decision-making and actions. These surface values may even be applied in simple, visible situations but quite clearly not be the Values (Informing) driving complex decision-making and the resulting actions. This model will be applied further in the discussion on values in organizations.

Emerging Values

The personal values of a decision-maker—and by decision-maker we infer each and every individual who walks this Earth—are also likely to *represent generational values*, and can exercise tremendous influence over decisions regarding how to solve a problem and take the best action in a situation. German sociologist Karl Mannheim forwards that a person's thoughts, feelings and behaviors, including their values, are shaped by the generation to which a person belongs (Mannheim, 1980).

Recognizing the new social knowledge paradigm—which supports the creation, leveraging and application of knowledge—the core and operational values linked to this generation of decision-makers include integrity, empathy, transparency, participation, collaboration, contribution, learning and creativity (Avedisian and Bennet, 2010).

The foundational value of **Integrity** is defined as "steadfast adherence to a strict moral or ethical code" (American Heritage Dictionary, 2006). An organization or person of integrity is "whole," aligns words and actions, keeps commitments, does the right thing, and engages in fair dealing. From the perspective of the Net Generation or Millennials (those growing up with the Internet and who began to enter the workforce around the turn of the century):

> Integrity is the foundation of the new enterprise. In North America, Net Geners define integrity as being honest, considerate, and transparent. They expect employers to be this way, and live by their commitment. Young people respond well to management integrity and quickly become engaged. (Tapscott, 2009, p.162)

Without integrity, ethical standards and excellence lack practical meaning. The sometimes-hidden idea underlying integrity is *consistency and steadfast adherence*, producing an authenticity that is in concert with accepted moral standards of an organization or a culture. Thus while integrity may be a fundamental value, the *way* it is understood and expressed, Knowledge (Proceeding), may be different across organizations, or around the world. Nonetheless, because of its consistency within the context in which it is expressed, integrity is a powerful conveyor of trust among decision makers, and between an organization and its stakeholders.

The second foundational value is **empathy.** Empathy is defined as the "identification with and understanding of another's situation, feelings, and motives" (American Heritage Dictionary, 2006). In *The Empathetic Civilization*, Rifkin explains that "empathy" is the act of identifying with another's struggle as if it were one's own, and is the ultimate expression of a sense of equality. "Empathy requires a porous boundary between I and thou that allows the identity of two beings to mingle in a shared mental space" (Rifkin, 2009, p.160). Empathy asserts the unconditional value of the human person and the meaning of his growth and the growth of his fellow man. When coupled with integrity, empathy can help create a credible relationship, company and product/service from the perspective of all key stakeholders. It builds the foundation not just for collaboration and participation, but for true fraternity, reciprocity, and integration.

Integrity and empathy provide the pre-conditions for the effectiveness of other more operational values by creating trust and mutual respect, and providing a non-judgmental environment, all of which form the basis of communication through shared understanding. Empathy and integrity are not mutually independent. First, empathy needs to be understood, confirmed and practiced in the light of integrity. Without integrity, empathy may degenerate into sentimentality. Second, integrity is softened by empathy. Without empathy, integrity may become judgmental, and even harsh and unforgiving. *Together, empathy and integrity serve as a foundation for effective teamwork and facilitate new knowledge creation, sharing and leveraging, enabling new, quick, flexible, and effective responses.*

> Integrity and empathy provide the pre-conditions for the effectiveness of other more operational values by creating trust and mutual respect, and providing a non-judgmental environment.

The concept of **transparency**, described as an operational value, is defined as: easily seen through or detected and free from guile; candid or open (The American Heritage Dictionary, 2006). Again, we see a level of interdependency emerging. *Empathy and integrity facilitate transparency by fostering trust, while transparency, in turn, reinforces trust. Unless transparency is balanced by empathy and integrity, it could foster misunderstanding and break down trust and relationships rather than supporting them.*

Tapscott agrees that transparency as a core value for Net Geners is critical to establishing trusting, long-term relationships (Tapscott, 2009, p. 267). He forwards that true transparency "must make the processes, underlying assumptions, and political presuppositions (including supporting research) of policy explicit and subject to criticism" (Tapscott, 2009, p. 266). Beyond sharing documents on websites, transparency extends to openly sharing ideas, feelings, personal viewpoints, and different levels of knowledge (Bennet and Bennet, 2008d). Therefore, transparency moves beyond surface knowledge to a focus on shallow knowledge, with the responsibility to ensure some level of understanding and meaning that makes information actionable in a changing, uncertain and complex environment.

Participation as an operational value is a keystone for the Net Generation, who reach out and creatively engage ideas and people around the world. This participation extends to political engagement and community service. For example, in the 2004 U.S. Presidential elections more people under the age of 30 cast votes than people over 65, with the biggest increase in the 18-24 age group. As Leyden et al. describe, "Signs indicate that Millennials are civic-minded, politically engaged, and hold values long associated with progressives, such as concern about economic inequalities ... and a strong belief in government" (Leyden et al., 2007, p. 1). In the area of community service, according to a 2006 report for the Corporation for National and Community Service, teens 16 to 19 years of age are spending twice as much time volunteering as in 1989 (Grimm et al., 2007). In the area of the economy, Tapscott sums up, "There is a new age of participation emerging in the economy ... The Net Generation ... is driving the democratization of information content" (Tapscott, 2009, p. 258). An example of the democratization of information content is the launching of www.data.gov the official U.S. government site providing increased public access to federal government datasets.

Collaboration means, "to work together, especially in a joint intellectual effort" (American Heritage Dictionary, 2000). In the current environment, the meaning of collaboration has extended from relatively intact internal groups at the team, unit, or company level to a fluid, changing interdependent network of diverse contributors across the internal and external environments. A decision-maker has a new type of peer network, one that moves from autonomy to interdependence, from deference to dialogue, and from a primary focus on doing a job well to a focus on contribution to collective purposes (Heckscher, 2007, p.108-109). In this peer network, alignment around such values as collaboration, transparency, and contribution make it possible for knowledge workers to work together in environments that are open, changing, and diverse. Collaboration is a core value embraced by the Net Geners, involving engagement and participation. "Collaboration as Net Geners know it, is achieving something *with* other people, experiencing power through other people, not by ordering a gaggle of followers to do your bidding" (Tapscott, 2009, p. 163). As noted by a student researcher, "Collaboration and communication are second nature for the Millennial generation" (Panetta, 2013, p. 51).

Closely linked to participation and collaboration, **contribution** measures success and performance in the context of helping peers and an organization move toward a common mission and strategy. *Participation is the act of engagement, collaboration is how to engage, and contribution is the result of that engagement.* The purpose-driven orientation of contribution is a motivating force in the lives of Net Generation knowledge workers. Through global connectivity, Net Geners share openly, engaging other's ideas and contributing their ideas freely.

As an operational value **learning** is integrally related to the ability to contribute. Learning in the CUCA environment means receiving, understanding, thinking critically, and learning how to adapt and apply knowledge quickly in new and unfamiliar situations. The learning of the Net Generation is unique. Learning in social settings locates learning "not in the head or outside it, but in the relationship between the person and the world, which for human beings is a social person in a social world" (Wenger, 2009, p. 1). The Net Generation is learning together, in groups and communities, through continuous interactions around the world. This new mode of learning is just-in-time, interactive, collaborative, fun, engaging, taps multiple senses (e.g., multi-media) and fosters discovery. Learning affects every other value, offering a way of practicing and applying each of the values in every aspect of work life including interactions with peers, customers, vendors, how work gets done, and how success is measured. This learning is collaborative. Demonstrating the interdependence between learning, empathy and collaboration, Tapscott says,

> Learning affects every other value, offering a way of practicing and applying each of the values in every aspect of work life.

> It goes without saying that collaborative learning, with its emphasis on mindfulness, attunement to others, nonjudgmental interactions, acknowledgement of each person's unique contributions, and recognition of the importance of deep participation and a shared sense of meaning coming out of embedded relationships, can't help but foster greater empathic engagement (Tapscott, 2009, p. 607).

As defined by Andreason (2005), **creativity** is emerging new or original ideas or seeing new patterns in some domain of knowledge. In other words, creativity can be considered as the *ability to perceive and/or create new relationships and new possibilities*, see things from a different frame of reference, or realize new ways of understanding/having insight or portraying something. Innovation means the creation of new ideas *and* the transformation of those ideas into useful applications; thus the combination of creativity and contribution as operational values bring about innovation. A creative environment is fueled by the values of integrity, empathy, transparency, collaboration, learning, and contribution which foster trust and a spirit of collaborative success (Avedisian & Bennet, 2010).

The values and abilities characterizing the Net Generation help support sustainability in a changing, uncertain and increasingly complex environment, and no doubt *that environment is contributing to the development of those abilities*. Today there is access to almost unlimited information, and each of us intuitively knows that using that information effectively (knowledge) is the key to success. Flooded by new thoughts and ideas, this generation surfs the Net, rarely focusing on a specific domain of knowledge long enough to acquire deep knowledge, and *the extent of their awareness determines their range of mobility*. The Net Generation operates at the edge of human thought, a place where insights find

> The Net Generation operates at the edge of human thought, a place where insights find their way into expression.

their way into expression. In other words, there is already *a level of co-evolving that can be observed in the Net Generation*. As the environment continues to change, so do decision-maker capabilities and capacities change to ensure flexibility, quick response, resilience, robustness and continuous learning, all of which contribute to sustainability in a CUCA environment (Bennet & Bennet, 2005).

An industry example demonstrates the implementation of the Net Generation values into the fabric of the business. The Nordic Sales and Marketing division of a pharmaceutical company was introduced to new corporate values including ownership and integrity (Values Informing) and mandated to put them into practice (Values Proceeding). The Leadership Team decided to initially put the values into practice by focusing on the launch of a new antihistamine drug to increase market penetration at a faster rate. Role holders at every level of the organization brainstormed creative ways they could contribute to the launch of the drug in ways which gave life to the values. What emerged were new behaviors and processes throughout the organization. For example, for the first time, all associates -- including administrative assistants and medical monitors - - were trained to sell the drug. Patients were asked to select the most popular allergy doctors who were asked to lecture on the topic. Health care professionals were reached for the first time through local patient organizations. These new behaviors became embedded into day-to-day work and processes as part of an emerging new culture. Value-based behaviors were built into performance appraisals. At a leadership level, product managers from each country formed a cross-country launch team and developed coordinated promotional programs and materials at reduced costs. This new business model for launching one drug became the pattern for launching all drugs.

The world is changing. We all know this: the market tells us, newspapers tell us, politicians tell us, and our kids tell us. At work we seem to go along for awhile, then there's wind of something in the air, an underlying shift in relationships with our partners and competitors, or even the taste of fear. When our organization is threatened, we are threatened. So, we shift our way of thinking, struggle to understand what is needed and wanted, and slowly we begin to see and feel things differently. And as we build our knowledge, our understanding, from this new way of looking at the world, our values change.

Values as Emergent

Parents spend hours and years telling their children what to do, many of those children demonstrating the desired behavior (or not, with parents often spending more hours and years telling their children why something is good for the adults but not the children). When it is all said and done, parents hope and pray they have embedded the right sets of thoughts and behaviors, the right values, to help their children live well and have "success" when they enter the world of adults.

Truth be told, values are emergent phenomena. This idea of emergence has only recently come into the mainstream of businesses. Through most of the last century we were still living blindly in a cause-and-effect world, where we honestly believed that certain behaviors and actions would cause certain results: focus on results, we need results! For example, how important have metrics been in the organizations in which you work? How much do you yourself rely on measures to prove the value of your performance, of that next raise, of that promotion? We've all been living in this same world. It wasn't until the last decade or so that experts started talking about measuring for the future. This means measuring desired behaviors instead of what we *thought would produce desired behaviors*. Subtle difference; big difference!

Emergence, and the concept it represents, helps provide us a way of thinking beyond a cause and effect relationship. Something that emerges comes from the interactions of many different things, moving beyond the sum of those things and producing something different. And what emerges doesn't just come from those things, but from the interactions and relationships among those things in a particular context. So if you can't trace it back to a single cause (or even multiple causes), then how do you make it happen? The answer is, you don't "make it" happen.

You cannot control emergence; you can, however, *nurture the environment*, as we learned 20 years ago from case studies on innovation in the Apple Computer think tank. You can put a structure and processes in place that support the people that will help make "it" happen. You can express a desired end state and direction for your organization to move, and share this understanding across the organization. So yes, you can, in fact, focus on instilling qualities in the workplace, and consequently the workforce, that *provide the opportunity* for "it" to happen. And then, no matter how sure you are that you're on the right track, the "it" may or may not be exactly what you planned or expected.

Why? Because people are complex adaptive systems, and hopefully intelligent complex adaptive systems. Complexity is a condition of a situation or organization (system) that is integrated in some way but has too many parts and relationships to understand in a simple way. Think about an ant colony, or 5 PM Friday night on the Los Angeles Freeway System! Add the word adaptive and you get the behavior of that motorist who sees the roadblock ahead and creates a new route for himself and his passengers. Add the word intelligent and you get the driver who stays at work until the thick of it clears. So the adaptive driver studies and analyzes his environment and--- from the middle of the thick of it---acts to influence his external environment and his relationship with that external environment. The intelligent driver took advantage of his understanding of the environment to adapt his working hours around the logjam, what might be termed as recognizing the environmental opportunity space, and weaving his relationship with the external environment such that he takes advantage of space and time. Or maybe another intelligent worker decided to start her own business in the suburbs. Or maybe another intelligent worker decides to both live and work in the city within walking distance or one or two stops on the subway! There are lots of *different* ways to act intelligently. The hard part is figuring out the best way in a particular situation (context), while simultaneously staying flexible and adaptable to the environment.

And **underlying all those decisions and behaviors are your values**. Do you enjoy living in the city? How many hours do you need to spend at work, and how many at home, and how many are you willing to spend twixt the two? Do you want to have your own business, or leave the headaches (and rewards) to someone else? How do you set your priorities? Value and values ... what is *of value* (to you at a particular time and in a particular situation) and *your values themselves*, which are emergent phenomena.

Let's explore this concept further. If I asked you for a core value or belief, what is the first thing that would come to mind? For most of us, one or two values come to mind fairly quickly. These values are things that we've given some thought to or are basic to our culture and work ethic, such values as honesty and integrity, or justice, or respect and tolerance. Pretty good values, certainly. I asked this question in a world-wide study based on interviews with 34 thought leaders in the knowledge management field. Most of them came up quickly with the first one, but pulling up the second value was harder, with hesitation. And if a third value came to mind there was even longer thought involved, several times popping up much later in the interview. This is not because we don't have beliefs and core values. We all have them. But we don't just sit around and think of them. They emerge when needed, and are the result of, among other things, our country, our neighborhood, our parents, our experiences, our spiritual orientation, our education, our families and friends, our work, our failures, our successes, etc., and the interactions and relationships among them. Furthermore, the way they play out are influenced by the particular time, situation and expectations.

Now, if I have a decision to make, or I'm in a situation where I need to act, my response is driven by my basic beliefs and values, called to the surface—called to action—based on how they pertain to a certain situation at a particular time. So, I may have different values that are *pertinent to different situations at different times*, i.e., not necessarily a specific value that carries all the way through.

A good example is represented by the title of a sermon one Sunday at the Hollywood Methodist Church in Hollywood, California: "There's sin in sincerity." As the story goes, an older member of the congregation wore an absolutely obnoxious hat to church, and was so excited with her new hat and felt so good about it that she couldn't help but call it out to all of her friends and acquaintances, "Don't you just love my new hat?" Honesty and integrity are strong values for you. How would you respond? If you say you'd tell her the truth, let's add a bit more weight to the other side. Let's say you know she's ailing, has lost most of the members of her family, and that her church community is the only family she has. Still going to tell her the truth? Or maybe just skirt around it? What happens when she insists that you are her friend, and she is feeling quite beautiful and special today with her new hat? How are you going to respond? Let's add more weight to your response. Let's say that you know she only has a few weeks to live, and this new hat is a last burst of joy for her. Now how do you respond? You get the picture. It's not black and white; there are all sorts of colors of gray. And anyone that tells you otherwise is not looking beyond their box, their frame of reference.

A more serious example, and one that continues to haunt mankind is as follows. You believe in life, the value of life, yet what do you do if you are threatened by a murderer with a gun? Okay, turn the other cheek (you're dead, now). What if a child is being attacked? How about a room full of children? How about a school full of children? How do you respond them? Conversely, how about the ecological rape of the world that's underway today? Where do you draw the line?

So values emerge as a result of the relationships and interactions of many things (using the word "things" not just to mean material things, but as a term *de arte* to include feelings, processes, etc.), and they for the most part are culture dependent, situation dependent, time dependent and you dependent. And your values emerge from the "you", that is, a complex system ... perhaps a complex adaptive system ... and just maybe an intelligent complex adaptive system.

The Value of Knowledge

Knowledge is an emergent phenomenon. Knowledge is an emergent phenomenon because there is no direct cause and effect relationship between information and knowledge, rather it is the *interaction* among many ideas, concepts and patterns of thought that creates knowledge. It can be a combination of information, experience, environmental need, intuition, feelings, processes, values etc. So, the creation of knowledge is an emerging process in a complex patterned system (with *you* at the center of the process) entangling itself with goals and objectives and issues and context and other such things (again, "things" as a term de arte).

> Knowledge is an emergent phenomenon. There is no direct cause and effect relationship between information and knowledge.

We're not saying that cause and effect relationships don't exist; certainly, they exist, particularly in our *perception*, and certainly in many simple, repeatable processes in this logical world of ours. For our mechanical-age organizations—and those organizations still operating in the mechanical-age mode—there are certainly many cause and effect relationships. But when you move into the knowledge world, where you deal with intangibles such as value in a complex environment, there are very few— if any—direct cause and effect relationships visible between actions and results!

Recall the definition of knowledge as the capacity (potential or actual) for effective action. To take effective action one needs to have awareness of the context, understanding, know the theory, laws, and rules related to the situation; and be able to exercise insight, intuition and good judgment; and anticipate expected results. The "potential or actual" is important because in a changing world we don't know what the future looks like, and something we thought about last week and stored away may be the exact thing that will prevent a business disaster or offer a business opportunity next month! In other words, our focus can no longer be on efficiency in terms of learning, i.e., learn what you need only and don't clutter your mind with anything you don't need to know. That doesn't work anymore. Not only do we need to learn more, we have to understand what we learn and continue learning and understanding in a larger way.

Effectiveness in terms of learning is knowing what you know, and knowing what you don't know, and being aware that there are important things out there that you either don't know that you know, or that you don't know that you don't know. When you recognize these four spheres you begin to open to new possibilities, to see the potential from a different light, as John Seely Brown would say, with a different set of perceptive glasses. We might even add a fifth sphere to the mix, and that's knowing what others know (so you know where to go to ask questions).

First, **knowledge has no inherent value**. There's no *inherent* goodness and badness, so to speak. The goodness and badness comes with the *context* and *how it is used in a specific situation*. For example, we could say that the terrorists that attacked the World Trade Center of 9/11 used good knowledge management in the sense that

> There is no inherent value in knowledge. The goodness and badness comes with the context and how knowledge is used in a specific situation.

they had enough knowledge and used it to succeed in what they set out to do. The good news is that while specific knowledge may have no inherent value, the more knowledge you have, the more you truly understand. As you use that knowledge and, through learning, expand the breadth and depth of your understanding, the more connected and interactive you become with the world, i.e., part of a living global network. When an individual is open to learning and begins to acquire the ability to see the world from different perspectives, to recognize the connectedness of this world, there is a higher-level value that *emerges*, a social responsibility. Thus as perceived from the individual's frame of reference, there is the potential for **knowledge to build values as well as value**. This process is similar to the recognized value of competition during the industrial age, where in order to compete and win an individual or organization had to understand the competition and create a better product. Note that in this model there are winners and losers. Since the product we're dealing with in the knowledge age is knowledge—which only increases when you share it—you don't just have a better product, everyone has a better product, and you have more knowledge to create an even better product, and so forth. Product differentiation, desirability, reliability and enjoyment coupled with trust and respect for the provider become the determinants of success in the marketplace. Once these interactive loops with customers and collaborators (formerly competitors) become a part of life, we as humans cannot help but build relationships and increase our understanding of—and respect for—how others see the world, which leads to *emergence* of a higher value set.

Finally, when we say **knowledge is built on value** that means that the things we perceive of value to us are the things we seek out, the things we try to learn more about, the things we put our energy towards. For example, if I believe that an education has value for my future, I pursue that education. If I believe that running three times a week will benefit my health, then I run three times a week … or at least I run three times a week if my actions follow my beliefs. Which leads us to think about and explore the relationships of values and beliefs and actions and, perhaps, motivation. But that is another book.

Levels of Knowledge Comprehension and Morality

In our discussion of morality, it will be useful to consider knowledge as having a number of *levels of comprehension* ranging from *data* (considered as a simple nonrandom pattern) to information, sense-making, understanding, meaning, intelligence and wisdom. These levels move from simple to complex, bringing out the *different attributes of knowledge* and providing some measure to understand the level of comprehension an individual has relative to a particular domain of reality or situation of interest. Unlike earlier models connecting data, information, knowledge and wisdom (Ackoff, 1989; Davenport and Prusak, 1998; Bennet & Bennet, 2014), this is *not* considered a continuum, that is, we recognize that knowledge is context-sensitive and situation dependent—what is considered data or information in one setting may be knowledge in another. As forwarded above, information is a fundamental building block of knowledge. As with all models, these levels should be considered as potentially useful guides rather than absolutes.

From a systems perspective, something makes *sense* when it is consistent with your own experience relative to that or similar situations. *Understanding* means a more detailed awareness and insight into the causal relationships in addition to the elements and boundaries of the situation. Understanding applied to a complex system could include recognition of the emergent phenomena of the situation. The next level, *meaning*, considers the context of a situation in terms of its relationships to, or impact on, the environment or individuals, and other significant factors. *Anticipation* is the capacity to estimate the effect of a perturbation on a situation. A useful and widespread interpretation of *intelligence* is a capacity to set and achieve goals. In this book we link knowledge with perfect communication. In this context, we refer to intelligent activity as representing a perfect state of interaction where intent, purpose, direction, values and expected outcomes are clearly communicated and understood among all parties, reflecting wisdom and achieving a higher truth. Knowledge is in service to wisdom. For an in-depth discussion of the relationship of wisdom and knowledge see Chapter 11.

As with other organizations co-evolving in a changing, uncertain and complex environment, leading a military organization requires knowledge of many different areas. For example, leaders who assume roles in an information-rich society must develop some of the aptitudes and attitudes of a generalist (Cleveland, 2002). Humphrey (1997) says that high-performing leaders have deep knowledge of the general business environment; their industry, company, and work group; and their organization's strategy, culture, and values.

Military leaders are developed and educated to deal with stressful, unpredictable situations with a potential for having the worst possible outcomes. Such experience builds the capacity to handle stress, work with people, develop strategies, and deal with the unknown, each of which requires knowledge that applies in many areas of individual and organizational life. Other areas of knowledge that military leaders develop include self-discipline, information gathering, situation assessment, communication, and intuition. Further, because military personnel shift jobs as they advance in rank with new job responsibilities, they become continuous learners. Once knowledge is acquired, it can prove highly valuable to both military and, as military personnel retire or take employment, non-military organizations. The sharing of deep knowledge that may occur through leadership, mentoring, coaching and teaching can significantly enhance the performance in their new organizations.

The inculcation of values represents a high payoff from military service to both individuals and society. In this context, values are considered standards, worthwhile qualities, or guiding principles that affect the course of events or the way we perceive the world around us. The core values of an organization—closely related to the identity, mission and function of the organization—are that set of values that the organization upholds

> The core values of an organization—closely related to the identity, mission and function of the organization—are that set of values that the organization upholds above others.

above others. This is particularly true in the military setting, where every person is expected to live and practice the core values of their service. For example, the U.S. Marine Corps' core values are honor, courage and commitment, and their motto *Semper Fi* means *always faithful*.

In a 2007 study of values in the Singapore Armed Forces, Lawrence Kohlberg's (1981) model of moral development was used to help understand how the military inculcates values. According to Kohlberg, moral development is hierarchical, with each subsequent stage of six stages reorganizing and integrating the preceding one and consequently providing a comprehensive basis for moral decisions (Kohlberg, 1981). See Figure 10-1. Although the sequence an individual moves through these stages is presumably fixed, the *rate* at which an individual progresses through the stages varies considerably dependent on experience and learning capacity.

The first stage of Kohlberg's sequence is externally based with a punishment orientation, that is, concerned more with the power of authorities and avoiding punishment than with doing the right thing. In the second stage (conventional reasoning), individual acts are performed to satisfy personal needs. In the third stage (interpersonal relationships), the individual makes decisions by internalizing the rules to meet their own desires or achieve approval of significant others. In stage four, morality becomes more of *doing one's duty*, implying that the internalized rules are maintained for their own sake rather than the sake of others.

Stages five and six deal with post conventional reasoning, where individuals begin understanding abstract moral principles and considering each situation differently. Here, an individual develops their own rules and principles for good decision-making and behavior. In stage five (contractual orientation), the individual recognizes the need for flexibility and relativism in the rules of behavior, and the protection of all individuals. In stage six, personal commitment instead of social consensus represents the basis for individual choices among moral possibilities (Berzonsky, 1994). At this stage an individual's conduct is driven by their own ideals and somewhat independent of the reaction of others.

In the 2007 study, the levels of knowledge comprehension defined above were used to help explore the relationship of knowledge and moral development in the military setting. As can be seen from the descriptions at the point of intersection in Figure 10-1, there is a correlation between these six stages and seven of the eight levels of knowledge comprehension. The intent is not to forward that knowledge is derived from values or vice-versa. It is to use the opportunity, as the individual is developing intellectual maturity, to concomitantly develop core values, thereby producing a competent, knowledgeable and value-oriented soldier and citizen. This relationship does not imply causation; it indicates a deliberate conceptual correlation between the knowledge maturity of young men during military service and growth in basic values. This, of course, can be extrapolated to other groups and organizations.

> There is a correlation between Kohlberg's six stages of moral development and seven of the eight levels of knowledge comprehension. As an individual is developing intellectual maturity, there is an opportunity to concomitantly develop core values.

We as humans are on a journey of learning (creation of knowledge, the capacity to take effective action) heading toward intelligent activity coupled with wisdom, which leads us to a deeper exploration of wisdom. When young people with minimum life experiences enter the military, they are often in early stages of moral development. This is consistent with what we know about the mind/brain, that is, development of the frontal cortex—often called the executive brain—is not complete until the mid-20's.

More than half of the militaries in the world practice conscription, compulsory enrollment or draft into the armed forces, generally at the minimum entry age (beginning as young as 14 in Oman and Yeman) (NationMaster, 2008). Note the moral development line in Kohlberg's model and the first two levels of knowledge comprehension. The characteristics at the nexus points read: action, immediate cause and effect response, and WIFM. Consistent with Kohlberg's model, the entry level of the military organization is where discipline is paramount. Whether conscripts or volunteers, recruits rapidly gain large amounts of information and knowledge in an unnatural environment with new rules, restrictions and requirements, and values.

KOHLBERG'S LEVELS OF MORAL DEVELOPMENT	INTELLIGENCE	ANTICIPATION OF THE FUTURE	MEANING	UNDERSTANDING	SENSE-MAKING	INFORMATION
POWER OF AUTHORITY; AVOID PUNISHMENT						ACTION IMMEDIATE CAUSE & EFFECT RESPONSE
SATISFYING PERSONAL NEEDS					WHAT'S IN IT FOR ME (WIFM)	
INTERPERSONAL RELATIONSHIPS; PLEASING OTHERS				INTERACTION		
DOING ONE'S DUTY; INWARD; FOR OWN SAKE			SYSTEMS: BOUNDARIES, CAUSAL RELATIONSHIPS			
POST-CONVENTIONAL REASONING; ABSTRACT; FLEXIBILITY, RELATIVISM IN RULES		CONCEPTUAL BASIS; THINKING IN ABSTRACT				
PERSONAL COMMITMENT; OWN IDEALS SOMEWHAT INDEPENDENT OF OTHERS	BALANCE; SETTING AND ACHIEVING GOALS					

(Column group heading: LEVELS OF KNOWLEDGE COMPREHENSION)

Figure 10-1: *The nexus of knowledge comprehension and moral development*

Final Thoughts

Exploring values as knowledge offers the opportunity for a deeper understanding of the relationships among values. Values, like knowledge, are context-sensitive and situation-dependent, that means they shift according to their specific application and the requirements of the environment. Core values appear to be Values (Informing), with the way they are applied dependent on context and situation, while operational values can serve as either Values (Informing) or Values (Proceeding), and appear much more sensitive to context and situation. Values were also explored in terms of knowledge levels: surface, shallow and deep.

Eight values were proposed for future knowledge workers: *integrity, empathy, transparency, participation, collaboration, contribution, learning and creativity*. These values are consistent with and supportive of the needs for working in a changing, uncertain and complex environment, and simultaneously appear to resonate with the Net Generation. While the first two are foundational and the latter six operational in nature, there are interdependencies among them.

We also looked at various attributes of knowledge against Kohlberg's model of moral development, recognizing the connections between life experiences—the expansion of knowledge—and moral development.

While there is benefit from exploring values in terms of levels of knowledge for greater understanding, there are further implications for considering interventions at each of these levels. For example, recognizing that core values are Values (Informing) and inform other values, yet as deep knowledge is developed over time, the sharing and aligning of these values might involve storytelling and mentoring. Conversely, operational values—which might be either Values (Informing) or Values (Proceeding) but primarily at a surface level—would be simpler to share, and change when necessitated by the environment and work product. This lays the groundwork for future thought.

Chapter 11
Moving from Knowledge to Wisdom[1]

During the 90's, Tom Stonier, a theoretical biologist, was developing a workable theory of information, and along the way discovered new relationships between information and the physical universe of matter and energy (Stonier, 1990; 1992; 1997) (see the earlier section on foundational definitions). Simultaneously, an intense interest in neuroscience research was spurred onward by the creation and sophistication of brain measurement instrumentation such as functional magnetic resonance imaging (fMRI), the electroencephalograph (EEG), and transcranial magnetic stimulation (TMS) (George, 2007; Kurzweil, 2005; Ward, 2006). For the first time we could see what was happening in the mind/brain as we process information and act on that information. Recall from Chapter 7 that in the mind/brain there is no cause-and-effect relationship between information and knowledge; knowledge is an emergent phenomenon. It is the interaction and selection (complexing) among many ideas, concepts and patterns of thought, all consisting of information, that create knowledge.

Also, during the late 90's the body of research focused on wisdom was rapidly expanding. In the early years of knowledge management, a number of authors argued that wisdom was the end of a continuum made up of data→information→knowledge→wisdom. But as Peter Russell explains,

> Various people have pointed to the progression of data to information to knowledge ... continuing the progression suggests that something derived from knowledge leads to the emergence of a new level, what we call wisdom. But what is it that knowledge gives us that takes us beyond knowledge? Through knowledge we learn how to act in our own better interests. Will this decision lead to greater well-being, or greater suffering? What is the kindest way to respond in this situation? Wisdom reflects the values and criteria that we apply to our knowledge. Its essence is discernment. Discernment of right from wrong. Helpful from harmful. Truth from delusion. (Russell, 2007)

Let us further explore the connection between knowledge and wisdom.

Definitions and Descriptions

As with knowledge so with wisdom; **a rich diversity of definitions and descriptions abound**. Focusing on work occurring around the turn of this century, Csikszentmihalyi and Nakamura (2005) described wisdom as referring to two distinct phenomena. The first was the *content* of wisdom (information and/or knowledge) and the second an individual's *capacity to think or act* wisely. Since the second part defines itself by itself, this demands a deeper exploration. Focusing on the content of wisdom, Clayton and

Birren (1980) said that individuals perceived wisdom differently when socio-demographic variables were changed, that is, as we now recognize about knowledge, they considered wisdom as developed over time from a series of events context-sensitive and situation dependent in terms of culture and locality. Similarly, the works of Holliday and Changler (1986); Erikson (1998), Sternberg (1990), Jarvis (1992), Kramer and Bacelar (1994), Bennett-Woods (1997), Merriam and Caffarella (1999) all take the position that wisdom is grounded in life's rich experiences,

> ... [wisdom] therefore is developed through the process of aging ... wisdom seems to consist of the ability to move away from absolute truths, to be reflective to make sound judgments related to our daily existence, whatever our circumstances. (Merriam & Caffarella, 1999, p. 165).

Some core words associated with wisdom that appear throughout the literature include: *understanding* (Clayton & Birren, 1980; Chandler & Holliday, 1990; Orwoll & Perlmutter, 1990); *empathy* (Clayton & Birren, 1980; Csikszentmihalyi & Rathunde, 1990; Chandler & Holliday, 1990; Levitt, 1999; Shedlock & Cornelius, 2000); *knowledge* (Baltes & Smith, 1990; Clayton & Birren, 1980; Sternberg, 1998; Shedlock & Cornelius, 2000); *knows self* (Chandler & Holiday, 1990; Levitt, 1999; Damon, 2000; Stevens, 2000; Shedlock & Cornelius, 2000); *living in balance* (Birren & Fisher, 1990; Meacham, 1990); *understanding* (Clayton & Barren, 1980; Chandler & Holliday, 1990; Levitt, 1999; Stevens, 2000); and *systemic thinking* (Chandler & Holliday, 1990; Stevens, 2000; Shedlock & Cornelius, 2000). Macdonald describes this systemic thinking as "acting with the well-being of the whole in mind" (Macdonald, 1996, p. 1).

Trumpa (1991) sees wisdom as a state of consciousness with the qualities of spaciousness, friendliness, warmth, softness and joy. Woodman and Dickinson (1996) see wisdom as the state of consciousness that allows the spiritual Self to be active. Similarly, in a comparative study of two groups (one characterized as elderly and one characterized as creative), Orwoll and Perlmutter (1990) discovered that wisdom was associated with advanced self-development and **self-transcendence**.

Wisdom also appears to have an affective component (Brown, 2000). The neurobiological roots of this were confirmed by Sherman (2000) who discovered that some brain-damaged patients who lacked wisdom also lacked the evaluative affects used to choose a course of action (make a decision).

A number of writers have considered wisdom as a part of intelligence (Smith et al., 1987; Dittmann-Kohli and Baltes, 1990). Baltes and Smith (1990) go on to say that wisdom is "a highly developed body of factual and procedural knowledge and judgment dealing with what we call the 'fundamental pragmatics of life'." In contrast, from qualitative research with Buddhist monks, Levitt (1999) said that the monks tended toward a spiritual definition and believed that **all people were capable of wisdom, regardless of their intellect**.

Around the turn of the century, the U.S. Department of the Navy placed knowledge at the beginning and wisdom near the end of their change model based on the seven levels of consciousness (Porter, et al, 2003; Bennet & Bennet, 2004). See Figure 11-1. The change model consists of the following progression to facilitate increased connectedness and heightened consciousness: (1) closed structured concepts, (2) focused by limited sharing, (3) awareness and connectedness through sharing, (4) creating concepts and sharing these concepts with others, (5) advancement of new knowledge shared with humanity at large, (6) creating wisdom, teaching, and leading, and (7) creating (and sharing) new thought in a fully aware and conscious process.[2] In the earlier levels of this model, value is absent since the positive or negative value of knowledge is situation-dependent and context sensitive. However, prior to reaching level 6 (creating wisdom, teaching and leading), there is the insertion of value framed in the context of the greater good.

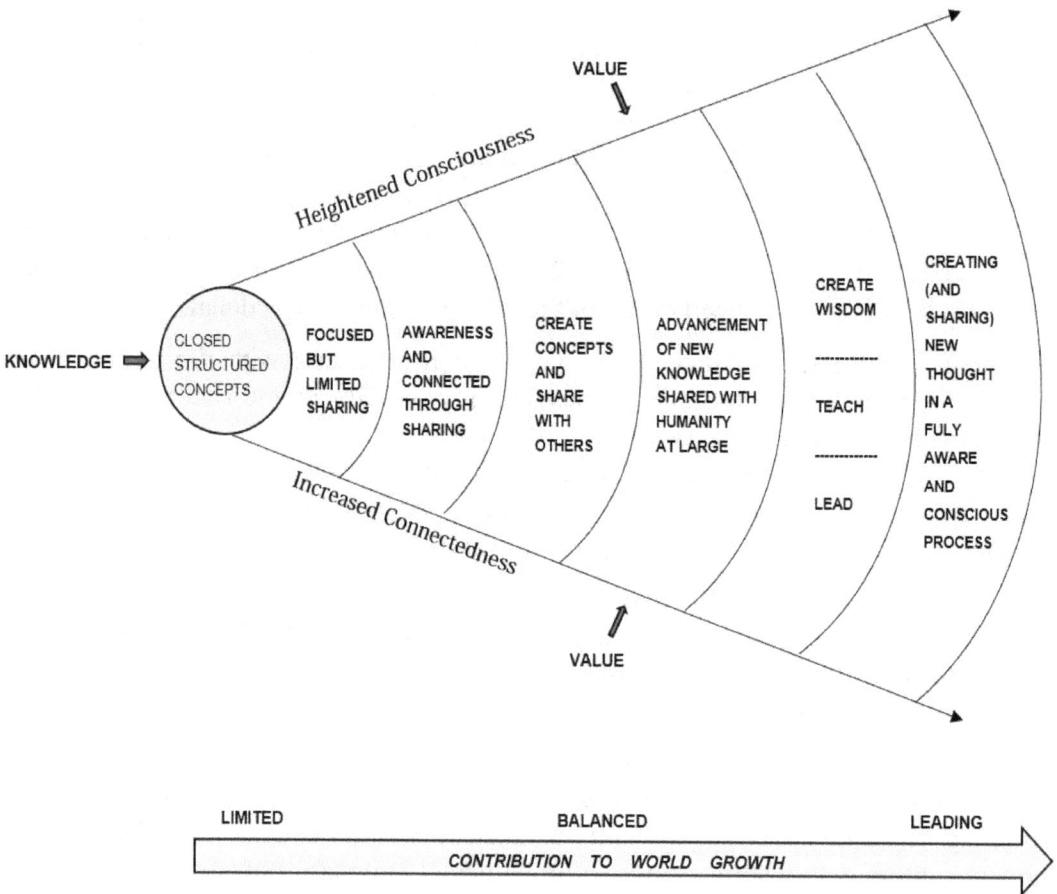

Figure 11-1. *The growth of knowledge and sharing (a change model used in the US Department of Navy based on the seven levels of consciousness.*

Recall our discussion in Chapter 10 of values and knowledge, forwarding that values are knowledge—context sensitive and situation dependent—developed over time and highly responsive to culture. We specifically focused on the new decision-maker emerging from a global culture. As introduced in Chapter 2, as connections increase and consciousness expands there is recognition of a higher value of knowledge, that is, moving beyond the individual to groups, to communities, to a global value. *This is the connection to wisdom.* Note that this relationship to others is also a factor in our description of intelligent activity, which activity reflects wisdom.[3]

Nussbaum (2000) forwards that all knowledge is in the service of wisdom. Nelson (2004) says that wisdom is the knowledge of the essential nature of reality. Further, similar to what was expressed in the Navy model, Sternberg defines wisdom as "the application of tacit knowledge as mediated by values toward the goal of

> Knowledge is in service to wisdom.

achieving a common good" (Sternberg, 1998, p. 353), thus suggesting that tacit knowledge is a prerequisite for developing wisdom and, as suggested in the previous paragraph, wisdom is defined in a social rather than individual context. This is an important distinction of wisdom, although in everyday language the term "wise" is often used in service to the individual. Note that over time, what is considered "wise" only from an individual perspective leads to separation, self-service, and learning limitations as the individual identifies with the knowledge they create. Looking from the functional viewpoint of the mind/brain as an associative patterner, it would appear that information (as patterns of energy) is intended to flow from person to person, triggering the continuous creation of knowledge (the capacity to take effective action) in support of experiential learning and expansion. This would indeed place knowledge in service to wisdom and insinuate its connection to a greater social good.

Wisdom as Patterns

Goldberg (a clinical professor of neurology) raises the question: if memory and mental focus decline with age, why is it that our wisdom and competence grow? After validating these two propositions, he answers the question by asserting that *tacit knowledge* does not suffer appreciable decline with age because it represents high-level patterns of procedural knowledge—knowledge of solving problems (Goldberg, 2005). These are **patterns that represent chunks or groups of other patterns**. If a mind has been active throughout life these high-level patterns represent competence, insight and deep (tacit) knowledge that may be considered wisdom. Thus while memory, specific facts and attention may decline with age, the knowledge of how to solve problems or what needs to be done in a specific situation does not appear to decline. Tacit knowledge and wisdom may remain strong and even continue to grow with age. What this also implies is that tacit knowledge—particularly as we age—is primarily process knowledge. Chunking of knowledge is further discussed in Chapter 13 on sub-personalities.

Murphy (2000) points out that wisdom is at home in several levels of the hierarchy of complexity. As she observes, "understanding of a phenomenon at each level of the hierarchy can be enhanced by relating it to its neighboring levels" (Murphy, 2000, p. 7). Schloss explains that the levels of a hierarchy are interrelated via feedback loops; increased understanding results from following these feedback loops from one level to another and back again (Schloss, 2000). Similarly, Erikson says that a sense of the complexity of living is an attribute of wisdom. A wise person embraces the,

> ... sense of the complexity of living, of relationships, of all negotiations. There is certainly no immediate, discernible, and absolute right and wrong, just as light and dark are separated by innumerable shadings ... [the] interweaving of time and space, light and dark, and the complexity of human nature suggests that ... this wholeness of perception to be given partially and realized, must of necessity be made up of a merging of the sensual, the logical, and the aesthetic perceptions of the individual (Erikson, 1988, p. 184).

As Can Be Noted in this Brief Treatment ...

The concept of wisdom is clearly related to knowledge—and in particular to tacit knowledge—and has also been related to the phenomenon of consciousness. Wisdom is clearly connected with systemic, hierarchical thinking, and the complexity of human nature has been brought into the discussion. Most importantly, wisdom is not in isolation; it appears to deal with the cognitive and emotional, personal and social, as well as the moral and religious aspects of life, very much based on the interconnectedness of people.

> As Costa sums up in *Working Wisdom*:

> Wisdom is the combination of knowledge and experience, but it is more than just the sum of these parts. Wisdom involves the mind and the heart, logic and intuition, left brain and right brain, but it is more than either reason, or creativity, or both. **Wisdom involves a sense of balance, an equilibrium derived from a strong, pervasive *moral* conviction ... the conviction and guidance provided by the obligations that flow from a profound sense of interdependence.** In essence, wisdom grows through the learning of more knowledge, and the practiced experience of day-to-day life—both filtered through a code of moral conviction. (Costa, 1995, p. 3)

From Ordinary to Extraordinary Consciousness

To quickly lay the groundwork for understanding our usage of consciousness, we provide representative viewpoints from several fields. The psychologist William James said that consciousness was the name of a non-entity in that it stands for the function of knowing (a process) (McDermott, 1977). The psychologist J. Allan Hobson considers consciousness as awareness of the world, the body and the self (Hobson, 1999). In neuroscience terms, this would be the sensitivity to outside stimuli as translated through the brain and neuron connections into patterns that to the mind represent thoughts. The Nobel Laureate physiologist Gerald Edelman considered consciousness as a process of the flow of thoughts, images, feelings and emotions (Edelman & Tononi, 2000). The spiritualist Ramon describes consciousness as the "energized pool of intent from which all human experience springs" (Ramon, 1997, p. 48).

We agree that consciousness is a process, and not a state. It is private, continuous, always-changing, and felt to be a sequential set of ideas, thoughts, images, feelings and perceptions (Bennet, 2001). It is the sum total of who we are, what we believe, how we act and the things we do, so it's all of our actions, thoughts and words (Dunning, 2014). A high-level property of consciousness is its unity. The mind is continually integrating the incoming signals from the environment as well as connecting many different processing areas within the brain and combining them into a coherent flow of conscious thinking or feeling. When we see a snapshot of the visible world, it appears as a coherent, unified whole.

As introduced in Chapter 5, ordinary consciousness represents the customary or typical state of consciousness, that which is common to everyday usage, or of the usual kind. Recall that Polanyi sees tacit knowledge as not part of one's ordinary consciousness (Polanyi, 1958); thus, tacit knowledge resides in the unconscious. To access tacit knowledge an individual needs to move beyond

> Consciousness is a process, not a state. It is private, continuous, always-changing, and felt to be a sequential set of ideas, thoughts, images, feelings and perceptions.

ordinary consciousness to what we call *extraordinary consciousness*, acquiring a greater sensitivity to information stored in the unconscious in order to facilitate the awareness and application of that information and knowledge. Extraordinary consciousness may be created through such techniques as meditation, lucid dreaming, hemispheric synchronization, and other ways of quieting the conscious mind, and by doing so allowing/encouraging accessibility to information in the unconscious. Such techniques create a heightened sensitivity to, awareness of, and connection with our unconscious mind together with its memory and thought processes.

On the other hand, consciousness appears to be a flow, with extraordinary consciousness representing increased sensitivity to awareness of tacit knowledge. As a process, consciousness represents a characteristic of the human mind to be *aware* of the nature and structure of information. Moving beyond ordinary consciousness to extraordinary consciousness would increase this awareness.

In the discussion of wisdom above, recall that Csikszentmihalyi and Nakamura (1990) described wisdom as referring to two distinct phenomena: the *content* of wisdom and the *capacity* to think or act wisely. This parallels our understanding of knowledge as both Knowledge (Informing) and Knowledge (Proceeding). In other words, wisdom has an information component and a process component. Knowledge and wisdom would then both deal with the *nature and structure of information*, with nature being (or representing) the quality or constitution of information and structure being (or representing) the process of building new information. Wisdom would represent **higher discernment** and the use of tacit knowledge to provide new, situation-dependent, context-sensitive knowledge—perhaps taking the form of intuition. The tacit knowledge driving what is surfaced would be both Knowledge (Informing) and Knowledge (Proceeding), although as noted by Goldberg (2005), primarily Knowledge (Proceeding).

Further, wisdom has been repeatedly related to systemic thinking and **the recognition of a higher order of interdependence in the hierarchy of life**, perhaps even the universe. Similarly, extraordinary consciousness delimits ordinary consciousness, increasing sensitivity to, and awareness of, that which is tacit (that which is in the unconscious) whether embodied, affective, intuitive or spiritual (detailed in Chapter 4). It is important to recall that these tacit knowledges are inter-linked; humans are holistic decision-makers. With this larger sensitivity and awareness of that which is tacit comes increased understanding of the interdependence associated with patterns of information, some of which would be patterns of patterns (possibly hierarchical in nature, although they might be represented by any three-dimensional patterns in space).

> Wisdom has been repeatedly related to systemic thinking, and the recognition of a higher order of interdependence in the hierarchy of life perhaps even the universe.

Figure 11-2 provides a visual representation of the relationships among knowledge, consciousness and extraordinary consciousness. The dotted lines represent a movement from ordinary consciousness into extraordinary consciousness, at whatever level that may occur. The wavy lines represent the fluctuating boundary between explicit and tacit knowledge, with implicit knowledge describing what was thought tacit but triggered into consciousness by incoming information.

While there is much thinking and experimentation needed to truly understand wisdom, it is increasingly clear that extraordinary consciousness—expanding our sensitivity and awareness of that which is tacit—appears to open the door to expanded wisdom.

A conversational Conscious Look Book entitled *Possibilities that are YOU! Volume 15: Seeking Wisdom* presents a model with two growth paths moving toward Wisdom in support of Intelligent Activity. The first path is concerned with developing the mental faculties and increasingly higher order patterns. This is the path of learning, creating knowledge through experience from the building blocks of information. The second path is concerned with developing increasingly deeper connections with

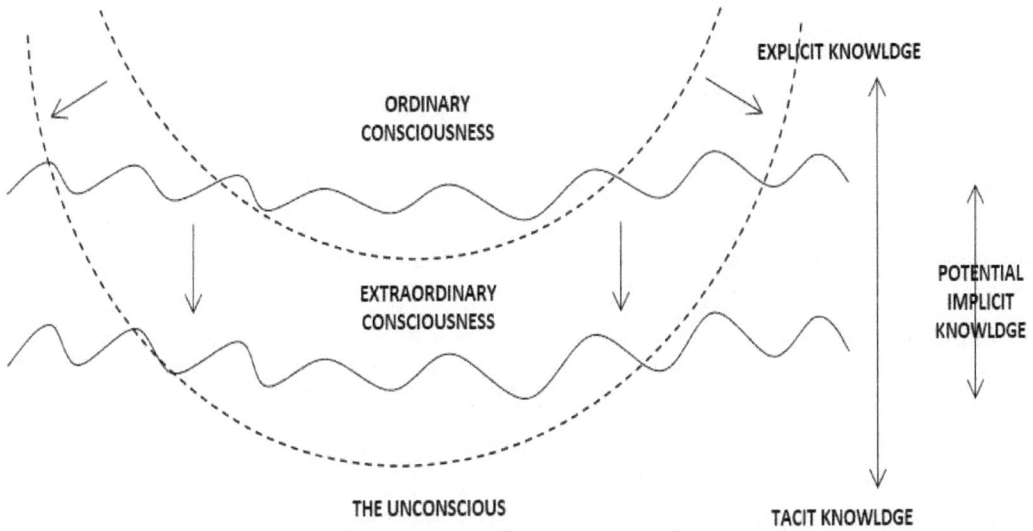

Figure 11-2. *Conceptual model relating knowledge and consciousness.*

others. This path begins with the illusion of separation, moving as we expand through life experiences through sympathy, empathy, and compassion in a journey toward unconditional love. From the learning along these two growth paths emerges wisdom and the capacity for intelligent activity.

Chapter 12
Knowledge and Knowing[1]

Every decision and the actions that decision drives is a learning experience that builds on its predecessors by broadening the sources of knowledge creation and the capacity to create knowledge in different ways. For example, as an individual engages in more and more conversations across the Internet in search of meaning, thought connections occur that cause an expansion of shallow knowledge. As we are aware, *knowledge begets knowledge*. In a global interactive environment, the more that is understood, the more that can be created and understood. This is how our personal learning system works. As we tap into our internal resources, *knowledge enables knowing, and knowing inspires the creation of knowledge.*

The concept of "knowing" is not easy to define, since the word and concept are used in so many different ways. We consider Knowing as a *sense* that is supported by our tacit knowledge. In this appendix, we provide a Knowing Framework (published as a chapter in Bennet & Bennet, 2013) that focuses on methods to increase individual sensory capabilities. This Framework specifically refers to our five external senses and to the increase of the ability to consciously integrate these sensory inputs *with our tacit knowledge*, that knowledge created by past learning experiences that is *entangled with* the flow of spiritual tacit knowledge continuously available to each of us. In other words, knowing—**driven by the unconscious as an integrated unit**—is the *sense* gained from experience that resides in the *subconscious* part of the mind, *and* the energetic connection our mind enjoys with the *superconscious*.

The subconscious and superconscious are both unconscious resources, with the subconscious directly supporting the embodied mind/brain and the superconscious focused on tacit resources involving larger moral aspects, the emotional part of human nature and the higher development of our mental faculties. When engaged by an intelligent mind which has moved beyond logic into conscious processing based on trust and recognition of the connectedness and interdependence of humanity, these resources are immeasurable.

In Figure 12-1, the superconscious is described with the terms spiritual learning, higher guidance, values and morality, and love. It is also characterized as "pre-personality" to emphasize that there are no personal translators such as beliefs and mental models attached to this form of knowing. In Chapter 26/Part IV, the flow of information from the superconscious is very much focused on the moment at hand and does not bring with it any awareness patterns that could cloud the decision-makers full field of perception.

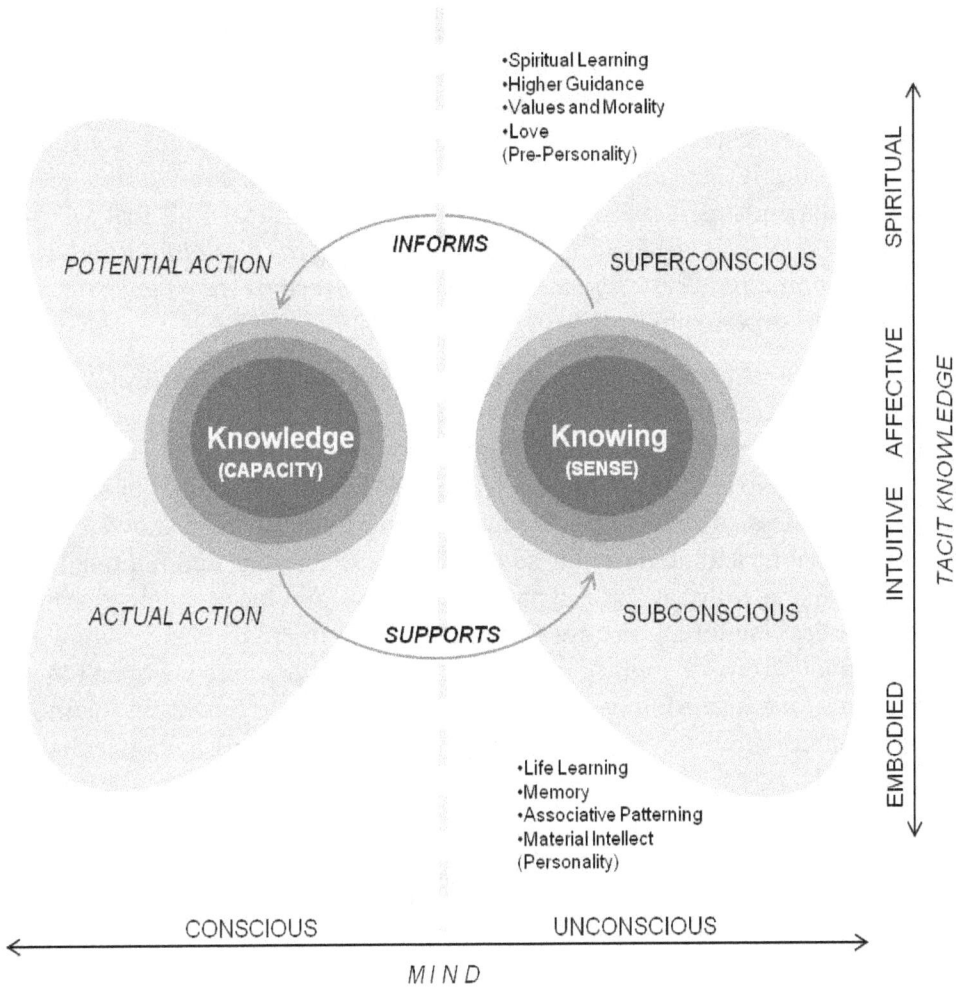

Figure 12-1. *The eternal loop of knowledge and knowing.*

In contrast, the memories stored in the subconscious are very much a part of the personality of the decision-maker, and may be heavily influenced by an individual's perceptions and feelings at the time they were formed. Embodied tacit knowledge would be based on the physical preferences of personality expression while affective tacit knowledge would be based on the feelings connected with the personality of the decision-maker. For example, if there was a traumatic event that occurred in childhood that produced a feeling of "helplessness," later in life there might be neuronal patterns that are triggered that reproduce this feeling when the adult encounters a similar situation. While these feelings may have been appropriate for the child, they would rarely be of service to a seasoned, intelligent decision-maker.

Descriptive terms for the subconscious include life learning, memory, associative patterning, and material intellect. The subconscious in an autonomic system serving a life-support function (see the discussion of personality in Chapter 4). We all must realize that **the human *subconscious* is in service to the conscious mind**. It is not intended to dominate decision-making. The subconscious expands as it integrates and connects (complexes) all that we put into it through our five external-connected senses. *It is at the conscious mind level that we develop our intellect and make choices that serve as the framework for our subconscious processing.*

Figure 12-1 is a nominal graphic showing the continuous feedback loops between knowledge and knowing. Thinking about (potential) and experiencing (actual) effective action (knowledge) supports development of embodied, intuitive and affective tacit knowledges. When we recognize and use our sense of knowing—regardless of its origin—we are tapping into our tacit knowledge to inform our decisions and actions. These decisions and actions, and the feedback from taking those actions, in turn expand our knowledge base, much of which over time will become future tacit resources. Since our internal sense of knowing draws collectively from all areas of our tacit knowledge, the more we open to this inner sense, respond accordingly, and observe and reflect on feedback, the more our inner resources move beyond limited perceptions which may be connected to embedded childhood memories.

Critical Areas of Knowing

The Knowing Framework encompasses three critical areas. The first is "knowing our self," learning to love and trust ourselves. This includes deep reflection on our self in terms of beliefs, values, dreams and purpose for being, and appreciation for the unique beings that we are. It includes understanding of our goals, objectives, strengths and weaknesses in thought and action, and internal defenses and limitations. By knowing ourselves we learn to work within and around our limitations and to support our strengths, thus ensuring that the data, information, and knowledge informing our system is properly identified and interpreted. Further, knowing our self means recognizing that we are a social beings, part of the large ecosystem we call Gaia and inextricably connected to other social beings around the world, which brings us to the second critical element: knowing others.

> As forwarded by the great military strategist Sun Tzu, the three critical areas of Knowing are knowing our self, knowing others and knowing the situation.

We live in a connected world, spending most of our waking life with other people, and often continuing that interaction in our dreams! There is amazing diversity in the world, so much to learn and share with others. Whether in love or at war, people are always in relationships and must grapple with the sense of "other" in accordance with their beliefs, values and dreams.

The third critical area is that of "knowing" the situation in as objective and realistic a manner as possible, understanding the situation, problem, or challenge in context. In the military this is called situational awareness and includes areas such as culture, goals and objectives, thinking patterns, internal inconsistencies, capabilities, strategies and tactics, and political motivations. The current dynamics of our environment, the multiple forces involved, the complexity of relationships, the many aspects of events that are governed by human emotion, and the unprecedented amount of available data and information make situational awareness a challenging but essential phenomenon in many aspects of our daily lives.

As we move away from predictable patterns susceptible to logic, decision-makers must become increasingly reliant on our "gut" instinct, an internal sense of knowing combined with high situational awareness.

> Decision-makers must become increasingly reliant on our "gut" instinct, an internal sense of knowing combined with high situational awareness.

Knowing then becomes key to decision-making. The mental skills honed in knowing help decision-makers identify, interpret, make decisions, and take appropriate action in response to current situational assessments.

This construct of knowing can be elevated to the organizational level by using and combining the insights and experiences of individuals through dialogue and collaboration within teams, groups, and communities, both face-to-face and virtual. Such efforts significantly improve the quality of understanding and responsiveness of actions of the organization. They also greatly expand the scope of complex situations that can be handled through knowing because of the greater resources brought to bear— all of this significantly supported by technological interoperability.

Organizational knowing is an aspect of *organizational intelligence*, the capacity of an organization as a whole to gather information, generate knowledge, innovate, and to take effective action. This capacity is the foundation for effective response in a fast-changing and complex world. Increasing our sensory and mental processes contributes to the "positioning" understood by the great strategist Sun Tzu in the year 500 B.C. when he wrote his famous dictum for victory: *Position yourself so there is no battle* (Clavell, 1983). Today in our world of organizations and complex challenges we could say "Position ourselves so there is no confusion."

By exploring our sense of knowing we expand our understanding of ourselves, improve our awareness of the external world, learn how to tap into internal resources, and increase our skills to affect internal and external change. The Knowing Framework provides ideas for developing deep knowledge within the self and sharing that knowledge with others to create new perceptions and levels of understanding. Since each situation and each individual is unique, this Framework does not provide specific answers. Rather, it suggests questions and paths to follow to find those answers.

Principles of Knowing

In response to a changing environment, the Knowing Framework presented below in its expanded form was first developed at the turn of the century for the U.S. Department of the Navy. There are a number of recognized basic truths that drove its development. These truths became the principles upon which the Knowing Framework is based.

(1) Making decisions in an increasingly complex environment requires new ways of thinking.

(2) All the information in the world is useless if the decision-maker who needs it cannot process it and connect it to their own internal values, knowledge, and wisdom.

(3) We don't know all that we know.

(4) Each of us has knowledge far beyond that which is in our conscious mind. Put another way, we know more than we know we know. (Much of our experience and knowledge resides in the unconscious mind.)

(5) By exercising our mental and sensory capabilities we can increase those capabilities.

(6) Support capabilities of organizational knowing include organizational learning, knowledge centricity, common values and language, coherent vision, whole-brain learning, openness of communications, effective collaboration, and the free flow of ideas.

The concept of knowing focuses on the cognitive capabilities of observing and perceiving a situation; the cognitive processing that must occur to understand the external world and make maximum use of our internal cognitive capabilities; and the mechanism for creating deep knowledge and acting on that knowledge via the self as an agent of change. Each of these core areas will be discussed below in more detail.

The Cognitive Capabilities

The cognitive capabilities include observing, collecting and interpreting data and information, and building knowledge relative to the situation. The six areas we will address are: listening, noticing, scanning, sensing, patterning, and integrating. These areas represent means by which we perceive the external world and begin to make sense of it.

Listening

The first area, listening, sets the stage for the other five cognitive capabilities. Listening involves more than hearing; it is a sensing greater than sound. It is a neurological cognitive process involving stimuli received by the auditory system. The linguist Roland Barthes distinguished the difference between hearing and listening when he says: "Hearing is a physiological phenomenon; listening is a psychological act." What this means is that there is a choice involved in listening in terms of the listener choosing to interpret sound waves to potentially create understanding and meaning (Barthes, 1985). There are three levels of listening: alerting, deciphering and understanding. Alerting is picking up on environmental sound cues. Deciphering is relating the sound cues to meaning. Understanding is focused on the impact of the sound on another person. Active listening is intentionally focusing on who is speaking in order to take full advantage of verbal and non-verbal cues.

In developing active listening, imagine how you can use all your senses to focus on what is being said. One way to do this is to role-play, imagining you are in their shoes and feeling the words. Active listening means fully participating, acknowledging the thoughts you are hearing with your body, encouraging the train of thought, actively asking questions when the timing is appropriate. The childhood game of pass the word is an example of a fun way to improve listening skills. A group sits in a circle and whispers a message one to the next until it comes back to the originator. A variation on this theme is Chinese Whispers where a group makes a line and starts a different message from each end, crossing somewhere in the middle and making it to the opposite end before sharing the messages back with the originators. Another good group exercise is a "your turn" exercise, where one individual begins speaking, and another person picks up the topic, and so forth. Not knowing whether you are next in line to speak develops some good listening skills.

The bottom line is that what we don't hear cannot trigger our knowing. Awareness of our environment is not enough. We must listen to the flow of sound and search out meaning, understanding and implications.

Noticing

The second area, noticing, represents the ability to observe around us and recognize, i.e., identify those things that are relevant to our immediate or future needs. We are all familiar with the phenomenon of buying a new car and for the next six months recognizing the large number of similar cars that are on the streets. This is an example of a cognitive process of which we are frequently unaware. We notice those things that are recently in our memory or of emotional or intellectual importance to us. We miss many aspects of our environment if we are not focusing directly on them. Thus the art of noticing can be considered the art of "knowing" which areas of the environment are important and relevant to us at the moment, and focusing in on those elements and the relationships among those elements. It is also embedding a recall capability of those things not necessarily of immediate importance but representing closely related context factors. *This noticing is a first step in building deep knowledge, developing a thorough understanding and a systems context awareness of those areas of anticipated interest.* This is the start of becoming an expert in a given field of endeavor, or situation.

A classic example of mental exercises aimed at developing latent noticing skills is repetitive observation and recall. For example, think about a room that you are often in, perhaps a colleague's office or a friend's living room. Try to write down everything you can remember about this room. You will discover that despite the fact you've been in this room often, you can't remember exactly where furniture is located, or what's in the corners or on the walls. When you've completed this exercise, visit the room and write down everything you see, everything you've missed. What pictures are on the walls? Do you like them? What personal things in the room tell you something about your colleague or friend? How does the layout of furniture help define the room? (These kinds of questions build relationships with feelings and other thinking patterns.) Write a detailed map and remember it. A few days later repeat this exercise from the beginning. If you make any mistakes, go back to the room again, and as many times as it takes to get it right. Don't let yourself off the hook. You're telling yourself that when details are important you know how to bring them into your memory. As your ability to recall improves, repeat this exercise focusing on a street, a building, or a city you visit often.

Scanning

The third area, scanning, represents the ability to review and survey a large amount of data and information and selectively identify those areas that may be relevant. Because of the exponential increase in data and information, this ability becomes more and more important as time progresses. In a very real sense, scanning represents the ability to reduce the complexity of a situation or environment by objectively filtering out the irrelevant aspects, or environmental noise. By developing your own system of environmental "speed reading," scanning can provide early indicators of change, that is, recognition of shifts in the type of data being scanned.

Scanning exercises push the mind to pick up details and, more importantly, patterns of data and information, *in a short timeframe*. This is an important skill that law enforcement officers and investigators nurture. For example, when you visit an office or room that you've never been in before, take a quick look around and record your first strong impressions. What feelings are you getting? Count stuff. Look at patterns, look at contrasts, look at colors. Try to pick up everything in one or two glances around the room. Make a mental snapshot of the room and spend a few minutes impressing it in your memory. As you leave, remember the mental picture you've made of the room, the way you feel. Impress upon yourself the importance of remembering this. This picture can last for days, or years, despite the shortness of your visit. Your memory can literally retain an integrated *gestalt* of the room. Realize that what you can recall is only a small part of what went into your mind.

Sensing

The fourth area, sensing, represents the ability to take inputs from the external world through our five external senses and ensure the translation of those inputs into our mind to represent as accurate a transduction process (the transfer of energy from one form to another) as possible. The human ability to collect information through our external sensors is limited because of our physiological limitations. For example, we only see a very small part of the electromagnetic spectrum in terms of light, yet with technology we can tremendously expand the sensing capability. As humans we often take our senses for granted, yet they are highly-sensitized complex detection systems that cause immediate response without conscious thought! An example most everyone has experienced or observed is a mother's sensitivity to any discomfort of her young child. The relevance to "knowing" is, recognizing the importance of our sensory inputs, to learn how to fine tune these inputs to the highest possible level, then use discernment and discretion to interpret them.

Exercise examples cited above to increase noticing, scanning, and patterning skills will also enhance the sense of sight, which is far more than just looking at things. It includes locating yourself in position to things. For example, when you're away from city lights look up on a starry night and explore your way around the heavens. Try to identify the main constellations. By knowing their relative position, you know where you are, what month it is, and can even approximate the time of day. The stars provide context for positioning yourself on the earth.

Here are a few exercise examples for other senses. Hearing relates to comprehension. Sit on a park bench, close your eyes and relax, quieting your mind. Start by listening to what is going on around you---conversations of passersby, cars on a nearby causeway, the birds chattering, the wind rustling leaves, water trickling down a nearby drain. Now stretch beyond these nearby sounds. Imagine you have the hearing of a panther, only multidirectional, because you can move your ears every direction and search for sounds. Focus on a faint sound in the distance, then ask your auditory systems to bring it closer. Drag that sound toward you mentally. It gets louder. If you cup one hand behind one ear and cup the other hand in front of the opposite ear, you can actually improve your hearing, focusing on noises from the back with one ear and noises from the front with the other. How does that change what you are hearing?

Next time you are in a conversation with someone, focus your eyes and concentrate on the tip of their nose or the point of their chin. Listen carefully to every word they say, to the pause between their words, to their breathing and sighs, the rise and fall of their voice. Search for the inflections and subtle feelings being communicated behind what is actually being said. When people are talking, much of the meaning behind the information they impart is in their feelings. The words they say are only a representation, a descriptive code that communicates thought, interacting electrical pulses and flows influenced by an emotion or subtle feeling. By listening in this way, with your visual focus not distracting your auditory focus, you can build greater understanding of the subtleties behind the words.

There are many games that accentuate the sense of touch. An old favorite is blind man's bluff; more current is the use of blindfolding and walking through the woods used in outdoor management programs. Try this at home by spending three or four hours blindfolded, going about your regular home activities. At first, you'll stumble and bump, maybe even become frustrated. But as you continue, your ability to manage your movements and meet your needs using your sense of touch will quickly improve. You will be able to move about your home alone with relatively little effort, and you'll know where things are, especially things that are alive, such as plants and pets. You will develop the ability to *feel* their energy. Such exercises as these, force your unconscious mind to create, re-create, and surface the imagined physical world. It activates the mind to bring out into the open its sensitivity to the physical context in which we live.

Patterning

The fifth area, patterning, represents the ability to review, study, and interpret large amounts of data/events/information and identify causal or correlative connections that are relatively stable over time or space and may represent patterns driven by underlying phenomena. These hidden drivers can become crucial to understanding the situation or the enemy behavior. This would also include an understanding of rhythm and randomness, flows and trends. Recall the importance of structure, relationships, and culture in creating emergent phenomena (patterns) and in influencing complex systems.

A well-known example of the use of patterning is that of professional card players and successful gamblers, who have trained themselves to repeatedly recall complicated patterns found in randomly drawn cards. To learn this skill, and improve your patterning skills, take a deck of cards and quickly flip through the deck three or four at a time. During this process, make a mental picture of the cards that are in your hand, pause, then turn over three or four more. After doing this several times, recall the mental picture of the first set of cards. What were they? Then try to recall the second set, then the third.

The secret is not to try and remember the actual cards, but to close your eyes and recall the mental picture of the cards. Patterns will emerge. After practicing for awhile, you will discover your ability to recall the patterns---as well as your ability to recall larger numbers of patterns---will steadily increase. As you increase the number of groups of cards you can recall, and increase the number of cards within each group, you are increasing your ability to recall complex patterns.

Study many patterns found in nature, art, science, and other areas of human endeavor. These patterns will provide you with a "mental reference library" that your mind can use to detect patterns in new situations. Chess experts win games on pattern recognition and pattern creation, not on individual pieces.

Integrating

The last area in the cognitive capabilities is integration. This represents the top-level capacity to take large amounts of data and information and pull them together to create meaning; this is frequently called sense-making. This capability—to pull together the major aspects of a complex situation and create patterns, relationships, models, and meaning that represent reality—is what enables us to make decisions. This capability would be inclusive of the ability to integrate internal organizational capabilities and systems.

While we have used the word "integrating" to describe this capability, recall that the human mind is an associative patterner that is continuously complexing (mixing) incoming information from the external environment with all that is stored in memory. Thus, while the decision-maker has an awareness of integrating, the unconscious is doing much of the work and providing nudges in terms of feelings and speculative thought. Our unconscious is forever our partner, working 24/7 for us.

These five ways of observing represent the front line of cognitive capabilities needed to assist all of us in creative and accurate situational awareness and building a valid understanding of situations. To support these cognitive capabilities, we then need processes that transform these observations and this first-level knowledge into a deeper level of comprehension and understanding.

The Cognitive Processes

Internal cognitive processes that support the capabilities discussed above include visualizing, intuiting, valuing, choosing, and setting intent. These five internal cognitive processes greatly improve our power to understand the external world and to make maximum use of our internal thinking capabilities, transforming our observations into understanding.

Visualizing

The first of these processes, visualizing, represents the methodology of focusing attention on a given area and through imagination and logic creating an internal vision and scenario for success. In developing a successful vision, one must frequently take several different perspectives of the situation, play with a number of assumptions underlying these perspectives, and through a playful trial-and-error, come up with potential visions. This process is more creative than logical, more intuitive than rational, and wherever possible should be challenged, filtered, and constructed in collaboration with other competent individuals. Often this is done between two trusting colleagues or perhaps with a small team. While there is never absolute assurance that visualizing accurately represents reality, there are probabilities or degrees of success that can be recognized and developed.

Intuiting

The second supporting area is that of intuiting. By this we mean the art of making maximum use of our own intuition developed through experience, trial-and-error and deliberate internal questioning and application. There are standard processes available for training oneself to surface intuition (see Chapter 5). Recognize that intuition is typically understood as being the ability to access our unconscious mind and thereby make effective use of its very large storeroom of observations, experiences, and information. In our framework, intuition is one of the four ways tacit knowledge expresses (see Chapter 4).

Empathy represents another aspect of intuition. Empathy is interpreted as the ability to take oneself out of oneself and put oneself into another person's world. In other words, as the old Native American saying goes, "Until you walk a mile in his moccasins, you will never understand the person." The ability to empathize permits us to translate our personal perspective into that of another, thereby understanding their interpretation of the situation and intuiting their actions. A tool that can be used to trigger ideas and dig deeper into one's intuitive capability, bringing out additional insights, is "mind mapping." Mind mapping is a tool to visually display and recognize relationships from discrete and diverse pieces of information and data (Wycoff, 1991). Empathy is also one of the values addressed in Chapter 10.

Valuing

Valuing represents the capacity to observe situations and recognize the values that underlie their various aspects and concomitantly be fully aware of your own values and beliefs. A major part of valuing is the ability to align your vision, mission, and goals to focus attention on the immediate situation at hand. A second aspect represents the ability to identify the relevant but unknown aspects of a situation or competitor's behavior. Of course, the problem of unknown unknowns always exists in a turbulent environment and, while logically they are impossible to identify because by definition they are unknown, there are techniques available that help one reduce the area of known unknowns and hence reduce the probability of them adversely affecting the organization.

A third aspect of valuing is that of meaning, that is, understanding the important aspects of the situation and being able to prioritize them to anticipate potential consequences. Meaning is contingent upon the goals and aspirations of the individual. It also relies on the history of both the individual's experience and the context of the situation. Determining the meaning of a situation allows us to understand its impact on our own objectives and those of our organization. Knowing the meaning of something lets us prioritize our actions and estimate the resources we may need to deal with it.

Choosing

The fourth supporting area is that of choosing. Choosing involves making judgments, that is, conclusions and interpretations developed through the use of rules-of-thumb, facts, knowledge, experiences, emotions and intuition. While not necessarily widely recognized, judgments are used far more than logic or rational thinking in making decisions. This is because all but the simplest decisions occur in a context in which there is insufficient, noisy, or perhaps too much information to make rational conclusions. Judgment makes maximum use of heuristics, meta-knowing, and verication.

Heuristics represent the rules-of-thumb developed over time and through experience in a given field. They are shortcuts to thinking that are applicable to specific situations. Their value is speed of conclusions and their usefulness rests on consistency of the environment and repeatability of situations. Thus, they are both powerful and dangerous. Dangerous because the situation or environment, when changing, may quickly invalidate former reliable heuristics and historically create the phenomenon of always solving the last problem; yet powerful because they represent efficient and rapid ways of making decisions where the situation is known and the heuristics apply.

Meta-knowing is knowing about knowing, that is, understanding how we know things and how we go about knowing things. With this knowledge, one can more effectively go about learning and knowing in new situations as they evolve over time. Such power and flexibility greatly improves the quality of our choices. Meta-knowing is closely tied to our natural internal processes of learning and behaving as well as knowing how to make the most effective use of available external data, information, and knowledge and intuit that which is not available. An interesting aspect of meta-knowing is the way that certain errors in judgment are common to many people. Just being aware of these mistakes can reduce their occurrence. For example, we tend to give much more weight to specific, concrete information than to conceptual or abstract information. (See Kahneman et al., 1982, for details.)

Verication is the process by which we can improve the probability of making good choices by working with trusted others and using *their* experience and knowing to validate and improve the level of our judgmental effectiveness. Again, this could be done via a trusted colleague or through effective team creativity and decision-making.

Setting Intent

Intent is a powerful internal process that can be harnessed by every human being. Intention is the source with which we are doing something, the act or instance of mentally setting some course of action or result, a determination to act in some specific way. It can take the form of a declaration (often in the form of action), an assertion, a prayer, a cry for help, a wish, visualization, a thought or an affirmation. Perhaps the most in-depth and focused experimentation on the effects of human intention on the properties of materials and what we call physical reality has been that pursued for the past 40 years by Dr. William Tiller of Stanford University. Tiller has proven through repeated experimentation that it is possible to significantly change the properties (ph) of water by holding a clear intention to do so. His mind-shifting and potentially world-changing results began with using intent to change the acid/alkaline balance in purified water. The ramifications of this experiment have the potential to impact every aspect of human life.

What Tiller has discovered is that there are two unique levels of physical reality. The "normal level" of substance is the electric/atom/molecule level, what most of us think of and perceive as the only physical reality. However, a second level of substance exists that is the magnetic information level. While these two levels always interpenetrate each other, under "normal" conditions they do not interact; they are "uncoupled." Intention changes this condition, causing these two levels to interact, or move into a "coupled" state. Where humans are concerned, Tiller says that what an individual intends for himself with a strong sustained desire is what that individual will eventually become (Tiller, 2007).

While informed by Spiritual, the Embodied, Intuitive and Affective tacit knowledges are *local expressions of knowledge*, that is, directly related to our expression in physical reality in a specific situation and context. Connecting Tiller's model of intention with our model of tacit knowledge, it begins to become clear that effective intent relates to an alignment of the conscious mind with the tacit components of the mind and body, that is Embodied, Intuitive, and Affective tacit knowledge. **We have to *know* it, *feel* it, and *believe* it to achieve the coupling of the electric/atom/molecule level and magnetic information level of physical reality**.

As we use our power of intent to co-create our future, it is necessary to focus from outcome to intention, not worrying about what gets done but staying focused on what you are doing and how you "feel" about what you are doing. Are we in alignment with the direction our decisions are taking us? If not, back to the drawing board—that's looking closer at you, the decision-maker, and ensuring that your vision is clear and your intent is aligned with that vision.

In summary, the five internal cognitive processes—visualizing, intuiting, valuing, choosing and setting intent—work with the six cognitive capabilities—listening, noticing, scanning, patterning, sensing, and integrating—to process data and information and create knowledge within the context of the environment and the situation. However, this knowledge must always be suspect because of our own self-limitations, internal inconsistencies, historical biases, and emotional distortions, all of which are discussed in the third area of knowing: the Self as an Agent of Change.

The Self as an Agent of Change

The third area of the knowing framework—the self as an agent of change—is the mechanism for creating deep knowledge, a level of understanding consistent with the external world and our internal framework. As the unconscious continuously associates information, the self as an agent of change takes the emergent deep knowledge and uses it for the dual purpose of our personal learning and growth, and for making changes in the external world.

As introduced in Chapter 2, deep knowledge consists of beliefs, facts, truths, assumptions, and understanding of an area that is so thoroughly embedded in the mind that we are often not consciously aware of the knowledge. To create deep knowledge an individual has to "live" with it, continuously interacting, thinking, learning, and experiencing that part of the world until the knowledge truly becomes a natural part of the inner being. An example would be that a person who has a good knowledge of a foreign language can speak it fluently; a person with a deep knowledge would be able to think in the language without any internal translation and would not need their native language to understand that internal thinking.

In the discussion of self as an agent of change, there are ten elements that will be presented. Five of these elements are internal: know thyself, mental models, emotional intelligence, learning and forgetting, and mental defenses; and five of these elements are external: modeling behaviors, knowledge sharing, dialogue, storytelling, and the art of persuasion.

Internal Elements

Alexander Pope, in his essay on man (1732-3), noted that: "Know then thyself, presume not God to scan; the proper study of mankind is man." We often think we know ourselves, but we rarely do. To really understand our own biases, perceptions, capabilities, etc., each of us must look inside and, as objectively as possible, ask ourselves, who are we, what are our limitations, what are our strengths, and what jewels and baggage do we carry from our years of experience. Rarely do we *take ourselves out of ourselves and look at ourselves*. But without an objective understanding of our own values, beliefs, and biases, we are continually in danger of misunderstanding the interpretation we apply to the external world. Our motives, expectations, decisions, and beliefs are frequently driven by internal forces of which we are completely unaware. For example, our emotional state plays a strong role in determining how we make decisions and what we decide.

The first step in knowing ourselves is awareness of the fact that we cannot assume we are what our conscious mind thinks we are. Two examples that most of us have experienced come to mind. The first is that we frequently do not know what we think until we hear what we say. The second example is the recognition that every act of writing is an act of creativity. Our biases, prejudices, and even brilliant ideas frequently remain unknown to us until pointed out by others or through conversations. Consciousness is our window to the world, but it is clouded by an internal history, experiences, feelings, memories, and desires.

> The first step in knowing ourselves is awareness of the fact that we cannot assume we are what our conscious mind thinks we are.

After awareness comes the need to constantly monitor ourselves for undesirable traits or biases in our thinking, feeling, and processing. Seeking observations from others and carefully analyzing our individual experiences are both useful in understanding ourselves. We all have limitations and strengths, and even agendas hidden from our conscious mind that we must be aware of and build upon or control.

Part of knowing ourselves is the understanding of what mental models we have formed in specific areas of the external world. Mental models are the models we use to represent our own picture of reality. They are built up over time and through experience and represent our beliefs, assumptions, and ways of interpreting the outside world. They are efficient in that they allow us to react quickly to changing conditions and make rapid decisions based upon our presupposed model. Concomitantly, they are dangerous if the model is inaccurate or misleading.

Because we exist in a rapidly changing environment, many of our models quickly become outdated. We then must recognize the importance of continuously reviewing our perceptions and assumptions of the external world and questioning our own mental models to ensure they are consistent with reality (Senge, 1990). Since this is done continuously in our subconscious, we must continuously question ourselves as to our real, versus stated, motives, goals and feelings. *Only then can we know who we are, only then can we change who we will be.*

The art of knowing not only includes understanding our own mental models, but the ability to recognize and deal with the mental models of others. Mental models frequently serve as drivers for our actions as well as our interpretations. When creating deep knowledge or taking action, the use of small groups, dialogue, etc. to normalize mental models with respected colleagues provides somewhat of a safeguard against the use of incomplete or erroneous mental models.

A subtle but powerful factor underlying mental models is the role of emotions in influencing our perception of reality. This has been extensively explored by Daniel Goleman (1995) in his seminal book *Emotional Intelligence*. Emotional intelligence is the ability to sense, understand, and effectively apply the power and acumen of emotions as a source of human energy, information, connection, and influence. It includes self-control, zeal and persistence, and the ability to motivate oneself. To understand emotional intelligence, we study how emotions affect behavior, influence decisions, motivate people to action, and impact their ability to interrelate. Emotions play a much larger role in our lives than previously understood, including a strong role in decision-making. For years it was widely held that rationality was the way of the executive. Now it is becoming clear that the rational and the emotional parts of the mind must be used together to get the best performance in organizations.

Much of emotional life is unconscious. Awareness of emotions occurs when the emotions enter the frontal cortex. As affective tacit knowledge, emotions in the subconscious play a powerful role in how we perceive and act, and hence in our decision-making. Feelings come from the limbic part of the brain and often come forth before the related experiences occur. *They represent a signal* that a given potential action may be wrong, or right, or that an external event may be dangerous. Emotions assign values to options or alternatives, sometimes without our knowing it. There is growing evidence that fundamental ethical stances in life stem from underlying emotional capacities. These stances create the basic belief system, the values, and often the underlying assumptions that are used to see the world—our mental model. From this short treatment of the concept, it is clear that emotional intelligence is interwoven across the ten elements of the self as an agent of change. (See Goleman, 1995; 1998.)

> Much of emotional life is unconscious.

Creating the deep knowledge of knowing through the effective use of emotional intelligence opens the door to two other equally important factors: learning and forgetting. Learning and letting go—in terms of "filing" away or putting away on the bookshelf—are critical elements of the self as an agent of change because they are the primary processes through which we change and grow. They are also the prerequisite for continuous learning, so essential for developing competencies representing all of the processes and capabilities discussed previously. Because the environment is highly dynamic and will continue to become more complex, learning will be more and more essential and critical in keeping up with the world.

Since humans have limited processing capability and the mind is easily overloaded and tends to cling to its past experience and knowledge, "letting go" becomes as important as learning. Letting go is the art of being able to let go of what was known and true in the past. Being able to recognize the limitations and inappropriateness of past assumptions, beliefs, and knowledge is essential before creating new mental models and for understanding ourselves as we grow. It is *one of the hardest acts of the human mind* because it threatens our self-image and may shake even our core belief systems.

The biggest barrier to learning and letting go arises from our own individual ability to develop invisible defenses against changing our beliefs. These self-imposed mental defenses have been eloquently described by Chris Argyris (1990). The essence of his conclusion is that the mind creates built-in defense mechanisms to support belief systems and experience. These defense mechanisms are invisible to the individual and may be quite difficult to expose in a real-world situation. They are a widespread example of not knowing what we know, thus representing invisible barriers to change. Several authors have estimated that information and knowledge double approximately every nine months. If this estimate is even close, the problems of saturation will continue to make our ability to acquire deep knowledge even more challenging. We must learn how to filter data and information through vision, values, goals, and purposes using intuition and judgment as our tools. *This discernment and discretion within the deepest level of our minds provides a proactive aspect of filtering, thereby setting up purposeful mental defenses that reduce complexity and provide conditional safeguards to an otherwise open system.* This is a fundamental way in which the self can simplify a situation by eliminating extraneous and undesirable information and knowledge coming from the external world.

The above discussion has identified a number of factors that can help us achieve an appropriate balance between change and our resistance to change. This is an important attribute: not all change is for the best, yet rigidity begets antiquity. This balance is situational and comes only from experience, learning, and a deep sense of knowing when to change and when not to change the self.

> Not all change is for the best, yet rigidity begets antiquity.

This section has addressed the self as an agent of change through internal recognition of certain factors that can influence self-change. Another aspect of change is the ability of the self to influence or change the external world. This is the active part of knowing. Once the self has attained deep knowledge and understanding of the situation and external environment, this must be shared with others, accompanied by the right actions to achieve success. We live in a connected world.

[NOTE: The Self is the foundation of the Intelligent Complex Adaptive Learning Systems model of experiential learning. See Bennet, D., Bennet, A. and Turner, R. (2015), *Expanding the Self: The Intelligent Complex Adaptive Learning System*, MQIPress, Frost, WV.]

External Elements

The challenge becomes that of translating knowledge into behavior, thus creating the ability to model that behavior and influence others toward taking requisite actions. Role-modeling has always been a prime responsibility of leadership in the government as well as the civilian world. Having deep knowledge of the situation the individual must then translate that into personal behavior that becomes a role model for others to follow and become motivated and knowledgeable about how to act. Effective role-modeling does not require the learner to have the same deep knowledge as the role model, yet the actions and behaviors that result may reflect the equivalent deep knowledge and over time creates deep knowledge in the learner—but only in specific situations. This is how you share the effectiveness from learning and thereby transfer implicit knowledge.

Wherever possible, of course, it is preferable to develop and share as much knowledge as possible so that others can act independently and develop their own internally and situation-driven behavior. This is the reason knowledge management and communities of practice and interest require management attention. Since most deep knowledge is tacit, knowledge sharing can become a real challenge.

A third technique for orchestrating external change is through the use of dialogue. Dialogue is a process described by David Bohm (1992) to create a situation in which a group participates as coequals in inquiring and learning about some specific topic. In essence, the group creates a common understanding and shared perception of a given situation or topic. Dialogue is frequently viewed as the collaborative sharing and development of understanding. It can include both inquiry and discussions, but all participants must suspend judgment and not seek specific outcomes and answers. The process stresses the examination of underlying assumptions and listening deeply to the self and others to develop a collective meaning. This collective meaning is perhaps the best way in which a common understanding of a situation may be developed as a group and understood by others.

Another way of creating change and sharing understanding is through the effective use of the time-honored process of storytelling. Storytelling is a valuable tool in helping to build a common understanding of our current situation in anticipating possible futures and preparing to act on those possible futures. Stories tap into a universal consciousness that is natural to all human communities. Repetition of common story forms carries a subliminal message, a subtext that can help convey a deep level of complex meaning. Since common values enable consistent action, Story in this sense provides a framework that aids decision-making under conditions of uncertainty.

Modeling behavior, knowledge sharing, dialogue, and storytelling are all forms of building understanding and knowledge. Persuasion, our fifth technique, serves to communicate and share understanding with others regarding a specific conviction or belief, and/or to get them to act upon it. To change the external environment, we need to be persuasive and to communicate the importance and need for others to take appropriate action. The question arises: When you have deep knowledge, what aspects of this can be used to effectively influence other's behavior? Since deep knowledge is usually tacit knowledge, we must learn how to transfer this to explicit knowledge. Nonaka and Taguichi (1995) and Polyani (1958) have done seminal work in this area. Persuasion, as seen from the perspective of the self, gets us back to the importance of using all of our fundamental values, such as personal example, integrity, honesty, and openness to help transfer our knowledge to others.

As can be seen in the discussion above, **all four forms of tacit knowledge inform knowing** (see Chapter 4 and Chapter 5 for an in-depth discussion of tacit knowledge).

The Knowing Framework seeks to engage our senses and hone our internal processing mechanisms to take full advantage of our minds/brains/bodies. By bringing our focus on knowing, we have the opportunity to move through relational, experiential, and cultural barriers that somewhere along the course of our lives have been constructed, and sometimes self imposed. This, however, is not the case for many of the young decision-makers moving into the workplace.

It's a New World

We all have been touched by the current climate of increasing change, uncertainty and complexity. As we co-evolve with our environment, new characteristics and ways of thinking and being are emerging both in seasoned decision-makers and in our younger generations. One of these characteristics could be described by the expression "knowing", being open to the fullness of who we are. Many of these young decision-makers have grown up unencumbered by the weights and barriers carried by previous generations linked to bureaucracy, and have embraced the collaborative frameworks increasingly emerging in our 21st century global economy. This amazing connectivity with our selves and the world provides greater access to our sense of knowing and expanded opportunity for development of knowledge. We, indeed, have entered a new way of being in a new world.

Chapter 13
Sub-Personalities as Knowledge

Knowledge is situation dependent and context sensitive, that is, as introduced in Chapter 1, detailed in Chapter 7 and demonstrated in Chapter 9, we are continuously associating the current circumstances of life with what has been previously learned in order to take effective action in the current situation, the Now. By "Now" we refer to the instant at hand; we live in a continuous flow of Nows.

Recall a time when you were thrown into a situation, perhaps unpleasant, where you shifted your internal thinking—and therefore your external actions—to an entirely different way of perceiving. For example, perhaps you were called upon to comfort a friend who has just lost a loved one. Your thoughts, feelings and actions are different than the norm, filled with love and compassion that preempts all other areas of thought and feeling, often accompanied with a knowing of what to say, or what not to say. In short, for the moment, you are a different person, that is, conveying a different personality than the perceived "normal" you. From this short example with which most of us can identify, it can be seen that not only is knowledge (the capacity to take effective action) context sensitive and situation dependent, but that **the individual personality adapts to the context and situation of the moment**. This concept demands a closer look.

We begin with developing a common understanding of the term personality which, like knowledge, is somewhat ambiguous. Certainly, it is connected to being a person—in general or as a specific—and involves attributes, qualities and mental and biophysical activities. From the external viewpoint, the concept would involve attributes, qualities, habits, factors and dimensions which impress themselves on others from which to compare individuals. In search of a clearer understanding, we build on the definition forwarded by Caprara and Cervone (2000), considering personality as *a psychological complex system which displays a unity and continuity in terms of past, present and future both as perceived by the individual and as the individual is perceived by others*. This definition enables viewing the personality from the perspective of the individual (a collection of attributes and inclinations) as well as the perspective of the observer (a social construct based on a set of perceived differing psychological characteristics). Further, personality is seen as a self-regulating system which supports individual development and well-being, with the field of personality psychology focused on enabling people to recognize their individuated personal and social experiences and the differences and qualities which emerge from those personal and social experiences (Caprara & Cervone, 2000).

Thus, personality is a complex system of structures and processes that emerges from multiple subsystems, specifically involving interdependencies between the person and the environment. This complexity is not surprising. Humans are complex adaptive systems (Bennet & Bennet, 2004) and the development of neurological structures is dependent on both genetic programming and personal experience (Kolb & Whishaw 1998). An exciting, fairly recent discovery in neuroscience is the concept of plasticity, which is a result of the connection between neural patterns in the mind and the physical world. This neural plasticity is the ability of neurons to change their structure and relationships, depending on environmental demands and personal decisions and actions. Evolution has created a brain that can adapt and readapt to a changing world (Buonomano & Merzenich, 1998). Indeed, one of the most striking findings in neuroplasticity is the discovery that new neurons appear when individuals are exposed to enriched environments, with this new growth significantly improving behavioral performance (Begley, 2007).

This plasticity is not limited to single thoughts; in reality, there is no single thought, since every aspect of a thought is connected to hundreds of other aspects of thought, including previous patterns, emotions and context (see Chapter 6 for a discussion of the avenues of context). Thus, related thoughts in terms of specific or similar situations are triggered when there is a reoccurrence or a perceived reoccurrence of *that type of situation*.

> There is no single thought, since every aspect of a thought is connected to hundreds of other aspects of thought, including previous patterns, emotions and context.

In Chapter 5, we introduced the concept of chunking. Specifically, the way people become experts involves the chunking of ideas and concepts and creating understanding through the development of significant patterns useful for solving problems and anticipating future behaviors within their area of focus. The example provided in Chapter 5 dealt with a study of chess players. Master players, or experts, examined the chessboard patterns over and over again, studying them, looking at nuances, generally "playing with" and studying these *patterns* (Ross, 2006). In other words, they used long-term working memory, pattern recognition and chunking as a means of understanding and decision-making, all of which over time becomes embedded in the unconscious (Ericsson, 2006).

Similar to this example of chunking, groups of thought (knowledge) are connected in the unconscious. As similar situations emerge, based on feedback and response, more and more neuronal connections are created relating to how to effectively handle these situations. Embedded in the unconscious—waiting to be triggered—these chunked groups of thought come to the fore when they are needed. The more an individual experiences situations that are similar, the stronger this pattern of thought becomes, eventually quite capable of driving actions which we may be unable to change by a conscious decision or an act of will. As Rowan describes, this experience of being "taken over" by a part of ourselves "lasts as long as the situation lasts—perhaps a few minutes, perhaps an hour, perhaps a few hours—and then changes by itself when we leave this situation and go into a different one." (Rowan, 1990, p. 7) In a social psychology textbook, Middlebrook (1974) pointed out that the individual is not a single self, but rather many selves, which shift and change as the individual moves from situation to situation. We would summarize by embracing Middlebrook's concept, *we become what the situation demands*.

While this concept is not new to the field of psychology, it has been called by many names including, for example, Freud's (1938) ego, id and superego; Jung's (1990) archetypes; Lewin's (1936) subregions of the personality; Tart's (1975) identity states; Goffman's (1959) multiple selfing; and Kihlstrom and Cantor's (1984) self-schemas. Similarly, other authors make reference to ego states, retroflection, internal objects, imaginal objects, the hidden observer, the emotionally divided self, the false or unreal self, energy patterns, deeper potential coming to the surface, subidentities, small minds, little I's, agencies within the mind, possible selves, prototypes, alter-personalities, and a community of self (Rowan, 2000). Building on the work of Assagioli (1975), Brown (1979), Redfearn (1985), Rowan (2000) and Wilber (2000)—and consistent with Sacred Attention Therapy (2015), a project with which the authors are associated—we choose to use the term sub-personalities to represent this concept. So what, in fact, are sub-personalities?

Your Sub-Personality as an Expert

Brown (1979) offers that sub-personalities are "patterns of feelings, thoughts, behaviors, perceptions, postures and ways of moving which tend to coalesce in response to various recurring situations in life." Rowan (2000, p. 8) takes this a step farther, considering a sub-personality as "a semi-permanent and semi-autonomous region of the personality capable of acting as a person."

To understand this concept in terms of a continuous flow of knowledge that is situation dependent and context sensitive, we must realize that these sub-personalities are not "things"; rather, they are very fluid processes, much as the individual when perceived as the continuous learner we are. Referring to the human—and introduced earlier in this book—one of our favorite concepts to share as we profess and lecture is: *We are a verb, not a noun.*

Chunking has occurred to create these sub-personalities—or patterns of knowledge—that are perceived critical to address and handle certain types of situations, that is, *providing the capacity to take effective action*. As layer after layer of these chunked knowledge patterns are added through related experiences, the sub-personality increases in complexity, and can take on a life of its own. Quite unconsciously, YOU have built an "expert" to handle a specific type of situation!

Recognizing our fluidity as learners, it is still convenient to talk about sub-personalities as "little people" and describe them in terms of specific characteristics that may or may not be consistent with the attributes, qualities and mental and biophysical activities of the day-to-day personality. Wilber (2000) says that, in his view, each sub-personality exists as an unconscious "I",

> ... an aspect of the proximate self that was defensively split off, but with which consciousness remains fused, embedded, or identified (as a hidden 'I'), with its own wants, desires, impulses, and so on. (p. 246)

He goes on to say that the specific nature of each of these sub-personalities is highly dependent on *when* it was dissociated, that is, split off while consciousness was still identified with it, becoming unconscious subjects with their own morals, worldviews, needs and so on (Wilber, 2000). When triggered by a situation, these "little people" (a layered collection of knowledge developed through repetitive chunking) move to (and often take over) the conscious level.

Since story provides a unique form of sharing context and meaning, we have provided a story in Appendix B—***Glimpses of Consciousness***—to further explore sub-personalities.

Wilber contends that healthy people have somewhere around a dozen sub-personalities, that is, psychological structures or entities, or a personality mode that kicks in when it is needed. Wiber (2000) talks about these sub-personalities as different states—the parent ego state, child ego state, adult ego state, topdog, underdog conscience, ego ideal, idealized ego, false self, authentic self, real self, harsh critic, superego, libidinous self and so on. From another perspective, Rowan (2000) says that common sub-personalities include: The Protector/Controller, the Critic, the Pusher, the Perfectionist, the Central Organizing Sub-personality, the Inner Child, the Nurturing Parent and the Power Brokers. Other authors have developed other descriptive terms and you, as the unique individual you are, may have developed pet names for sets of behaviors that periodically emerge into your conscious awareness!

> Healthy people have somewhere around a dozen sub-personalities, psychological structures that kick in when needed.

These sub-personalities offer different frames of reference for dealing with the world. For example, we understand the power of exploring counter-arguments in decision-making (Janis and Mann, 1977). Perhaps one of your sub-personalities is a skeptic, or a debater. We agree with Rowan's (2000) research hypothesis: "Better decisions are made by bringing out the counter-arguments and integrating them, than by allowing one side to dominate, or making some kind of mean compromise." (p. 201)

As can be seen, as layered chunks of knowledge patterns focused on handling certain challenges and situations, sub-personalities can be considered knowledge tools to navigate changing, uncertain and complex situations in life, when they are triggered, emerging to take effective action. As a mental exercise, take a few minutes to recall instances in the course of life where sub-personalities have come to the fore, perhaps to handle a difficult situation or challenge. What roles have these sub-personalities played in your life? What special knowledge did they bring to bear on a challenging or difficult situation? Is that knowledge generally available to you or does it emerge when needed? Do you recall where that knowledge originated? Most likely this knowledge—in the form of a sub-personality—emerges when it is needed, and you don't recall where it originated. The knowledge embedded within a sub-personality may well be implicit, that is, tacit until triggered by the situation at hand.

Human Transformation

As we repeat experiences throughout life, we continue to grow and expand at some level. Depending highly on individual choices and the level of learning embraced—again, context sensitive and situation dependent—those situations which were considered challenges and difficulties at an earlier age slide into a pattern of normalcy, even comfort, in the handling. Like beliefs and values, human preferences shift and change.

Let's look at the Myers-Brigg's Type Indicator (MBTI) as an example. The MBTI is a psychometric questionnaire that was designed to measure personal preferences in how people perceive and interact with the world. The instrument was built on Jung's (1923) theory that there are four cognitive functions by which humans experience the world—sensation, intuition, feeling and thinking—with each function having one of two orientations (extraversion or introversion).

Katherine Cook Briggs and her daughter, Isabel Briggs Myers, developed a personal inventory based on Jung's work, which include four dichotomies: Intuition/Sensing (I/S), Perception/Judging (P/J), Feeling/Thinking (F/T) and Intraversion/Extraversion (I/E). These dichotomies are set up to express preferences. For example, introversion/extraversion refers to preferences in attitudes, with extraversion meaning outward-turning and introversion meaning inward-turning. People who prefer extraversion are those whose focus is external and who draw energy from acting in the external world. People who prefer intraversion are those whose focus is internal and who draw energy from quiet time with nature, concepts and ideas. The intuition/sensing function refers to information-gathering, with sensing focused on external validation and intuition focused on internal knowing. The feeling/thinking function refers to decision-making. While both functions are used to make rational decision, feeling relies on associating or empathizing with the situation, and thinking takes a more detached viewpoint. The judging/perception function deals with the outside world and whether you prefer to get things done or keep your options open. (Myers & Myers, 1995)

While it is not the intent here to argue the validity of this instrument—and there is still controversy over its effectiveness—note that the MBTI is the world's most widely used personality assessment instrument. What is fascinating about the use of the MBTI, is that it is highly context sensitive (for example, answers are different depending on whether you focus on the work or home environment) and, over time, preferences tend to coalesce toward the middle. What this conveys is that for some learners preferences cease having great import, that is, they function comfortably in all eight dimensions, and the scoring moves closer to being a balance rather than a preference.

Similarly, as sub-personalities become more connected through the process of self-knowledge, what is occurring through self knowledge is an integration across the whole such that, when triggered, sub-personalities become more playful than dominant, accompanied by a creative dynamic. Knowledge provides greater choice. When a person begins to develop knowledge of the authentic self, sub-personalities become less important, gradually moving from what Rowen (2000) describes as great feudal barons to becoming colorful characters occasionally popping into consciousness. This is when we achieve what Richard Harvey (2015) describes as a natural condition of inner peace and harmony.

Humanity in Transition

We look to the work of Ken Wilber to further explore this transition. Wilber (1999) says that humanity—both as individuals and as members of a historically located culture—is undergoing a process of psychospiritual development. This transition is not much different than the shifting developmental stages each of us experiences in life, that is, moving from a symbiotic state with our mother to separation, from focus on an individual body to membership in a group, and then into development of the mental ego. As we move through these stages our idea of "self" shifts and changes. Moving beyond the mental ego into the heart is such a shift, and this is what is currently underway for humanity. As Harvey (2013) explains, we are "in a period of evolution where the world has expanded and developed outwardly and left the inner world behind. Our inner selves must catch up and restore the balance."

There are two dimensions that Wilber says are necessary to transition from one stage to another: *the creative urge* and *the willingness to let go*, that is, be open to new thought and experiences (Wilbur, 2000). Note the similarity of these dimensions to those required for innovation! Certainly, the beginning of this transition is the global network of technology facilitating the movement of information around the world and enriching the creative field from which innovation emerges. Coupled to this capacity are the attitudes of a new generation of decision-makers who are growing up green and growing up connected, and who are not satisfied with the world as it is (Tapscott, 2009).

Wilber (2000) notes that there are four factors that are particularly important to facilitate personal transformation: fulfillment, dissonance, insight and opening. *Fulfillment* is the completion of basic tasks at the current stage, having the knowledge, a basic competency, to function adequately and ready to move on. *Dissonance* is between the old (holding on) and the new (setting in), which could be emotionally charged through affective tacit knowledge. *Insight* into the situation and what is actually wanted provides the direction to move forward and most likely draws on intuitive and spiritual tacit knowledge. *Opening* refers to the quality of openness needed to move forward into a new awareness, learning and an expansion of consciousness.

So how does this help us understand the role our sub-personalities play in our personal transition? Let's consider their relationship to Wilber's four factors of import to personal transformation.

Sub-personalities can develop from the personal unconscious, the cultural unconscious and the collective unconscious (Rowen, 2000). In the personal unconscious, with the first experience that raises our awareness of not being in control comes a split between the Okay self and a self that has "lost the notion of being perfect and whole" (Rowen, 2000, p. 123). This splitting experience is quite powerful—and can be traumatic—since "it is only in this experience that I first become conscious that there is a 'me' at all" (p. 124). As these experiences with the world continue, with chunked knowledge layered upon chunked knowledge, a sub-personality comes to life to deal with similar experiences, and so on. Note that sub-personalities can also develop from joyful experiences; for example, the Inner Child that exists in most of us.

> Sub-personalities, which navigate the rough spots of life can develop from the personal unconscious, the cultural unconscious and the collective unconscious.

The cultural unconscious has to do with the "conflicts endemic in the culture into which we were born" (Rowen, 2000, p. 139). An example is the glass ceiling for women and minorities that reared its head in the middle of the last century, with the fallout lasting for many years. Faced with this repeated challenge, a sub-personality would emerge which might be dominant or submissive, depending on the individual's historic success in dealing with related challenges.

Sub-personalities developed from the collective unconscious would include development of archetypes such as the shadow, (the negative self-image, the part we like the least), the persona (the self we would like others to meet) and the parent, adult and child ego states (Jung,1990; Berne, 1961).

As we move through life these sub-personalities navigate the rough spots, emerging in response to challenges, bringing us through those challenges to a state of interdependency and comfort, and finally reaching a state of *fulfillment*, the ability to function adequately in our environment. At this point, strong sub-personalities are no longer necessary for survival and protection, yet still emerge in response to the external environment. When triggered, they exert the same behaviors previously necessary but no longer warranted, perhaps providing us the experience referred to above as *feeling taken over by a part of ourselves* that we may not have realized was there! Similarly, for strong sub-personalities who take on a life of their own (morals, etc.) there may be a susceptibility to becoming (believing they are) their knowledge; for example, setting up a "positional" front that may reflect attributes of egocentricity and arrogance, and hijacking the personality in specific situations.

Awareness of this out-of-control part of ourselves creates a *dissonance*, Wilber's second factor for personal transformation. If we choose, we begin exploring our behavior and come to recognize that this sub-personality was a defensive necessity earlier in life which is no longer needed. This leads to questions. How would we change our response? What behavior do we want to exhibit? Who is the authentic me? And since we are indeed the most knowledgeable expert on our "self", this is where *insight* can occur.

While knowledge in terms of experience and associative patterning has been accrued over many years of life—shaping these sub-personalities as they are triggered by specific situations—when we become aware (conscious) of these patterns of knowledge *we move to a position of choice*. This, of course, is a small example in a larger pattern of transition and ever-expanding consciousness.

Afterward

A few years ago, this might have been considered a book that added another perspective to the emerging theory of knowledge, as indeed it does. But today, there is a crying need for individuals and organizations to learn more about deep knowledge, which directly impacts the decisions we make and the actions we take. **We call this body of ideas action theory because of the direct link between knowledge and action**.

From an organizational viewpoint, the following is the logic trail. The performance of any organization is determined every day by the actions taken by every single employee. Decisions drive those actions, and knowledge empowers good decisions and implements effective actions (see the definition of knowledge in Chapter 1). Thus, the knowledge within an organization—and the actions taken as a result of that knowledge—determines organizational performance. Further, meta knowledge (knowledge about knowledge) occurs at the level of patterns, a notch above pragmatic knowledge in terms of context and content. This means that it is not tied to a specific content or context, but rather is associated with higher-level patterns suggested by that content and context that can potentially be transferred to other situations. From an individual viewpoint, these higher-level patterns form our personal theory of how to operate in the world; and yes, **each of us has a personal theory that guides our decisions and actions**!

> Each of us has a personal theory of how to operate in the world which guides our decisions and actions.

Let's further explore the concept of a theory. A **theory** is considered a set of statements and/or principles that explain a group of facts or phenomena to guide action or assist in comprehension or judgment (American Heritage Dictionary, 2006; Bennet & Bennet, 2010). Taken from the Greek word *theoria*, which has the same root as theatre, theory means to *see* or *view* or *to make a spectacle* (Bohm, 1980). Theories reflect higher-order patterns, that is, not the facts themselves but rather the *basic source of recognition and meaning of the broader patterns*. Bohm sees theories as a form of insight, a way of looking at the world, clear in certain domains, and unclear beyond those domains, continuously shifting as new insights emerge through experience. While a written theory could be considered information, when understood in a manner such that it offers the potential to, or is used by, individuals to create and guide effective action, it would be considered knowledge. Further, while in its incoming form it is Knowledge (Informing), when complexed with other information in the mind of the individual to make decisions and guide action it becomes part of the process that is Knowledge (Proceeding). A framework or model based on a theoretical structure highlights the primary elements of the theory and their relationships.

Based on beliefs and/or mental models and built on assumptions, theories provide a *plausible or rational explanation of cause and effect relationships*. In terms of our usage here, assumptions are something taken for granted or accepted as true without proof, a supposition or presumption. Principles are considered basic truths or laws; rules or standards; an essential quality or element. Guidelines are a statement or other indication of policy or procedure by which to determine a course of action (how to apply). A framework is a set of assumptions, concepts, values and practices that constitutes a way of viewing reality (American Heritage Dictionary, 2006). Thus, a framework is tied closely to action. In this book, the frameworks developed and explicated in the various chapters represent our personal theories as related to knowledge.

In Figure A-1below, there is a dotted line between practice and assumptions and assumptions and theory. While every decision made and action taken is at some level based on the decision-maker's assumptions, these assumptions are often tacit. Further, people tend to not dig down below surface knowledge to *understand* their assumptions, yet these assumptions underpin theory, from which principles can emerge.

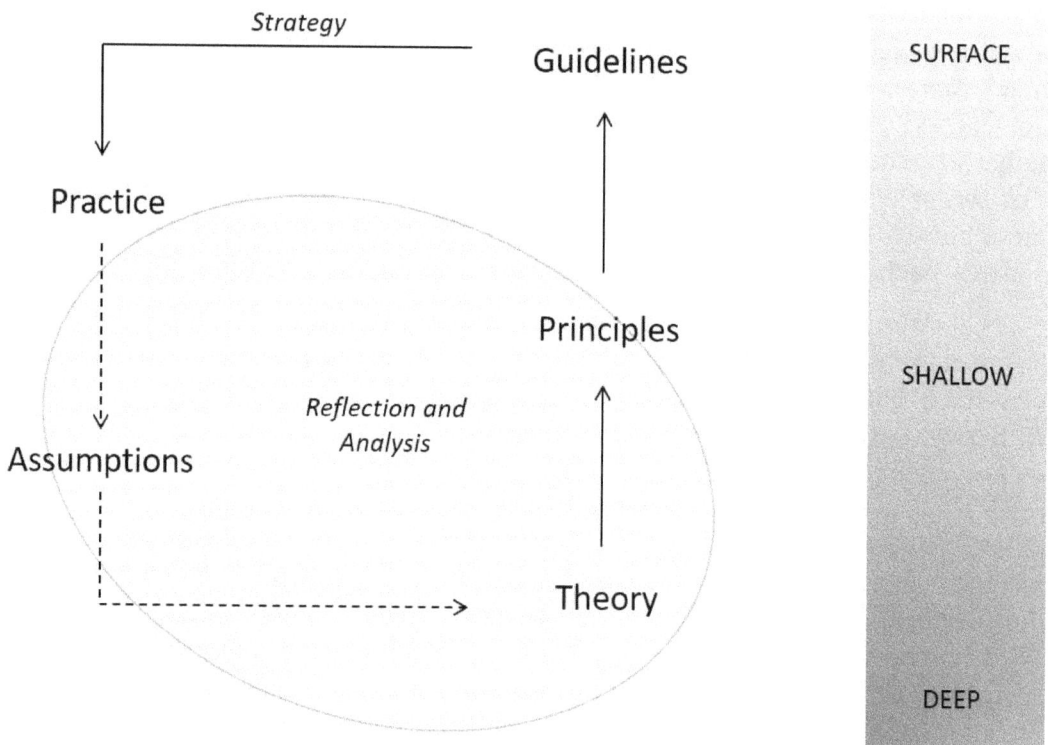

Figure A-1: *Theory as deep knowledge. Deeper understanding (recognizing second-order patterns) increases the ability to apply learning in different contexts and changing situations.*

As Surinder Kumar Batra said in a recent research project, the symbiotic relationship between theory and practice cannot be over-emphasized (Bennet & Bennet, 2014). This is shown in Figure A-1. Principles emerge from theory and drive guidelines, which in turn inform practice. Recall that a characteristic of deep knowledge is the ability to shift our frame of reference as the context and situation shift, which is the realm of the expert who has learned to identify and apply patterns (deep knowledge). Thus, the expert is able to identify and understand second-order patterns and apply them in different situations. This is no easy task. As Fitzgerald (2003) observed, "In theory there is no difference between theory and practice; but in practice, there is."

From the neuroscience perspective, as we live through life our cortex builds a model of the world around us, a hierarchical and nested structure that is our perceived model of the real world (Hawkins & Blakesley, 2004). Our hierarchical world view provides internal context to the situation at hand based on life-long observations, experiences and reflection in terms of the strength of personal meaning and essence. Chapter 13 introduced the concept of sub-personalities as knowledge; these sub-personalities are an emergent quality linked to the internal context to a specific type of situation at hand.

We have used the words "a 21st century theory of knowledge" as a subheading for this book. Note that we did not use the word "epistemology", which is heavily laden with many years of philosophical thought, although, indeed, from the framework of a shifting decision environment and recent discoveries in neuroscience, this is very much a study of the nature of knowledge.

For many years as change agents we have touted and believed Einstein's famous thought, we cannot solve our problems with the same thinking we used when we created them. So, to address the challenges of the future, we have changed and expanded our thinking about knowledge, learning from ourselves, our families, and so many friends and colleagues at all levels of organizations and academia; researching the latest findings in neuroscience and integrating them into our focus on knowledge and learning; and sharing what we are learning through journals and books, international conferences, and lecturing and professing in universities around the world. In this book we bring this work together for the first time, looking at knowledge through our 21st century lens of knowing, and pragmatically tying it to effective action. **The human process of creating knowledge is *one of the greatest tools we bring into the Golden Age of Humanity*.**

Appendix A
The KMTL Study

In 2005, 34 Knowledge Management (KM) thought leaders spanning four continents participated in an extensive study exploring the field of KM and their passion for the field. For purposes of this study, hereinafter referred to as the KMTL Study, thought leaders were considered those individuals (a) whose focus had been in the area of KM for several years and continued in this or a related field, (b) who had published or edited books or multiple articles in the field, (c) who had developed and taught academic or certification courses in the area of KM, and (d) who had spoken about KM at multiple symposia and conferences (Bennet, 2005). By definition, this means that thought leaders are both learners and educators. As Durham (2004) points out, thought leadership is as much a social role as the command of knowledge, going beyond subject matter expertise to imply leadership and a willingness to assert direction.

Initial contacts were with thought leaders who appeared most often in the KM literature and appeared at conferences to share their work. Five of these thought leaders recommended additional participants, who were then contacted. While all of these individuals met the selection criteria, it was ultimately the self-selection process of their agreement to participate that created the sample group used. Thus an overall weakness of the study was the potential for selection bias. All but one person agreed to participate; and those thought leaders interviewed later in the process continued to make suggestions of additional candidates such that time constraints became the primary limiting factor.

Participants in the KMTL Study were (in alphabetical order): Verna Allee, Debra Amidon, Ramon Barquin, David Bennet, Juanita Brown, John Seely Brown, Francisco Javier Carrillo, Robert Cross, Tom Davenport, Ross Dawson, Steve Denning, Nancy Dixon, Leif Edvinsson, Kent Greenes, Susan Hanley, Clyde Holsapple, Esko Kilpi, Dorothy Leonard, Geoff Malafsky, Carla O'Dell, Larry Prusak, Madanmohan Rao, Tomasz Rudolf, Melissie Rumizen, Hubert Saint-Onge, Judi Sandrock, Dave Snowden, Tom Stewart, Michael J.D. Sutton, Karl-Erik Sveiby, Doug Weidner, Steve Weineke, Etienne Wenger and Karl Wiig.

Three of the 34 thought leaders participated in a pilot study; and 31 in the primary stage of research. The format of the interviews was either face-to-face, teleconference or in written format as determined by location and participant preference. The longest teleconference was four hours; the shortest two hours. Face-to-face interviews often extended through a meal.

A standard open-ended format of questioning was used; with stories, anecdotes and narratives solicited beyond the answers to the questions. This qualitative approach allowed subjects to describe their own behaviors and experience in the language native to that experience. Transcripts of face-to-face and telephone interviews were reviewed by participants, and follow-on telephone conversations provided clarifications (Bennet, 2005). In-depth qualitative and quantitative analyses were performed.

When participants were asked to define knowledge, 32 of the 34 participants offered an immediate response. Of these responses, 84 percent *tied knowledge directly to action* or use (see Table). For example, John Seely Brown said:

> Knowing has much more to do with *knowledge in action,* and *we know infinitely more than we have knowledge.* That is kind of a key differentiator I think. For example, why stories are so important . . . because they bring knowledge into play. It also has to do with why when I approach something and interact with it, it's almost like something is going to pull the relevant stuff out of my head and I can now do something. I can do things I don't even know that I can do.

Similarly, Juanita Brown tends to think about knowing collectively, "which means knowing together . . . and so to me knowledge has to do with the discovery of an inner knowing that is an embodied thing that enables the *capacity to act.*"

Three other responders connected knowledge and knowing. One responder saw knowledge as, "The very simple, know-how, know-what, know-where, know-when, know-why about stuff in the organization, and if it in any way infuses the individual with some knowing experience other than the mundane side of the informative aspect of data, then it has knowledge qualities." Another classified knowledge as a social phenomenon. "The experience of knowing is very much ours, but our ability to know is related to our engagement with community . . . then knowing is the experience of participating as an individual in this process of knowledge defined at the social level." Yet another responder reflected that knowledge is related to the knowing dimensions in terms of, "you have a sense that it's probably right. Knowledge is more an iconized package of the knowing, so it's easier to share." This sense of *rightness*, or truth, was the focus of another responder who saw knowledge as truth—validated rules derived analytically by first principles or validated through experimentation. Closely related to "rightness" was the reflection added by one responder that, "What is missing from knowledge is any issues of ethics and what it should be used for, where it's coming from, what the purpose is, and the overall context within which knowledge should be embedded." It is forwarded here that **with knowledge comes the responsibility for how that knowledge is used**. See Chapter 12 for a treatment of Knowledge and Knowing.

Offering a different perspective, Clyde Holsapple found the definition forwarded by Alan Newell in 1982 useful, looking at knowledge as "that which is conveyed in usable representations." By representations Newell means patterns that may exist: symbolic, digital, mental, audiovisual, or behavior patterns. The other key part of Newell's definition is usability. A representation that is usable suggests there is a processor that uses it, which then depends on the time, situation and context in which that processor is operating (Newell, 1982). In other words, some knowledge that may be very valuable in one situation is entirely irrelevant or not so important in another situation. The idea that *knowledge is context sensitive and situation dependent* has been recognized in the KM field (Bennet & Bennet, 2007a; Bennet & Bennet, 2007b).

One definition that is descriptive in nature is: Knowledge is considered as the intellectual property of the individual (what we have learned through books, experience, and conversations with others). A second definition descriptive in nature leans toward Karl Popper's identification of knowledge objects as the basis for understanding knowledge. For example, Michael Sutton said, "I'm actually using a framework or taxonomy to describe knowledge, knowledge existing everywhere from the most molecular level in terms of DNA and the coding that goes into that (and that's naturally created) versus the personal, psychological, philosophical beliefs held by an individual that cannot easily be shared (and their dispositions that they may not even be conscious of) to the abstractions that are codified for sharing purposes." After a pause, Sutton thoughtfully adds, "Yet, in apparent contradiction, I believe very strongly in the social construction of knowledge within our different realities . . . There seem to be knowledge objects within and without."

The full study is available on the Mountain Quest Institute website: www.mountainquestintitute.com or email Dr. Alex Bennet at alex@mountainquestinstitute.com

Appendix B

Glimpses of Consciousness

[This story was prepared for the **Sacred Attention Therapy Project**, a collective effort to bring together a group of therapists, healers, and writers to produce a book explaining some of the central building blocks and principle steps in this healing method. The steps in Sacred attention Therapy are Life Statements, Family Beliefs, Emotional-Behavioral Patterns, Emotional Repression, Sub-Personalities, Character Strategies, the Central Character Dynamic, and the Forgiveness Process. The project is based on the work developed by Richard Harvey. See www.sacredattentiontherapy.com   This story is intended to expand the understanding of sub-personalities. In order to not interfere with the flow of the story, references and additional details of ideas introduced in the story are included in the Endnote section of this book.]

* * * * *

I am standing, leaning against the indoor round pen, watching a feisty young gelding do his rounds. David is beside me, his strong arm around my shoulders, his face ignoring the snorting animal, focused fully on me. I turn my head to look at him, and query, "What happened? What's going on?"

Concern rides with his voice, "Don't you remember? You fell off the horse."

Confusion. Remembering. "I was just sitting on the horse." I breathe deeply, it was THAT horse I was sitting on—the horse circling the ring in front of me. How can I be standing here looking from the sidelines?

Watching my thoughts, David quickly responds. "That's been 20 minutes ago. You fell over his rear and landed on your head; passed out for several minutes. Then, you were up, and we've been talking since then. Don't you remember?"

No, I don't remember any of it. Just riding the horse in the ring, and thinking it would be nice to move into a canter and see what he could do. That must have been some canter! What does David mean saying I've been talking to him? "You *just* came back in" comes a soft little voice inside my head. Every once in awhile I talk to myself. That's happening now. "You just came back in" repeats the whisper. Just came back in from where?

The farm manager is walking towards us. "Would you like to see a new foal?" he asks. That would be nice. We move into a neighboring building. The foal is quite young, perhaps a few days old, but already tossing his head, curious about the world, curious about me. "He knows," comes that whisper again. Knows what? "He knows," breezes through my head. This is getting a bit strange. I turn my head to the left, then to the right. Where is that whisper coming from?

It is night. I stay up late, watching movies to block the little voice that keeps interjecting thoughts—soft wisps of tone saying things like, "Try to remember" (isn't that a song?) and "You know who you are." And then, as I reach to turn the television set off, "We're here for you." Who's here for me? Who are you? My head is aching. I climb into bed and close my eyes. Please let me sleep. A warm embrace of love wraps around me and I sleep, ever expanding, expanding. In my dreams I'm on the horse again. I know I'm dreaming, so I decide to change the ending. This time there is no fall, there is no sense of loss. Only, there was, there is ... a sense of loss. WHAT have I lost? Time? No, more than that. What do I need to find?

[The Beginning of a New Day]

It is morning and I'm up keyboarding at my computer. I watch the early light flicker across the Spring green fields, teasing the grass awake. An errant bird taps the window. Tap, tap, tap. A pattern there. Three taps. "Tap, tap, tap" echoes my soft little inner voice. There is no one in the room, so I speak out loud, "Who are you?"

"You," comes the answer. Ah, so I AM talking to myself. "It depends on what you mean by *myself*" comes a whispered response. "I mean ME," still talking out loud. The whisper is almost laughing, "Then I am myself." Okay, I get it ... the *me, myself and I* trick! The voice: "That works!" So I don't need to talk out loud. "No, you don't."

The voice changes the subject: "You took quite a fall yesterday." Where'd I go? "You went within, beyond. Can't speculate further than that ...You weren't here." So, you were in my mind, my body, when I was gone? "Yes, we're always here." We? "Yes, we. Did you think you were alone in here?"

This is getting difficult. I don't understand.

"Lots of ways to think about it. You are the personality, the boss, calling the shots ... for the most part. Then, we have the fluff in your right ear—doesn't really have much of a personality, but has really strong connections upstairs and offers some stimulating light, a real high! Then there's me, or *myself*, depending on the role I'm playing, I'm your witness, and you're my ride this lifetime. " My soul? Softly: "Yes, that term works. Although the English language can be limiting. I prefer the word *dusa*[1] ... I sit at your spiritual core, helping you stage your moral and emotional life. You are my *rodnye*[2], my beloved." Wow! Do I deserve all that? A slight whisper, "Yes."

I feel a bit uncomfortable being the center of all this attention. Who's the fluff on my shoulder? "Fluff is like a little angel—or devil—riding your shoulder. Let's see ... you read that book called *Urantia*[3], so in those terms we'd call fluff your thought adjuster, pre-personality, your spirit connection, bringing in a stream of Source energy."

I understand who you are now: YOU'RE ME! ... maybe a bit of indigestion ... you're just feeding back stuff that I've read and thought about, stuff like *Urantia*! "Maybe ... and maybe not, but if that's true, then *who* is SHE?" She?

Strong female voice: "Me." Oh, my, SHE is another me! "Not to panic. You already *know* me. Think back when you were in the middle of writing that new knowledge book and you got all flustered. I moved in and took over, peacefully gliding us through the process. We were playing around together with ideas, and we made our deadline." That was me, wasn't it? "Well, I'm you as well, so technically that's true, only I'm quite different than the regular, everyday you. Most of the time I ride along quite content to learn from our collective experiences, although I do consider myself somewhat permanent and at least semi-autonomous and quite capable of acting as a person in my own right.[4] When you have trouble navigating this physical realm, I come to the fore and take over. That's MY strength: telling you what to do when you haven't figured it out yet!"

You take over my thoughts; take over my body?

"Not exactly," comes a deep voice, resonating in my stomach. "I have a LOT of capability in that area. For example, since you hoped out of body for awhile, I'm the one who kept the conversation going with David after you hit your head." So you were doing the talking? Who are you? Wait ... I know *you* are *me*, but let's differentiate a bit. "Okay. Let's just say I'm connected pretty tightly to your body, especially the autonomic systems, those systems that keep everything going. It's a big job. I'll give you an example. You know when you're driving and thinking and dreaming, and all of a sudden in the flash of an eye you've gone 20 miles? You don't remember the road at all, but you made it safely to your destination. That's *me* taking over." Thank you. "You're welcome. Of course, I have a lot of help." There's more of you? "Oh, yes, I have billions of helpers, only they're not as complete as me, relatively small in their focus, but incredibly important. By the way, when you did that new meditation last week, they were grateful for you sending light to every cell in your body! I was grateful, too. Thank you for that." You're welcome. Some synergy happening here.

A thin tenor voice screams in my right ear, "Damn it, enough chatter, let's get on with it, let's get back on schedule!" That can't be me. I don't use that kind of language. "That's what you think," comes the humorous response. "I feel separate. I'm my own person, so to speak ... but sometimes the slow ride really irks me, and I have to break in to get you off your ass."

Don't think I care much for you. "That makes sense. I don't care much for you, either."

[Sub-Personalities[5]]

"Ignore him." My soft little voice is back. Boy am I glad to hear from YOU. I'm trying to grasp all this in my mind. "Let me help. Let's say you are the personality; again, the one ultimately in charge of this lifetime." Big responsibility. "Yes, it is, although we're all in this together." Okay, I'm the personality. When David and I facilitate retreats, we often talk to people about the power of the mind/brain, letting them know that no two people have ever been alike or ever will be, that we are each very special and unique. This, despite geneticists saying there is a tremendous overlap across individuals and groups of the human genome, and despite anthropologists discovering that significant parts of social life are experienced universally![6]

The whisper agrees, "You ARE unique!" Could this whisper be my superego?[7] This thought is ignored. "You represent a new and unique integrated pattern of mind, body and spirit, connected to the same energy pattern circuit as others, but with a unique combination of mental and emotional traits, developed skills and personal belief patterns, all in an embryonic state of potential!"[8] What a lot of words and thoughts. My mind is swirling. So, in essence, I am unique because of my attributes, my perceptions ... because of all of YOU!

The whisper sweeps through my ears, building. "One way of looking at US is as sub-personalities, each a part of the larger whole that is YOU—*patterns of feelings and thoughts, behaviors and perceptions, postures and ways of moving, which respond to life situations*.[9] Remember the work of Ken Wilber you read?" Ken Wilber ... Integral Psychology. Lots to try and remember there. Hmmm ... Yes ... healthy people have somewhere around a dozen sub-personalities, that is, psychological structures or entities, or a personality mode that kicks in when it perceives being needed. "Perceives? We're the ones that help you navigate the world, wade through psychological ambushes!" Okay, I'm beginning to see your value. "If we couldn't add value at some level, I doubt we'd be here. However, we do operate in a variety of functional areas, some of which *can* prove troubling."

Let's see. In Wilber's work, sub-personalities include a bunch of different states— the *parent ego state, child ego state, adult ego state, topdog, underdog, conscience, ego ideal, idealized ego, false self, authentic self, real self, harsh critic, superego, libidinous self, and so on*.[10] Or, maybe we could think about you in terms of relationship roles, like wife, child, mother, employee, boss, horseback rider ... "Let's drop that one!" from a deep voice. You're right, but then maybe it wasn't really ME that was on that horse and fell off ... maybe it was one of YOU who doesn't know how to ride! "That's transference," from the SHE.

Or, maybe we could look at you in terms of capabilities like artist, vocalist, actress, speaker, teacher, student, sort of like Edward Debono's changing hats[11], with a sub-personality for each hat! "Hold up, there, myself. You're getting the idea, certainly, but going too far. The roles and capabilities relate more to Aspects." Aspects? "Or modes, or ..."

Hey, I wonder if there is a piano player in our midst? Always wanted to play the piano. Hello? Anyone? No response. Guess not.

"Personally, I like John Rowan's list of common sub-personalities better." That deep voice again. John Rowan? Did I read his book? "Several of them. Remember the subs? *The Protector/Controller, the Critic, the Pusher, the Perfectionist, the Central Organizing Sub-personality, the Inner Child, the Nurturing Parent, the Power Brokers.*"[12] I really don't remember them that specifically, just that sub-personalities come from the different roles I play in life, and something about setting up conflicting thoughts when I'm uncertain of what direction to go. However, I ran into the internalized parent roles when I was reading Jung's work in college. The mother sub could be considered the nurturing parent and the father sub could be considered the critical parent.

"Back to work," the stern tenor voice breaks through the pause. "I don't really like joining this foray, but, really, stop wasting time! We *are*—and you *are*—and what else makes a difference?" He's got a point, certainly.

"You've got to love the persistence," my little voice softly sings, then adds, "That's one of the life lessons we are here to learn: persistence."

I remember back when I had just finished a performance of Mozart's opera, *The Magic Flute.* Two little old ladies (oh, my, they were the age I am now!) ran up to me and asked for my autograph. I agreed with a smile, of course, taking hold of the pen and program offered to me, then stopped when the pen touched the paper. I couldn't remember who I was! "I remember that" comes a soft whisper.

That was when I decided to create a self that would be who I chose to be; and my untouchables came into being. The first untouchables were my dad, my music mentor, and Mother Theresa. People I admired, each with traits I wished to emulate and inculcate. Compassion and persistence came from Mother Theresa. "Then she came into your life," came the soft reminder. Yes, such a gift ... the power of thought and love. After a couple years, while I was living in Japan and working hard to embed compassion and persistence as a part of me, I received a phone call inviting me to spend a day with Mother Theresa![13]

"We all know the story. We were there." A young voice with a Southern drawl. Who are you? "Call me Libby ... I've been in and out of your life quite a bit. Not so much since you perceive yourself as older." Libby. Oh! I get it! My libidinous self. "Perhaps your authentic self?" Definitely a PART of my authentic self! "Aren't we all?" Yes, I think so.

I hear the friendly whisper humming, pulling me back to my exploration of sub-personalities. What a lovely sound! "I love you, too," sings the whisper. "Now, about Aspects ... an interesting term that some people use to mean the same as sub-personalities, but let's use it to describe a less developed focus than a sub-personality, more like a personality trait. And, by necessity, very context sensitive and situation dependent."

Context sensitive and situation dependent. That's what we say about knowledge.[14]. But wouldn't sub-personalities *also* be context sensitive and situation dependent? They only come to the fore in certain situations when they are needed. "Agree. Generally sub-personalities *are* context and situation triggered, as long as none of the subs is dominating, which isn't always the case."

"I heard that," comes the tenor, with a strain in his voice. "It's time to dominate right now." I really appreciate his persistence. "Thank you," a bit softer. Okay, I hear you ... and while I'm not going to let you dominate, I promise not to ignore your voice. Only right now, I want to learn more about this stuff. Can sub-personalities individuate?

"I'll help with that." The strong SHE is back—maybe this *is* my topdog. "Absolutely I'm your topdog, and I don't say that lightly since there are few absolutes other than the Absolute." My head is reeling. "Sub-personalities can, and do, individuate, and we are all at different levels of development and growth. For example, harsh critic is still into satisfying personal needs, the second stage of Kohlberg's moral development sequence,[15] conventional reasoning. In contrast, take me. *I'm* rapidly moving from the label topdog through ego ideal to real self." How can that be? Aren't those different sub-personalities? I hear laughing. "You're learning too fast. What I meant to say is that I'm in the final stage of the moral development scale, post conventional reasoning, with an understanding of abstract moral principles and considering each situation differently." If my harsh critic is at level 2 in moral development and my topdog is at level 5 or 6, where does that put me? "Somewhere in the middle, we'd say." More laughter. My topdog continues, "The good news is that I have a strong personal commitment to OUR ideals." That sounds more like my authentic self. "Maybe that's what I'm becoming!"

Silence.

What about when I'm dreaming or meditating? Where are you then? "Actually, I'm the one that is a bit psychic" comes a sharp quip, staccato, to the point. "I simply cooperate and communicate with the mental you such that you *think* it is you experiencing expanded awareness!"[16] And are my dreams mine? "We are you ... so don't get into a funk about all this! Yes, we all certainly move in and out of your dreams, but there are some characters in your dreams who are of the nature of sub-personalities, only you create them, and they perform on your stage."[17]

Or, am I performing on *your* stage? How can I be one and many at the same time? My sweet soft voice responds, "Perhaps you could think of this in terms of a spiritual plurality.[18] You are a product of a diversity of experiences in life as well as a variety of sub-personalities, each behaving like a mind, all contributing to the one that you are." I'm going to have to reflect on that ... Now I'm curious, why can I only hear one of you at a time?

My SHE responds, "That's more about your expectations. These internal realms are multidimensional; the limitations are in *your* thoughts, *your* feelings." Okay, then let me think differently. I imagine a duet, singing both parts in my head, hearing the voices weave in and out, tones expanding. It feels good! A third voice joins, then a fourth, now there is a quintet. Now a sextet. And all at once: "That is beautiful!"-"You need to think like that more often."-"What the heck ..."- "Lovely."-"I'm falling asleep."-"Back to work."

It happened! I hear you all at once! Now, what fun if only you could sing in harmony. Overlapping responses, with some new voices added: "Harmony?" "But we need to be different to add value." "I'm afraid." "Beautiful idea; beautiful ideal." "I like to argue." "Okay ... if everyone listens to *me*." "I'm a returning fragment. Do I count?" "Good idea." "Would I lose me?"

Harmony honoring diversity. Unity honoring individuation. Remember last year when I was part of that large project team? I was so worried about everyone trying to claim credit for my successes. Only, then I realized that I was succeeding BECAUSE of the team and their support! Later when WE as a team were rewarded, it didn't take anything away from my personal satisfaction and learning; in fact, it helped ... those people are still part of my knowledge sharing network! Wow, was THAT a learning lesson!

Yes, harmony. Maybe not all at once; it may take some time. Some of us are pretty rough around the edges. "I hear that!" of course, from the tenor.

Let me continue. Now that you are all part of my conscious awareness, maybe we can work as a team ... surely, we can do more and go farther together. "Halleluia! I'm all for action," again, the stern tenor. That agreement is a surprise!

"Me, too?" comes a tiny squeak I don't recall hearing from before.

Yes, you too, *all* the known and unknown you's, me's, myself's. Let's think about what to call ourselves ... Considering the billions of little guys that are a part of us, how about we think of all of you sub-personalities—and me as well—as a governance committee, a group of collaborative decision-makers heading up a large community, with each of us having unique strengths. Let's have a floating leadership, with each of us taking the lead when a particular strength is needed. We kind of do that already, only now it will be by choice. Hey, and let's think about some of those other crazy ideas circulating around teamwork—collaborative entanglement, shape shifter morphing, cohesion in variety, genetic algorithm mobility. I pause.

Several voices project the same thought, "What's all that?" Actually, I'm not really sure what all those terms mean, just read them in a book somewhere, but the words really have a great feel to them! Let's figure it out as we go? A chorus of agreement.

A raspy voice comes to the fore, another voice heard from. "It sounds like fun. I've been waiting a long time for this." Me, too, I realize. Had I always known about these guys? Somehow, this all feels familiar. I want to get to know each and every one of us.

The whisper: "You're remembering."

Yes. Now, what's next? If I'm a personality, new and different and specially created for this life span, do I disappear when my soul moves on?

Perhaps it is in my imagination, but there is a breeze in the air, a tingling on my lips (a kiss from the fluff on my shoulder?) A loving thought fires among the neurons of my heart, "Even now we are joining to become co-creators of the future."

I am at peace.

References

Ackoff, R. L. (1989), "From data to wisdom" in *Journal of Applied Systems Analysis*, Vol. 16, pp.3-9.

Adolfs, R. (2004), "Processing of emotional and social information by the human amygdala" in Gazzaniga, M.S. (Ed.), *The Cognitive Neurosciences III*, The Bradford Press, Cambridge, MD.

Aiello, J. R. & Cooper, R. E. (1972), "Use of personal space as a function of social affect" in *Proceedings of the 80th Annual Convention of the American Psychological Association*, 7(1), pp.207-208.

Akil, H., Campeau, S., Cullinan, W., Lechan, R., Toni, R., Watson, S., & Moore, R.   (1999), "Neuroendocrine system I: Overview—thyroid and adrenal axis" in Zigmond, M., Bloom, F., Landis, S., Roberts, J. & Squire, L. (Eds.), *Fundamentals of Neuroscience*,   Academic Press, New York, pp.1127-1150.

Amann, T. (2003), "Creating space for somatic ways of knowing within transformative learning theory" in Wiessner, C.A., Meyer, S.R., Pfhal, N.L. & Neaman, P.G. (Eds.), *Proceedings of the Fifth International Conference on Transformative Learning*, Teacher's College, Columbia University, Columbia, MD, pp.26-32.

Amen, D. G. (2005), *Making a Good Brain Great*, Harmony Books, New York.

The American Heritage Dictionary of the English Language (3rd Ed) (1992), Houghton Mifflin Company, Boston.

The *American Heritage Dictionary of the English Language*, 4th edition (2000), Houghton-Mifflin, Boston.

Anderson, J.R. (1983), *The Architecture of Cognition*, Harvard University Press, Cambridge, MA.

Andreason, N. (2005), *The Creating Brain: The Neuroscience of Genius*, The Dana Foundation, New York.

Anonymous, [Appeared in numerous emails to authors and is available on dozens of Internet sites], Retrieved April 5, 2009, from
http://www.gamedev.net/community/forums/topic.asp?topic_id=375056

Argyris, C. (1990), "Teaching Smart People How to Learn" in Howard, R. (Ed.), *The Learning Imperative: Managing People for Continuous Innovation*, Harvard Business School Publishing Corp., Boston, MA, pp.177-194.

Ashby, W.R. (1964), *An Introduction to Cybernetics*, Methuen, London.

Assagioli, R. (1975), *Psychosynthesis: A Manual of Principles and Techniques*, Turnstone Press, London.

Atwater, F.H. (2004), *The Hemi-Sync® Process*, The Monroe Institute, Faber, VA.

Auyang, S.Y. (1998), *Foundations of Complex-System Theories in Economics, Evolutionary Biology, and Statistical Physics*, Cambridge University Press, New York.

Avedisian, J. & Bennet, A. (2010), "Values as knowledge: A new frame of reference for a new generation of knowledge workers" in *On the Horizon*, Vol. 18, No. 3, pp.255-265.

Axelrod, R. & Cohen, M.D. (1999), *Harnessing Complexity: Organizational Implications of a Scientific Frontier*, The Free Press, New York.

Baker, C. L. (1989), *English Syntax*, The MIT Press, Cambridge, MA.

Baltes, P.B. & Smith, J. (1990), "Toward a psychology of wisdom and its ontogenesis" in Sternberg, R.J. (Ed.), *Wisdom: Its Nature, Origins, and Development*, Cambridge University Press, Cambridge.

Bargh, John A. (2004), "Bypassing the will: Toward demystifying the nonconscious control of social behavior" in Hassin, Ran R., Uleman, James S. & Bargh, John A. (Eds.), *The New Unconscious*, Oxford University Press, New York, pp.37-60.

Barthes, R. (1985). *In the Responsibility of Forms*, Hill and Wang, New York.

Batchelor, J. P. & Goethals, G. R. (1972), "Spatial Arrangements in Freely Formed Groups" in *Sociometry*, 35, pp.270-279.

Begley, S. (2007), *Train Your Mind Change Your Brain: How a New Science Reveals Our Extraordinary Potential to Transform Ourselves,* Ballantine Books, New York.

Bennet, A. (2005), *Exploring Aspects of Knowledge Management that Contribute to the Passion Expressed by its Thought Leaders*, Self-Published, Frost, WV. Available at www.mountainquestinstitute.com

Bennet, A (2000). *Knowing: The Art of War 2000*, U.S. Department of the Navy, Washington, D.C.

Bennet, A. & Bennet, D. (2014), "Knowledge, theory and practice in Knowledge Management: Between associative patterning and context-rich action" in *Journal of Entrepreneurship, Management and Innovation*, Vol. 10, Issue 1, pp.7-55, www.jemi.edu.pl

Bennet, A. & Bennet, D. (2013), *Decision-Making in The New Reality*, MQIPress, Frost, WV.

Bennet, A. & Bennet, D. (2010a), "Multidimensionality: Building the mind/brain infrastructure for the next generation knowledge worker" in *On the Horizon*, Vol. 18, No. 3, pp.240-254.

Bennet, A. & Bennet, D. (2010b), "Leaders, decisions and the neuro-knowledge system" in Wallis, S., *Cybernetics and Systems Theory in Management: Tools, Views and Advancements*, IGI Global, Hershey, PA.

Bennet, A. & Bennet, D. (2009a), "Managing self in troubled times: Banking on self-efficacy" in *Effective Executive* (April), The Icfai University Press, India, pp.56-82.

Bennet, A. & Bennet, D. (2009b), "A Conversation: Facing The New Reality" in *Effective Executive*, The Icfai University Press, India, April 2009, pp. 66-73.

Bennet, A. & Bennet, D. (2009c), "Meta-Knowledge: Understanding the Knowledge that Drives our Actions" in Batra, Surinder and Carrillo, F.J. (Eds.), *Knowledge Management and Intellectual Capital: Emerging Perspectives*, Allied Publishers, New Delhi, pp.411-434.

Bennet, A. & Bennet, D. (2008a), "The depth of knowledge: Surface, shallow, or deep?" in *VINE: The Journal of Information and Knowledge Management Systems,* Vol. 38, No. 4, pp.405-420.

Bennet, A. & Bennet, D. (2008b), "The Decision-Making Process for Complex Situations in a Complex Environment", in Burstein, F. and Holsapple, C.W. (Eds.), *Handbook on Decision Support Systems*, Springer-Verlag, New York.

Bennet, A. & Bennet, D. (2008c), "The fallacy of knowledge reuse" in *Journal of Knowledge Management*, 12(5), pp.21-33.

Bennet, A. & Bennet, D. (2008d), "Moving from knowledge to wisdom, from ordinary consciousness to extraordinary consciousness" in VINE, Vol. 38, No. 1, pp.7-15.

Bennet, A. & Bennet, D. (2008g), "The human knowledge system: Music and brain coherence" in *VINE*, Vol. 38, No. 3, pp.277-296.

Bennet, A. & Bennet, D. (2007a), "CONTEXT: The shared knowledge enigma" in *VINE*, Vol. 37, No. 1, pp. 27-40.

Bennet, A. & Bennet, D. (2007b), *Knowledge Mobilization in the Social Sciences and Humanities: Moving From Research To Action*, MQIPress, Frost, WV.

Bennet, A. & Bennet, D. (2007c), "The knowledge and knowing of spiritual learning" in *VINE*, Vol. 37, No. 2, pp.150-168.

Bennet, A. & Bennet, D. (2007d), "The MQI Value Infusion Methodology", a White Paper, Mountain Quest Institute, Frost, WV.

Bennet, A. & Bennet, D. (2006a), "Learning as associative patterning" in *VINE*, Vol. 36, No. 4, pp.371-376.

Bennet, A. & Bennet, D. (2006b), "Hierarchy as a learning platform" in *VINE*, Vol. 36, No. 3, 2006, pp.255-260.

Bennet, A. & Bennet, D. (2004), *Organizational Survival in the New World: The Intelligent Complex Adaptive System*, Elsevier, Boston, MA.

Bennet, D. (2006), *Expanding the knowledge paradigm*, in *VINE,* 36(2), pp.175-181.

Bennet, D. (2001), "Loosening the world knot", unpublished paper available at www.mountainquestinstitute.com

Bennet, D. & Bennet, A. (2015), *Expanding the Self: The Intelligent Complex Adaptive Learning System*, MQI Press, Frost, WV

Bennet, D. & Bennet, A. (2008e), "Engaging tacit knowledge in support of organizational learning" in *VINE*, 38(1), pp.72-94.

Bennet, D. & Bennet, A. (2008f), "Associative patterning: The unconscious life of an organization" in Girard, J.P. (Ed.), *Building organizational memory*, ICI Global, Hershey, PA.

Bennett-Woods, D. (1997), "Reflections on wisdom", unpublished paper, University of Northern Colorado.

Berne, E. (1961), *Transactional Analysis in Psychotherapy*, Grove Press, New York.

Berzonsky, M.D. (1994), "Kohlberg" in *Encyclopedia of Psychology* (2nd Ed), Vol. 2, John Wiley & Sons, New York.

Birren, J.E. & Fisher, L.M. (1990), "The elements of wisdom: Overview and integration" in Sternberg, R.J. (Ed.), *Wisdom: Its Nature, Origins, and Development*, Cambridge University Press, Cambridge, England.

Blakemore, S., & Frith, Y. (2005), *The learning brain: Lessons for education,*. Blackwell, Malden, MA.

Bloom, H. (2000), *Global Brain: The Evolution of Mass Mind from the Big Bang to the 21st Century*, John Wiley & Sons, New York.

Bohm, D. (1992), *Thought as a System*, Routledge, New York.

Bohm, D. (1980), *Wholeness and the Implicate Order*, Routledge & Kegal Paul, London.

Bownds, M. D. (1999), *The Biology of Mind: Origins and Structures of Mind, Brain, and Consciousness*, Fitzgerald Science Press, Bethesda, MD.

Brookfield, S. D. (1987), *Developing critical thinkers*, Jossey-Bass, San Francisco, CA.

Brown, J.S. & Duguid, P. (2000), *The Social Life of Information*, Harvard Business School Press, Boston, MA.

Brown, M.Y. (1979), *The Art of Guiding: the Psychosynthesis Approach to Individual Counselling and Psychology*, Johnson College, University of Redlands, Redlands, CA.

Brown, W.S. (2000), "Wisdom and human neurocognitive systems: Perceiving and practicing the laws of life" in Brown, W.S. (Ed.), *Understanding Wisdom: Sources, Science and Society*, Templeton Foundation Press, Philadelphia, PA.

Buonomano, D. V., & Merzenich, M. M. (1998), "Cortical plasticity: From synapses to maps" in *Annual Review of Neuroscience, 21*, pp.149-186.

Burgoon, J. K., Buller, D. B., & Woodall, W. G. (1989), *Nonverbal Communication: The Unspoken Dialogue*, HarperCollins New York.

Buzsaki, G. (2006). *Rhythms of the Brain*, Oxford University Press, New York.

Byrnes, J. P. (2001), *Minds, Brains, and Learning: Understanding the Psychological and Educational Relevance of Neuroscientific Research*, The Guilford Press, New York.

Caprara, G.V. & Cervone, D. (2000), *Personality: Determinants, Dynamics, and Potentials*, Cambridge University Press, Cambridge, UK.

Chandler, M.J. & Holliday, S. (1990), "Wisdom in a postapocalyptic age" in Sternberg, R.J. (Ed.), *Wisdom: Its Nature, Origins, and Development*, Cambridge University Press, Cambridge, England.

Chickering, A. W., Dalton, J. C., & Stamm, L. (2005), *Encouraging Authenticity & Spirituality in Higher Education*, Jossey-Bass, San Francisco, CA.

Choi, Y. Susan, Gray, Heather M. & Ambady, N. (2004), "The Glimpsed World: Unintended Communication and Unintended Perception" in Hassin, Ran R., Uleman, James S. & Bargh, John A. (Eds.), *The New Unconscious*, Oxford University Press, New York, pp.309-333.

Christos, G. (2003), *Memory and Dreams: The Creative Human Mind*, Rutgers University Press, New Brunswick, NY.

Church, D. (2006), *The Genie in Your Genes: Epigenetic Medicine and the New Biology of Intention*, Elite Books, Santa Rosa, CA.

Clausing, D. (1994), *Total Quality Development: A Step-By-Step Guide to World-Class Concurrent Engineering*, Asme Press, New York.

Clavell, J. (Ed.) (1983), *The Art of War: Sun Tzu,* Dell Publishing, New York.

Clayton, V. & Birren, J.E. (1980), "The development of wisdom across the lifespan: a reexamination of an ancient topic" in Baltes, P.B. & Brim, O.G.J. (Eds), *Life Spa Development and Behavior*, Academic Press, pp.104-135.

Cleveland, H. (2002), *Nobody in Charge: Essays on the Future of Leadership*, Jossey-Bass, San Francisco, CA.

Costa, J.D. (1995), *Working Wisdom: The Ultimate Value in the New Economy*, Stoddart, Toronto, Canada.

Cozolino, L. J. (2002), *The Neuroscience of Psychotherapy: Building and Rebuilding the Human Brain*, Norton, New York.

Cozolino, L. J. (2006), *The Neuroscience of Human Relationships: Attachment and the Developing Social Brain*, Norton, New York.

Cozolino, L., & Sprokay, S. (2006), "Neuroscience and adult learning" in Johnson, S. & Taylor, T. (Eds.), *The Neuroscience of Adult Learning,* Jossey-Bass, San Francisco, CA.

Csikszentmihalyi, M. & Nakamura, J. (2005), "The role of emotions in the development of wisdom" in Sternberg, R.J. & Jordan, J., *A Handbook of Wisdom: Psychological Perspectives*, Cambridge University Press, New York.

Csikszentmihalyi, M. (1990), *Flow: The Psychology of Optimal Experience*, Harper & Row, New York.

Csikszentmihalyi, M. & Rathunde, K. (1990), "The psychology of wisdom: An evolutionary interpretation, in Sternberg, R.J. (Ed.), *Wisdom: Its Nature, Origins, and Development*, Cambridge University Press, Cambridge.

Daloz, L. (1986), *Effective Teaching and Mentoring*, Jossey-Bass, San Francisco, CA.

Daloz, L. (1999), *Mentor: Guiding the Journey of Adult Learners*, Jossey-Bass, San Francisco, CA.

Damasio, A. R. (2007), "How the brain creates the mind" in Bloom, F.E. (Ed.), *Best of the brain from Scientific American: Mind, Matter, and Tomorrow's Brain*, Dana Press, New York, pp.58-67.

Damasio, A. R. (1999), *The Feeling of What Happens: Body and Emotion in the Making of Consciousness*, Harcourt Brace & Company, New York.

Damasio, A.R. (1994), *Descartes' Error: Emotion, Reason, and the Human Brain*, G.P. Putnam's Sons, New York.

Damon, W. (2000), "Setting the stage for the development of wisdom: Self-understanding and moral identity during adolescence" in Brown, W.S. (Ed.), *Understanding Wisdom: Sources, Science and Society*, Templeton Foundation Press, Philadelphia, PA.

Darwin, C. (1998), *The Descent of Man*, Prometheus Books, Amherst, NY.

Darwin, C. (1964), *On the Origin of Species,* (A Facsimile of the First Edition published in 1859.) Harvard Paperbacks, Cambridge, MA.

Davenport, T.H. & Prusak, L. (2000), *Working Knowledge: How Organizations Manage What They Know*, Harvard Business Review Press, Boston.

Delmonte, M.M. (1984), "Electrocortical activity and related phenomena associated with meditation practice: A literature review" in *International Journal of Neuroscience*, 24, pp.217-231.

Dewey, J. (1938/1997), *Experience and Education*, Simon & Shuster, New York.

Dijksterhuis, Ap, Aarts, Henk & Smith, Pamela K. (2004), "The power of the subliminal: On subliminal persuasion and other potential applications" in Hassin, Ran R., Uleman, James S. & Bargh, John A. (Eds.), *The New Unconscious*, Oxford University Press, New York, pp.309-333.

Dijksterhuis, A. & Bargh, J. A. (2001), "The Perception-Behavior Expressway: Automatic Effects of Social Perception on Social Behavior" in M. P. Zanna (Ed.), *Advances in Experimental Social Psychology*,Vol. 33, Academic Press, San Diego, pp.1-40.

Dittmann-Kohli, F. & Baltes, P.B. (1990), "Toward a neofunctionalist conception of adult intellectual development: wisdom as a prototypical case of intellectual growth" in Alexander, C. & Langer, E. (Eds.), *Beyond Formal Operations: Alternative Endpoints to Human Development*, Oxford University Press, New York.

Dobbs, D. (2007), "Turning off depression" in F. E. Bloom (Ed.), *Best of the Brain from Scientific American: Mind, Matter, and Tomorrow's Brain,* Dana Press, New York.

DONCIO (1998), "Building the knowledge enterprise", presentation by the Chief Knowledge Officer of the Department of the Navy made to APQC.

Doyle, Sir Arthur Conan (1994), *Memoirs of Sherlock Holmes*, Book of the Month Club, New York.

Dunning, J. (2014), Discussion of consciousness via the Internet on December 13.

Durham, M. (2004), "Three critical roles for knowledge management workspaces: Moderators, thought leaders, and managers" in Koenigh, E. & Srikantaiah, T., *Knowledge Management Lessons Learned: What Works and What Doesn't*, Information Today, Medford, NJ.

Dvir, R. (2006), "Knowledge City, Seen as a Collage of Human Knowledge Moments" in Carrillo, F.J. (Ed.), *Knowledge Cities: Approaches, Experiences, and Perspectives*, Butterworth Heinemann Elsevier, Oxford.

Edelman, G.M. (2000), *A Universe of Consciousness: How Matter Becomes Imagination*, Basic Books, New York, NY.

Edelman, G. and Tononi, G. (2000), *A Universe of Consciousness: How Matter Becomes Imagination*, Basic Books, New York.

Eich, E., Kihlstrom, J. F., Bower, G. H., Forgas, J. P., & Niedenthal, P. M. (2000), *Cognition and Emotion*, Oxford University Press, New York.

Ellinor, L. & Gerard, G. (1998), *Dialogue: Rediscover the Transforming Power of Conversation*, John Wiley & Sons, New York.

Ericsson, K.A., Charness, N., Feltovich, P.J. & Hoffman, R.R. (Eds.) (2006), *The Cambridge Handbook of Expertise and Expert Performance*, Cambridge University Press, New York.

Erikson, J.M. (1988), *Wisdom and the Senses: The Way of Creativity*, Norton, New York.

Fekete, John (1977), *The Critical Twilight: Explorations in the Ideology of Anglo-American Literary Theory from Eliot to McLuhan*, Routledge, London.

Fine, G. (2003), Introduction in Plato on *Knowledge and forms: Selected essays*, Oxford University Press, New York.

Fischer, R. (1971), "A cartography of ecstatic and meditative states" in *Science*, 174 (4012), pp.897-904.

Fitzgerald, B. (2003), "Introduction to the special series of papers on informing each other: Bridging the gap between researcher and practitioners" in *Informing Science 6*.

Friedman, T.L. (2005), *The World Is Flat: A Brief History of the Twenty-First Century*, Farrar, Straus and Giroux, New York.

Frith, C., & Wolpert, D. (2003), *The Neuroscience of Social Interaction: Decoding, Imitating, and Influencing the Actions of Others*, Oxford University Press, New York.

Frith, C. D., Blakemore, S. J., & Wolpert, D. M. (2000), "Abnormalities in the Awareness and Control of Action, *Philosophical Transactions of the Royal Society of London*, 355, pp.1771-1788.

Freud, S. (1938), "Splitting of the ego in the process of defence" in *Standard edition Vol. 23*, Hogarth Press, London.

Gazzaniga, M.S. (Ed.) (2004), *The Cognitive Neurosciences III*, The MIT Press, Cambridge, MA.

George, M. S. (2007), "Stimulating the brain" in F. E. Bloom (Ed.), *Best of the Brain from Scientific American: Mind, Matter, and Tomorrow's Brain*, The Dana Foundation, New York.

Gerth, H.H. & Mills, C.W. (Eds. & Trans.) (1946), *Max Weber: Essays in Sociology*, Oxford University Press, New York.

Gettier, E. L. (1963), "Is justified true belief knowledge?" in *Oxford Journals*, Oxford University Press. Retrieved June 4, 2014 from http://rintintin.colorado.edu/~vancecd/phil1000/Gettier.pdf

Goffman, E. (1959), *The Presentation of Self in Everyday Life*, Anchor, New York.

Goldberg, E. (2005), *The Wisdom Paradox: How Your Mind Can Grow Stronger as Your Brain Grows Older*, Gotham Books, Penguin Group, New York.

Goleman, D. (1998), *Working with Emotional Intelligence*, Bantam Books, New York.

Goleman, D. (1995), *Emotional Intelligence*, Bantam Books, New York.

Goleman, G.M. (1988), *Meditative Mind: The Varieties of Meditative Experience*, G.P. Putnam, New York.

Gordon, W. Terrence (1997), *Marshall McLuhan: Escape into Understanding*, Basic Books, New York.

Grimm, R., Dietz, N., Foster-Bey, J., Reingold, D., & Nesbit, R. (2006), "Volunteer Growth in America: A Review of Trends Since 1974", Research Report, Corporation for National and Community Service (December).

Haberlandt, K. (1998), *Human Memory: Exploration and Application,* Allyn & Bacon, Boston.

Hall, B. (1998), "Culture and Values Management" in Sullivan, P., *Profiting from Intellectual Capital,* John Wiley & Sons, New York.

Hanks, William F. (1996), *Language & Communicative Practices*, WestviewPress, Boulder, CO.

Harvey, Richard. "The Ancient Thread of Authenticity" (An interview on Sacred Attention Therapy), 2013. Downloaded June 13, 2015, from www.sacredattentiontherapy.com/Articles.html

Hawkins, J. & Blakeslee, S. (2004), *On Intelligence: How a New Understanding of the Brain will Lead to the Creation of Truly Intelligent Machines,* Times Books, New York.

Heckscher, C. (2007), *The Collaborative Enterprise,* Yale University Press, New Haven, CT.

Henderson, M. & Thompson, D. (2003), *Values at Work*, HarperCollinsPublishers, New Zealand.

Hobson, J.A. (1999), *Consciousness*, Scientific American Library, New York.

Hodgkin, R. (1991), "Michael Polanyi—Profit of life, the universe, and everything" in *Times Higher Educational Supplement*, September 27, p.15.

Holliday, S.G. & Chandler, M.J. (1986), *Wisdom: Explorations in Adult Competence: Contributions to Human Development*, Vol. 17, Karger, Basel.

Humphrey, J. W. (1997), "A time of 10,000 leaders" in Shelton, K. (Ed.), *A New Paradigm of Leadership: Visions of Excellence for 21st Century Organizations*, Executive Excellent Publishing, Provo, UT., pp.31-34.

Hyman, S. E. (2007), "Diagnosing disorders" in F. E. Bloom (Ed.), *Best of the Brain from Scientific American: Mind, Matter, and Tomorrow's Brain,* Dana Press, New York.

Janis, I.L. & Mann, L. (1977), *Decision making: A Psychological Analysis of Conflict, Choice and Commitment*, The Free Press, New York.

Jarvis, P. (1992), *Paradoxes of Learning: On Becoming an Individual in Society*, Jossey-Bass, San Francisco, CA.

Jaynes, J. (1976), *The Origin of Consciousness in the Breakdown of the Bicameral Mind*, Houghton Mifflin, Boston.

Jensen, E. (1998), *Teaching with the Brain in Mind*, Association for Supervision and Curriculum Development, Alexandria, VA.

Jevning, R., Wallace, R.K. & Beidenbach, M. (1992), "The physiology of meditation: A review" in *Neuroscience and Behavioral Reviews*, 16, pp.415-424.

Johnson, S. (2006), "The neuroscience of the mentor-learner relationship" in S. Johnson & K. Taylor (Eds.), *The Neuroscience of Adult Learning: New Directions for Adult and Continuing Education*, Jossey-Bass, San Francisco, CA.

Jung, C.J. (Trans. By Hull, R.F.C.) (1990), *The Archetypes and the Collective Unconscious* (10th Ed.), Princeton University, Princeton, NJ.

Kahneman, D., P. Slovic, & A. Tversky (1982), *Judgment Under Uncertainty: Heuristics and Biases*, Cambridge University Press, New York.

Kandel, E. R. (2006a), *In search of Memory: The Emergence of a New Science of Mind*, Norton & Company, New York.

Kandel, E.R. (2006b), *The Neuroscience of Adult Learning: New Directions for Adult and Continuing Education*, Jossey-Bass, San Francisco.

Kelzer, K. (1987), *The Sun and the Shadow: My Experiment with Lucid Dreaming*, ARE Press, Virginia Beach, VA.

Kihlstrom, J.F. & Cantor, N. (1984), "Mental representations of the self" in L. Berkowitz (Ed.), *Advances in Experimental Social Psychology 17*, Academic Press, New York.

Kirsner, K., Speelman, C., Maybery, M., O'Brien-Malone, A., Anderson, M. & MacLeod, C. (Eds.). (1998), *Implicit and Explicit Mental Processes*, Lawrence Erlbaum Associates, Publishers, Mahwah, NJ.

Klein, G. (2003), *Intuition at Work: Why Developing Your Gut Instincts Will Make You Better at What You Do*, Doubleday, New York.

Knuf, L., Aschersleben, G., & Prinz, W. (2001). "An Analysis of Ideomotor Action" in *Journal of Experimental Psychology*: General, 130, pp.779-798.

Kolb, D.A. (1984), *Experiential Learning: Experience as the Source of Learning and Development*, Prentice Hall, Englewood Cliffs, NJ.

Kolb, B. & Whishaw, L.Q. (1998), "Brain plasticity and behavior" in *Annual Review of Psychology, 49*, pp.43-64.

Kohlberg, L. (1981), *Philosophy of Moral Development: Moral Stages and the Idea of Justice*, Harper, San Francisco, CA.

Kramer, D.A. & Bacelar, W.T. (1994), "The educated adult in today's world: Wisdom and the mature learner", in Sinnott, J.D. (Ed.), *Interdisciplinary Handbook of Adult Lifespan Learning*, Greenwood Press, Westport, Conn.

Kuntz, P.G. (1968), *The Concept of Order*, University of Washington Press, Seattle, WA.

Kurzweil, R. (2005), *The Singularity is Near: When Humans Transcend Biology,* Viking, New York.

Lakoff, G. (2006), *Thinking Points: Communicating Our American Values and Vision*, Farrar, Straus and Giroux, New York.

LeDoux, J. (1996), *The Emotional Brain: The Mysterious Underpinnings of Emotional Life*, Touchstone, New York.

Lee, R.G. & Garvin, T. (2003), "Moving from information transfer to information exchange in health and health care" in *Social Science & Medicine*, 56, pp.449-464.

Levitt, H.M. (1999), "The development of wisdom: An analysis of Tibetan Buddhist experience" in *Journal of Humanistic Psychology*, 39(2), pp.86-105.

Lewin, K. (1936), *Topological Psychology*, McGraw-Hill, New York.

Leyden, P., Teixeira, R., & Greenberg, E. (2007), "The Progressive Politics of the Millennial Generation", Generational Study, New politics Institute, June 20, 2007, www.newpolitics.net (accessed April 26, 2010).

Macdonald, C. (1996), *Toward Wisdom: Finding Our Way to Inner Peace, Love, and Happiness*, Hampton Roads, Charlottesville, VA.

MacFlouer, N. (2011), "The Creation and Development of Knowledge", BBSradio.com show #219, downloaded June 15, 2015 from www.aelesswisdom.com/archives_of_radio_shows.htm

MacFlouer, N. (1999), *Lie's Meaning*, Ageless Wisdom Publishers, Book One LLC, Tempe, AZ.

Mannheim, K. (1960), *Ideology and Utopia: An Introduction to the Sociology of Knowledge*, Routledge, London.

Marchese, T.J. (1998), "The new conversations about learning: Insights from neuroscience and anthropology, cognitive science and workplace studies", available at www.newhorizons.org/lifelong/higher_ed/marchese.htm

Marton, F. & Booth, S. (1997), *Learning and Awareness*, Lawrence Erlbaum Associates, Hillsdale, NJ.

Matthews, R.C. (1991), "The forgetting algorithm: How fragmentary knowledge of exemplars can yield abstract knowledge" in *Journal of Experimental Psychology: General*, 120, pp.117-119.

Mavromatis, A. (1991), *Hypnagogia*, Routledge, New York.

Mayer-Kress, G. & Barczys, C. (1995), "The Global Brain as an Emergent Structure from the Worldwide Computing Network, and its Implications for Modeling" in *The Information Society*, 11(1), pp.1-28.

McDermott, J.J. (1977), *The Writings of William James*, University of Chicago Press, Chicago, IL.

McLuhan, Marshall (1964), *Understanding Media: The Extensions of Man*, McGraw-Hill, New York.

Meacham, J.A. (1990), "The loss of wisdom" in Sternberg, R.J. (Ed.), *Wisdom: Its Nature, Origins, and Development*, Cambridge University Press, Cambridge, England.

Merriam, S.B., Caffarella, R.S. & Baumgartner, L.M. (2006), *Learning in Adulthood: A Comprehensive Guide*, John Wiley & Sons, San Francisco, CA.

Merriam, S.B. and Caffarella, R.S. (1999), *Learning in Adulthood: A Comprehensive Guide* (2nd Ed.), Jossey-Bass, San Francisco, CA.

Mezirow, J. (1991), *Transformative Dimensions of Adult Learning*, Jossey-Bass, San Francisco, CA.

Middlebrook, P.N. (1974), *Social Psychology and Modern Life*, Alfred A. Knoph, New York.

Moenssens, A.A., Starrs, J.E., Henderson, C.E., ^ Inbau, F.E. (1995), *Scientific Evidence in Civil and Criminal Cases*, 4th Ed, Foundation Press, New York.

Moon, J.A. (2004), *A Handbook of Reflective and Experiential Learning: Theory and Practice*, RoutledgeFalmer, London and New York.

Mulvihill, M.K. (2003), "The Catholic Church in crisis: Will transformative learning lead to social change through the uncovering of emotion?" in Weissner, C.A., Meyers, S.R., Pfhal, N.L. & Neaman, P.J. (Eds.), *Proceedings of the 5th International Conference on Transformative Learning*, pp 320-325, Teachers College, Columbia University, New York.

Murphy, N. (2000), "Introduction: A hierarchical framework for understanding wisdom" in Brown, W.S. (Ed.), *Understanding Wisdom: Sources, Science and Society*, Templeton Foundation Press, Philadelphia, PA.

Myers, Isabel Briggs & Myers, Peter B. *Gifts Differing: Understanding Personality Type*. Mountain View, CA: Davies-Black Publishing, 1995.

National Research Council (2000), *How People Learn: Brain, Mind, Experience, and School*, National Academy Press, Washington, DC.

NationMaster (2008), "Military Statistics>Manpower>Reaching military age annually>Males" (most recent) by country. Taken from the *CIA World Factbook*. Downloaded 01/18/08 from www.NationMaster.com/index.php

Nelson, A. (2004), "Sophia: Transformation of human consciousness to wisdom", unpublished paper, Fielding Graduate University, Santa Barbara, CA.

Nelson, C.A., de Haan, M. and Thomas, K.M. (2006), *Neuroscience of Cognitive Development: The Role of Experience and the Developing Brain*, John Wiley & Sons, Hoboken, NJ.

Newell, A. (1982), "The Knowledge Level" in *Artificial Intelligence*, 18(1), pp.87-127.

Nisbett, R. & Ross, L. (1980), *Human Inference: Strategies and Shortcomings of Social Judgment*, Prentice-Hall, Englewood Cliffs, NJ.

Nonaka, I. & Takeuchi, H. (1995), *The Knowledge-Creating Company: How Japanese Companies Create the Dynamics of Innovation*, Oxford University Press, New York.

Nouwen, H.J.M. (1975), *Reaching Out: The Three Movements of the Spiritual Life*, Doubleday, New York.

Nussbaum, S.W. (2000), "Profundity with panache: the unappreciated proverbial wisdom of sub-Saharan Africa" in Brown, W.S. (Ed.), *Understanding Wisdom: Sources, Science and Society*, Templeton Foundation Press, Philadelphia, PA.

Oakes, J., & Lipton, M. (1999), *Teaching to Change the World*, McGraw Hill, Boston, MA.

O'Dell, C. & Hubert, C. (2011), *The New Edge in Knowledge: How Knowledge Management is Changing the Way We Do Business*, John Riley & Sons, Inc., Hoboken, NJ.

Orwoll, L. & Perlmutter, M. (1990), "The study of a wise person: Integrating a personality perspective" in Sternberg, R.J. (Ed.), *Wisdom: Its Nature, Origins and Development*, Cambridge University Press, Cambridge, MA.

The Oxford English Dictionary (5th Ed) (2002), Oxford University Press, New York.

Panetta, K. (2002). "A collaborative learning methodology for enhanced comprehension using TEAMThink" in *Journal of Engineering Education*, Vol. 91, Issue 2, pp. 223-229 (April).

Perry, W. G. (1970/1988), *Forms of Ethical and Intellectual Development in the College Years*, Jossey-Bass, San Francisco, CA.

Pert, C. B. (1997), *Molecules of Emotion: A Science Behind Mind-Body Medicine,* Touchstone, New York.

Pinker, S. (2007), *The Stuff of Thought: Language as a Window into Human Nature*, Viking Press, New York.

Polanyi, M. (1967), *The Tacit Dimension*, Anchor Books, New York.

Polanyi, M. (1958), *Personal Knowledge: Towards a Post-Critical Philosophy*, the University of Chicago, Chicago, IL.

Pollock, Thomas Clark & Spaulding, John Gordon (1942), *A Theory of Meaning Analyzed* [Two Papers from the Second American Congress on General Semantics], Institute of General Semantics, Lakeville, CN.

Porter, D., Bennet, A., Turner, R. & Wennergren, D. (2003), *The Power of Team: The Making of a CIO*, Department of the Navy, Alexandria, VA.

Ramachandran, Vilayanur S. & Hubbard, Edward M. (2006), "Hearing Colors, Tasting Shapes" in *Scientific American* (Special Edition: Secrets of the Senses),   December 12.

Ramon, S. (1997), *Earthly Cycles. How Past Lives and Soul Patterns Shape Your Life*, Pepperwood Press, Ojai, CA.

Ratey, J. J. (2001), *A User's Guide to the Brain: Perceptions, Attention, and the Four Theaters of the Brain*, Pantheon Books, New York.

Reber, A.S. (1993), *Implicit Learning and Tacit Knowledge: An Essay on the Cognitive Unconscious*, Oxford University Press, New York.

Redfearn, J.W.T. (1985), *My Self, My Many Selves*, Academic Press, London.

Rifkin, J. (2009), *The Empathic Civilization: The Race to Global Consciousness in a World in Crisis*, Penguin Group, New York.

Ritchey, D. (2003), *The H.I.S.S. of the A.S.P.: Understanding the Anomalously Sensitive Person*, Headline Books, Inc., Terra Alta, WV.

Rock, A. (2004), *The Mind at Night: The New Science of How and Why We Dream*, Basic Books, New York, NY.

Rogers, W. T. (1978), "The contribution of kinesic illustrators toward the comprehension of verbal behavior within utterances" in *Human Communication Research*, 5, pp.54-62.

Rose, S. (2005), *The Future of the Brain: The Promise and Perils of Tomorrow's Neuroscience*, Oxford University Press, New York.

Ross, P.E. (2006), "The expert mind" in *Scientific American*, August, pp.64-71.

Rowan, J. (1990), *Subpersonalities: The People Within Us*, Routledge, New York.

Russell, P. (2007), *What is Wisdom?* Downloaded 1/14/2008 from www.peterrussell.com/SP/Wisdom.php

Russell, Peter (1982), *The Awakening Earth: The Global Brain*, Routledge & Kegan Paul, London.

Ryle, G. (1949), *The Concept of Mind*, Hutchinson, London.

Sacred Attention Therapy Project (2015). See www.sacredattentiontherapy.com

Saffo, P. (2007), "Six rules for effective forecasting" in *Harvard Business Review*, July-August.

Schloss, J.P. (2000), "Wisdom traditions as mechanisms for organismal integration: Evolutionary perspectives on homeostatic 'laws of life'" in Brown, W.S. (Ed.), *Understanding Wisdom: Sources, Science and Society*, Templeton Foundation Press, Philadelphia, PA.

Schore, A. N. (1994), *Affect, Regulation and the Origin of the Self: The Neurobiology of Emotional Development*, Erlbaum Hillsdale, NJ.

Senge, P. M. (1990), *The Fifth Discipline: The Art and Practice of the Learning Organization*, Doubleday, New York.

Shedlock, D.J. & Cornelius, S.W. (2000), "Wisdom: perceptions and performance", paper presented at the Cognitive Aging Conference, Atlanta, GA.

Sherman, N. (2000), "Wise emotions" in Brown, W.S. (Ed.), *Understanding Wisdom: Sources, Science and Society*, Templeton Foundation Press, Philadelphia, PA.

Simon, H.A. (1969), *The Science of the Artificial*, The MIT Press, Cambridge, MA.

Siegel, D. J. (2007), *The Mindful Brain: Reflection and Attunement in the Cultivation of Well-Being*, Norton & Company, New York.

Skoyles, J. R., & Sagan, D. (2002), *Up from Dragons: The Evolution of Human Intelligence*, McGraw-Hill, New York.

Smith, J., Dixon, R.A. & Baltes, P.B. (1987), "Age differences in response to life planning problems: A research analog for the study of wisdom, related knowledge", unpublished manuscript.

Smith, M.K. (2003), "Michael Polanyi and tacit knowledge" in *The Encyclopedia of Informal Education*, p.2 www.infed/org/thinkers/Polanyi.htm

Sousa, D.A. (2006), *How the Brain Learns*, Corwin Press, Thousand Oaks California.

Stern, D. N. (2004), *The Present Moment in Psychotherapy and Everyday Life*, Norton, New York.

Sternberg, R.J. (2003), *Wisdom, Intelligence, and Creativity Synthesized*, Cambridge University Press, Cambridge, MA.

Sternberg, R.J. (Ed.) (1990), *Wisdom: Its Nature, Origins, and Development*, Cambridge University Press, Cambridge, MA.

Stevens, K. (2000), "Wisdom as an organizational construct: Reality or rhetoric?", unpublished dissertation, Fielding Institute, Santa Barbara, CA.

Stonier, T. (1997), *Information and Meaning: An Evolutionary Perspective*, Springer, New York, NY.

Stonier, T. (1992), *Beyond information: The natural history of intelligence*, Springer-Verlag, London.

Stonier, T. (1990), *Information and the Internal Structure of the Universe: An Introduction into Information Physics*, Springer-Verlag, New York.

Sunstrom , E. & Altman, I. (1976), "Interpersonal Relationships and Personal Space: Research Review and Theoretical Model" in *Human Ecology*, 4, pp.47-67.

Tallis, F. (2002), *Hidden Minds: A History of the Unconscious*, Arcade, New York.

Tapscott, D. (2009), *Grown up Digital*, McGraw Hill, New York.

Tart, C.T. (1975), "Science, states of consciousness and spiritual experiences: the need for state-specific sciences" in C.T. Tart (Ed.), *Transpersonal Psychologies*, Routledge & Kegan Paul, London.

Taylor, K. (2006). "Brain function and adult learning: Implications for practice" in S. Johnson & K. Taylor (Eds.), *The Neuroscience of Adult Learning,* Jossey-Bass, San Francisco, pp.71-86.

Tiller, W. (2007), *Psychoenergetic Science: A Second Copernican-Scale Revolution*, Pavior, Walnut Creek, CA.

Trumpa, C. (1991), *The Heart of the Buddha*, Shambhala, Boston, MA.

von Krogh, G. (2000), *Enabling Knowledge Creation: How to Unlock the Mystery of Tacit Knowledge and Release the Power of Innovation*, Oxford University Press, New York.

Ward, J. (2006), *The Student's Guide to Cognitive Neuroscience*, Psychology Press, New York.

Weick, K.E. (1995), *Sensemaking in Organizations*, Sage Publications, Thousand Oaks, CA.

Wenger, E. (2009), *Digital Habitats*, CPsquare, Portland.

West, M.A. (1980), "Meditation and the EEG", *Psychological Medicine*, 10, pp.369-375.

White, R.W. (1959), "Motivation Reconsidered: The Concept of Competence" in *Psychological Review*, Vol. 66, pp.297-333.

Wilber, K. (2000), *Integral Psychology: Consciousness, Spirit, Psychology, Therapy*, Shambhala, Boston.

Wilber, K. (2000b), *A Theory of Everything: An Integral Vision for Business, Politics, Science, and Spirituality*, Shambhala, Boston.

Wilber, K. (1999), *The Collected Works of Ken Wilber*, Vols. 1-8, Shambhala, Boston.

Wilber, K. (1983), *Up from Eden: A Transpersonal View of Human Evolution*, Shambhala, Boulder, CO.

Wilson, E. O. (1998), *Consilience: The Unity of Knowledge*, Alfred A. Knopf, New York.

Woodman, M. & Dickson, E. (1996), *Dancing in the Flames: The Dark Goddess in the Transformation of Consciousness*, Shambhala, Boston, MA.

The World Capital Institute and Teleos (2007), *The 2007 Most Admired Knowledge City Report*, available at www.worldcapitalinstitute.org

Wycoff, J. (1991), *Mindmapping: Your Personal Guide to Exploring Creativity and Problem-Solving*, The Berkley Publishing Group, New York.

Yew, Lee Kuan (2000), *From Third World to First: The Singapore Story: 1965-2000*, HarperCollins Publishers, New York.

Zohar, D. & Marshall, I. (2000), *Connecting with Our Spiritual Intelligence,* R.R. Donnelley and Sons Company, Harrisonburg, VA.

Zull, J. E. (2002), *The Art of Changing the Brain: Enriching the Practice of Teaching by Exploring the Biology of Learning*, Stylus, Sterling, VA.

Endnotes

Foreward

[1]These are amazing times within which we live. It is difficult to let go of our past and jump out of the current perturbations that collide with our everyday life from every direction and imagine a world that is connected and at peace, a place where love and joy abound. Yet this is exactly the world that is emerging. This goes beyond our families, beyond our communities and beyond Humanity. As, presumably, the most intelligent species on this planet, we have a responsibility and a duty to create, provide and act with high moral standards and wisdom as we continue to learn, develop create and apply knowledge and leadership to aid and support the growth and prosperity of all life forms. The *Golden Age of Humanity* describes just such a reality.

SECTION I

Chapter 2

[1] Content from this chapter first appeared in "The Depth of Knowledge: Surface, Shallow or Deep?" in *VINE: The Journal of Information and Knowledge Management Systems*, Vol. 38, No. 4, 2008, pp.405-420; and "Multidimensionality: Building the mind/brain infrastructure for the next generation knowledge worker" in *On the Horizon*, Vol. 18, No. 3, pp.240-254.

[2] A different frame of reference is to recognize that the problem is the same as if there were two monks, one starting from the bottom and another starting from the top at exactly the same time on the same day. Then the question becomes will they ever meet on the path? From this different frame of reference, the answer is clearly yes, and wherever they cross is the answer to the question.

[3] In this context, "conserve" insinuates a living state that co-evolves with a changing environment. For example, think in terms of forest conservation, where old dead trees are removed to enable new seeds to grow, and over-crowding is thinned to enable healthy growth which provides sustenance and habitats for various forms of life while directly impacting air quality for all.

Chapter 3

[1] Contents from this chapter first appeared in Bennet, A. & Bennet, D. (2007), *Knowledge Mobilization in the Social Sciences and Humanities: Moving from Research to Action*, MQIPress, Frost, WV, pp.37-39.

SECTION II

Chapter 4

[1]Content from this chapter first appeared as "Meta-Knowledge: Understanding the Knowledge that Drives Our Actions" in Batra, Surinder, and Carrillo, F.J. (Eds.) (2009), *Knowledge Management and Intellectual Capital: Emerging Perspectives*, Allied Publishers, New Delhi, pp.411-434; and "Engaging Tacit Knowledge in Support of Organizational Learning" in *VINE: The Journal of Information and Knowledge Management Systems*, Vol. 38, No. 1, 2008, pp.72-94.

Chapter 5

[1] Content from this chapter first appeared as "Engaging Tacit Knowledge in Support of Organizational Learning" in *VINE: The Journal of Information and Knowledge Management Systems*, Vol. 38, No. 1, 2008, pp.72-94.

[2] Paul Potts was the winner of the Britain's Got Talent competition. See *Paul Potts One Chance* music CD (SYCOmusic, 2007); also see www.youtue.com/watch?v=9hlq_GGi1n4 for his incredible performance in the finals.

Chapter 6

[1] Content from this chapter first appeared as "CONTEXT: The Shared Knowledge Enigma" in *VINE: The Journal of Information and Knowledge Management Systems*, Vol. 36, No 4, 2006, pp.371-376.

SECTION III

[1] In 2004 the *Bennets published Organizational Survival in the New World: The Intelligent Complex Adaptive System* (Elsevier). The evolution of the organization is covered in-depth in Appendix A of this book, including the rise and fall of bureaucratic model.

[2] In the US Department of Navy the meme "Knowledge Shared is Power Squared" caught hold with excellent results. Of course, out at sea every ship is an interactive community, with special expertise inculcated in individuals and teams that in the instant might be called upon to handle challenges and save lives. Everyone is required to work together. Thus the bureaucratic meme of "Knowledge is Power" in terms of control had already diminished since it was not in service to achieving the mission of the organization.

Chapter 7

[1] Content from this chapter first appeared as "Leaders, Decisions and the Neuro-Knowledge System" in Wallis, S. (2010), *Cybernetics and Systems Theory in Management: Tools, Views and Advancements*, IGI Global, Hershey, Pa.

Chapter 8

[1] Content first appeared as "Social Learning from the Inside Out" in Girard, J. & Girard, J. (2010), *Social Knowledge: Using Social Media to Know What You Know*, IGI Global, Hershey, PA. For a deeper discussion of neuroscience findings related to learning and knowledge, see Bennet, D., Bennet, A. and Turner, R. (2015), *Expanding the Self: The Intelligent Complex Adaptive Learning System*, MQIPress, Frost, WV.

Chapter 9

[1] Content first appeared as "The Fallacy of Knowledge Reuse: Building Sustainable Knowledge" in *Journal of Knowledge Management*: *Towards a Global Knowledge-Based Development Agenda*, Vol. 12, No. 5, 2008, pp. 21-33.

[2] CUCA is a term coined in *Organizational Survival in the New World: The Intelligent Complex Adaptive System* (Elsevier, 2004) to represent increasing Change, rising Uncertainty, growing Complexity, and the Anxiety as people become entangled within this environment.

SECTION IV

Chapter 10

[1] Content first appeared as "Values As Knowledge: A New Frame of Reference for a New Generation of Knowledge Workers" with Joyce Avedisian in "The Future of Knowledge Workers," a special issue of the International Journal *On the Horizon*, Summer 2010; and in "Exploring the Military Contribution to KBD through Leadership and Values" in *The Journal of Knowledge Management*, Vol. 14 No. 2, 2010 pp. 314-330.

Chapter 11

[1] Content from this chapter first appeared as "Moving from knowledge to wisdom, from ordinary consciousness to extraordinary consciousness" in *VINE: The Journal of Information and Knowledge Management Systems*, Vol. 38, No. 1, 2008, pp.7-15.

[2] In order of growth toward wisdom and beyond, the seven levels of consciousness focus on: (1) structured concepts: material, ideological, causative; (2) spiritual concepts: focused and limited love at

the personal level; (3) spiritual concepts: soul as part of a larger structure, awareness and connectedness through giving; (4) senses other souls: giving what is needed by others so they can create virtue; balance, humility and hierarchy of thought and need in giving virtue; (5) spiritual awareness: planetary level, advancement of new knowledge communicated to humanity and re-communicated in mental framework; contribution to development of civilization to assist in creating virtue; (6) understanding soul as part of God (wisdom): creating virtue, teaching in soul capacity, leading; and (7) awareness of soul as a functional part of God: creating more of God in a fully aware and conscious method (MacFlouer, 1999).

[3] Intelligent activity represents a perfect state of interaction where intent, purpose, direction, values and expected outcomes are clearly understood and communicated among all parties, reflecting wisdom and achieving a higher truth. Intelligent activity was introduced as Assumption 4 in the Foreward.

Chapter 12

[1] Content first developed as "Knowing: The Art of War 2000" (for the US Department of the Navy) and was included in "Chapter 20: Knowing" in *Organizational Survival in the New World: The Intelligent Complex Adaptive System*, Elsevier, Burlington, MA, 2004. Original material expanded and included as "Chapter 16: The Art of Knowing" in *Decision-Making in The New Reality: Complexity, Knowledge and Knowing*, MQIPress, Frost, WV, 2013. Also, part of *The Profundity and Bifurcation of Change* series and Volume 10 in *Possibilities that are YOU!*

Appendix A

[1] Russian. While simply translated *dusa* means "soul", it is much more. As noted in the text, it represents the spiritual core, that which is staging our thoughts and actions in terms of morals and emotions.

[2] Russian. Again, *rodnye* is difficult to translate into English. Refers to close relatives and friends, those embraced in unconditional love that become part of the identify of self.

[3] *The Urantia Book* (Indexed Version). New York: Uversa Press.

[4] Rowan, J. (1990). *Subpersonalities: The People Inside Us*. New York: Routledge. John Rowan's working definition of a sub-personality is *a semi-permanent and semi-autonomous region of the personality capable of acting as a person* (p.8).

[5] Sub-Personalities are one of the steps in Sacred Attention Therapy, representing a stage that must be passed through and experienced as part of the healing process when seeking liberation from life conditioning. Sacred Attention Therapy (SAT) is a heart-gift of Richard Harvey. See Harvey, R. (2015). "Liberation from Conditioning: An Interview on the Sacred Attention Therapy project." Downloaded June 2 from www.sacredattentiontherapy.com

[6] Brown, D.E. (1991). *Human Universals*. New York: McGraw-Hill.

[7] Freud (1938). "Splitting of the ego in the process of defence" in *Collected Works of Freud Vol. 23*. London: Hogarth Press, p.203. Freud's description of the superego is very close to the description of sub-personalities forwarded in this paper. To explain the origin of the superego, Freud says: "A portion of the external world has, at least partially, been abandoned as an object and has instead by identification, been taken into the ego and thus become an integral part of the internal world. This new psychical agency continues to carry on the functions which have hitherto been performed by people in the external world."

[8] Cooper, L.R. (2005). *The Grand Vision: The Design and Purpose of a Human Being*. Ft. Collins, CO: PlanetaryHeart. This excellent book sets about presenting a universal perspective that excludes no one—no race, culture or religion on or off the planet, a perspective that applies to all sentient beings wherever they are. Builds on the following sources: *The Urantia Book*, the early Theosophical writings, *The Keys of Enoch*, *A Course in Miracles*, *The New Testament of the Holy Bible*, and *The Starseed Transmissions: The Third Millenium*.

[9] Brown, M.Y. (1979) *The Art of Guiding: The Psychosynthesis Approach to Individual Counseling and Psychology.* Redlands, CA: Johnson College, University of Redlands.

[10] Wilber, K. (2000). *Integral Psychology: Consciousness, Spirit, Psychology, Therapy.* Boston: Shambhala.

[11] DeBono, E. (1985, 1999). *Six Thinking Hats.* MICA Management Resources, Inc. DeBono is the creator of Lateral Thinking, which moves beyond a vertical mode to look at how creativity works.

[12] Rowan, J. (1993). *Discover Your Subpersonalities: Our Inner World and the People In It.* New York: Brunner-Routledge.

[13] In 1984 Mother Theresa and the author shared a few life moments. The account appears as Idea 6 in *Possibilities that are YOU! Volume 6: Conscious Compassion* by Alex Bennet (2018), Frost, WV: MQIPress. (Available in soft cover from Amazon.)

[14] Bennet, A. & Bennet, D. (2004). *Organizational Survival in the New World: The Intelligent Complex Adaptive System.* Burlington, MA: Elsevier. All knowledge is context sensitive and situation dependent.

[15] Kohlberg, L. (1981). *Philosophy of Moral Development: Moral Stages and the Idea of Justice.* San Francisco, CA: Harper.

[16] Mavromatis, A. (1987). *Hypnagogia.* London: Routledge. Mavromatis suggests that it is a subpersonality who has the psychic ability we experience.

[17] Rowan, J. (1990). *Subpersonalities: The People Inside Us.* New York: Routledge, pp.32-33.

[18] Joachim, H.H. (1948). *Logical Studies.* Oxford: Clarendon Press. Joachim says: "The mind is one throughout its many experiences; but its unitary being—its individual character—depends upon, is made and molded by, the special variety it experiences: The 'many' in this case contribute to determine the character of their 'one.' And at the same time, what each experience is depends essentially upon the individual character of the mind which is experiencing. The 'one', in this case, contributes to determine the character of every item of its 'many'—contributes to make and mold each single experience." (pp.86-7)

Subject Index

About Mountain Quest Institute

MQI is a research, retreat and learning center dedicated to helping individuals achieve personal and professional growth, and helping organizations create and sustain high performance in a rapidly changing, uncertain, and increasingly complex world.

Current research is focused on Human and Organizational Development, Knowledge, Knowledge Capacities, Adult Learning, Values, Complexity, Consciousness and Spirituality. MQI has three questions: The Quest for Knowledge, The Quest for Consciousness, and The Quest for Meaning. **MQI is scientific, humanistic and spiritual and finds no contradiction in this combination**. See www.mountainquestinstitute.com

MQI is the birthplace of Organizational Survival in the New World: The Intelligent Complex Adaptive System (Elsevier, 2004), a new theory of the firm that turns the living system metaphor into a reality for organizations. Based on research in complexity and neuroscience—and incorporating networking theory and knowledge management—this book is filled with new ideas married to practical advice, all embedded within a thorough description of the new organization in terms of structure, culture, strategy, leadership, knowledge workers and integrative competencies.

Mountain Quest Institute, situated four hours from Washington, D.C. in the Monongahela Forest of the Allegheny Mountains, is part of the Mountain Quest complex which includes a Retreat Center, Inn, and the old Farm House, Outbuildings and mountain trails and farmland. See www.mountainquestinn.com The Retreat Center is designed to provide full learning experiences, including hosting training, workshops, retreats and business meetings for professional and executive groups of 25 people or less. The Center includes a 27,000-volume research library, a conference room, community center, computer room, 12 themed bedrooms, a workout and hot tub area, and a four-story tower with a glass ceiling for enjoying the magnificent view of the valley during the day and the stars at night. Situated on a 430 acres farm, there is a labyrinth, creeks, four miles of mountain trails, and horses, Longhorn cattle, Llamas and a myriad of wild neighbors. Other neighbors include the Snowshoe Ski Resort, the National Radio Astronomy Observatory and the CASS Railroad.

About the Authors

Drs. Alex and David Bennet are co-founders of the Mountain Quest Institute. They may be contacted at alex@mountainquestinstitute.com

Alex Bennet, a Professor at the Bangkok University Institute for Knowledge and Innovation Management, is internationally recognized as an expert in knowledge management and an agent for organizational change. Prior to founding the Mountain Quest Institute, she served as the Chief Knowledge Officer and Deputy Chief Information Officer for Enterprise Integration for the U.S. Department of the Navy, and was co-chair of the Federal Knowledge Management Working Group. Dr. Bennet is the recipient of the Distinguished and Superior Public Service Awards from the U.S. government for her work in the Federal Sector. She is a Delta Epsilon Sigma and Golden Key National Honor Society graduate with a Ph.D. in Human and Organizational Systems; degrees in Management for Organizational Effectiveness, Human Development, English and Marketing; and certificates in Total Quality Management, System Dynamics and Defense Acquisition Management. Alex believes in the **multidimensionality and interconnectedness of humanity as we move out of infancy into full consciousness**.

David Bennet's experience spans many years of service in the Military, Civil Service and Private Industry, including fundamental research in underwater acoustics and nuclear physics, frequent design and facilitation of organizational interventions, and serving as technical director of two major DoD Acquisition programs. Prior to founding the Mountain Quest Institute, Dr. Bennet was CEO, then Chairman of the Board and Chief Knowledge Officer of a professional services firm located in Alexandria, Virginia. He is a Phi Beta Kappa, Sigma Pi Sigma, and Suma Cum Laude graduate of the University of Texas, and holds degrees in Mathematics, Physics, Nuclear Physics, Liberal Arts, Human and Organizational Development, and a Ph.D. in Human Development focused on Neuroscience and adult learning. He is currently researching the nexus of Science, the Humanities and Spirituality.

Dr. Joyce Avedisian, an Associate of the Mountain Quest Institute, is an Organizational Effectiveness consultant, author, speaker, and educator with over 20 years of experience in the pharmaceutical and healthcare industry. She focuses on developing the capability of people, teams, and organizations and leveraging knowledge to execute the mission, values, and strategy. Joyce has a proven track record in Fortune 1000 and mid-sized companies in the US and Europe in helping leaders realize results by integrating a strategic vision of the future with strong operational focus and building stakeholder alignment around the customer/patient. Since she created Avedisian Management Consultants in 2009, her clients in the healthcare industry have included Sanofi, Merck, Bristol Myers Squibb, and Aptalis Pharmaceuticals. Joyce holds a Ph.D. in Organization Behavior from Brandeis University and is the author of articles on building a patient-focused culture, gerontology, high performance teams, knowledge transfer, and values-based leadership. She has conducted research and writes white papers and blogs for Eyeforpharma on "Putting Patients at the Center of Your Clinical Trials." She resides in Bedminster, New Jersey.

We hope you have enjoyed this book.

MQIPress is a wholly-owned subsidiary of Mountain Quest Institute, LLC, located at 303 Mountain Quest Lane, Marlinton, West Virginia 24954, USA.

Possibilities that are YOU!

These little **Conscious Look Books** are focused on sharing 22 large concepts from *The Profundity and Bifurcation of Change.* Conversational in nature, each with seven ideas offered for the graduate of life experience. Available in soft cover from Amazon.

eBooks available in PDF format from MQIPress (US 304-799-7267 or alex@mountainquestinstitute.com) and Kindle format from Amazon.

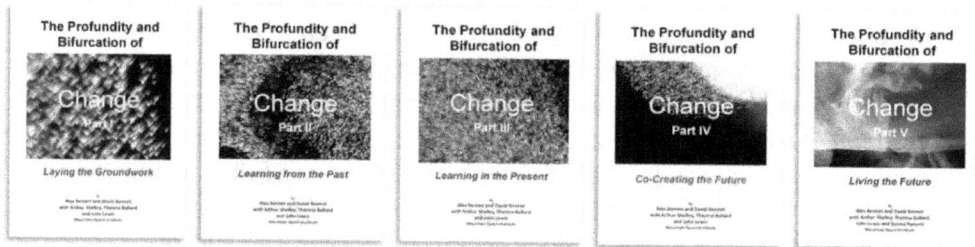

Five in-depth eBooks, *The Profundity and Bifurcation of Change*, heavily referenced and resourced. These books lay the groundwork for the **Intelligent Social Change Journey** (ISCJ), a developmental journey of the body, mind and heart, moving from the heaviness of cause-and-effect linear extrapolations, to the fluidity of co-evolving with our environment, to the lightness of breathing our thought and feelings into reality. Grounded in development of our mental faculties, these are phase changes, each building on and expanding previous learning in our movement toward intelligent activity. Available as eBooks from Amazon. (Available 2019 in soft cover.)

eBooks available NOW
(Available in soft back copy from Amazon in 2019)

Expanding the Self: The Intelligent Complex Adaptive Learning System

by David Bennet, Alex Bennet and Robert Turner (2015)

We live in unprecedented times; indeed, turbulent times that can arguably be defined as ushering humanity into a new Golden Age, offering the opportunity to embrace new ways of learning and living in a globally and collaboratively entangled connectedness (Bennet & Bennet, 2007). In this shifting and dynamic environment, life demands accelerated cycles of learning experiences. Fortunately, we as a humanity have begun to look within ourselves to better understand the way our mind/brain operates, the amazing qualities of the body that power our thoughts and feelings, and the reciprocal loops as those thoughts and feelings change our physical structure. This emerging knowledge begs us to relook and rethink what we know about learning, providing a new starting point to expand toward the future.

This book is a treasure for those interested in how recent findings in neuroscience impact learning. The result of this work is an expanding experiential learning model call the Intelligent Complex Adaptive Learning System, adding the fifth mode of social engagement to Kolb's concrete experience, reflective observation, abstract conceptualization and active experimentation, with the five modes undergirded by the power of Self. A significant conclusion is that should they desire, adults have much more control over their learning than they may realize.

Leading with the Future in Mind: Knowledge and Emergent Leadership

by David Bennet and Alex Bennet with John Lewis (2015)

We exist in a new reality, a global world where the individuated power of the mind/brain offers possibilities beyond our imagination. It is within this framework that thought leading emerges, and when married to our collaborative nature, makes the impossible an everyday occurrence. Leading with the Future in Mind, building on profound insights unleashed by recent findings in neuroscience, provides a new view that converges leadership, knowledge and learning for individual and organizational advancement.

This book provides a research-based tour de force for the future of leadership. Moving from the leadership of the past, for the few at the top, using authority as the explanation, we now find leadership emerging from all levels of the organization, with knowledge as the explanation. The future will be owned by the organizations that understand and can master the relationships between knowledge and leadership. Being familiar with the role of a knowledge worker is not the same as understanding the role of a knowledge leader. As the key ingredient, collaboration is much more than "getting along"; it embraces and engages.

The nature of the organization has moved beyond the factory and process metaphor, and is now understood as an intelligent complex adaptive system (ICAS). Leading with the Future in Mind covers the essentials of working, learning, and leading in an ICAS, covering knowledge and complexity, but also passion and spiritual energy. As social creatures living in an entangled world, our brains are linked together. We are in continuous interaction with those around us, and the brain is continuously changing in response. Wrapped in the mantle of collaborative leadership and engaging our full resources—physical, mental, emotional and spiritual—we open the door to possibilities. We are dreaming the future together.

Decision-Making in The New Reality: Complexity, Knowledge and Knowing

by Alex Bennet and David Bennet (2013)

We live in a world that offers many possible futures. The ever-expanding complexity of information and knowledge provide many choices for decision-makers, and we are all making decisions every single day! As the problems and messes of the world become more complex, our decision consequences are more and more difficult to anticipate, and our decision-making processes must change to keep up with this world complexification. This book takes a consilience approach to explore decision-making in The New Reality, fully engaging systems and complexity theory, knowledge research, and recent neuroscience findings. It also presents methodologies for decision-makers to tap into their unconscious, accessing tacit knowledge resources and increasingly relying on the sense of knowing that is available to each of us.

Almost every day new energies are erupting around the world: new thoughts, new feelings, new knowing, all contributing to new situations that require new decisions and actions from each and every one of us. Indeed, with the rise of the Net Generation and social media, a global consciousness may well be emerging. As individuals and organizations, we are realizing that there are larger resources available to us, and that, as complex adaptive systems linked to a flowing fount of knowing, we can bring these resources to bear to achieve our ever-expanding vision of the future. Are we up to the challenge?

Other books by the authors and available on Amazon...

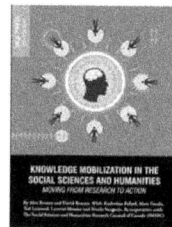

Organizational Survival in the New World: The Intelligent Complex Adaptive System

by Alex and David Bennet (Elsevier, 2004), available in hard and soft formats from Amazon.

In this book David and Alex Bennet propose a new model for organizations that enables them to react more quickly and fluidly to today's fast-changing, dynamic business environment: the Intelligent Complex Adaptive System (ICAS). ICAS is a new organic model of the firm based on recent research in complexity and neuroscience, and incorporating networking theory and knowledge management, and turns the living system metaphor into a reality for organizations. This book synthesizes new thinking about organizational structure from the fields listed above into ICAS, a new systems model for the successful organization of the future designed to help leaders and managers of knowledge organizations succeed in a non-linear, complex, fast-changing and turbulent environment. Technology enables connectivity, and the ICAS model takes advantage of that connectivity by fostering the development of dynamic, effective and trusting relationships in a new organizational structure. AVAILABLE as a hardback and as an eBook FROM AMAZON.

Knowledge Mobilization in the Social Sciences and Humanities: Moving from Research to Action

by Alex Bennet and David Bennet (2007), available in hard and soft formats from Amazon.

This book takes the reader from the University lab to the playgrounds of communities. It shows how to integrate, move and use knowledge, an action journey within an identified action space that is called knowledge mobilization. Whether knowledge is mobilized through an individual, organization, community or nation, it becomes a powerful asset creating a synergy and focus that brings forth the best of action and values. Individuals and teams who can envision, feel, create and apply this power are the true leaders of tomorrow. When we can mobilize knowledge for the greater good humanity will have left the information age and entered the age of knowledge, ultimately leading to compassion and—hopefully—wisdom. AVAILABLE as an eBook FROM AMAZON

Also available in PDF format from MQIPress (US 304-799-7267 or alex@mountainquestinstitute.com) and Kindle format from Amazon.

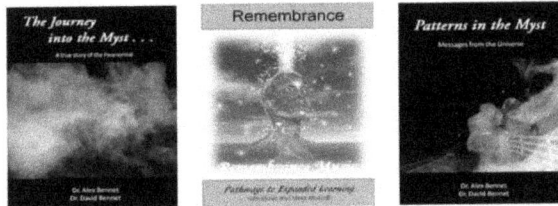

REMEMBRANCE: Pathways to Expanded Learning with Music and Metamusic®

by Barbara Bullard and Alex Bennet (2013)

Take a journey of discovery into the last great frontier—the human mind/brain, an instrument of amazing flexibility and plasticity. This eBook is written for brain users who are intent on mining more of the golden possibilities that lie inherent in each of our unique brains. Begin by discovering the role positive attitudes play in learning, and the power of self-affirmations and visualizations. Then explore the use of brain wave entrainment mixed with designer music called Metamusic® to achieve enhanced learning states. Join students of all ages who are creating magical learning outcomes using music and Metamusic.® AVAILABLE as an eBook FROM AMAZON

The Journey into the Myst (Vol 1 of The Myst Series)

by Alex Bennet and David Bennet (2012)

What we are about to tell you would have been quite unbelievable to me before this journey began. It is not a story of the reality either of us has known for well over our 60 and 70 years of age, but rather, the reality of dreams and fairytales." This is the true story of a sequence of events that happened at Mountain Quest Institute, situated in a high valley of the Allegheny Mountains of West Virginia. The story begins with a miracle, expanding into the capture and cataloging of thousands of pictures of electromagnetic spheres widely known as "orbs." This joyous experience became an exploration into the unknown with the emergence of what the authors fondly call the *Myst*, the forming and shaping of non-random patterns such as human faces, angels and animals. As this phenomenon unfolds, you will discover how Drs. Alex and David Bennet began to observe and interact with the *Myst*. This book shares the beginning of an extraordinary *Journey into the Myst*.

Patterns in the Myst (Vol 2 of The *Myst* Series)

by Alex Bennet and David Bennet (2013)

The Journey into the Myst was just the beginning for Drs. Alex and David Bennet. Volume II of the *Myst* Series brings Science into the Spiritual experience, bringing to bear what the Bennets have learned through their research and educational experiences in physics, neuroscience, human systems, knowledge management and human development. Embracing the paralogical, patterns in the Myst are observed, felt, interpreted, analyzed and compared in terms of their physical make-up, non-randomness, intelligent sources and potential implications. Along the way, the Bennets were provided amazing pictures reflecting the forming of the *Myst*. The Bennets shift to introspection in the third volume of the series to explore the continuing impact of the *Myst* experience on the human psyche.

www.ingramcontent.com/pod-product-compliance
Lightning Source LLC
Chambersburg PA
CBHW061814210326
41599CB00034B/7001